UNCIV

THE ISRAEL C(

JEWISH C(

KEITH KAHN-HARRIS

WITH FOREWORDS BY CLIVE LAWTON AND

GABRIELLE RIFKIND

DAVID
PAUL

First published in Great Britain in 2014

By David Paul

25 Methuen Park

London N10 2JR

www.davidpaulbooks.com

A CIP catalogue record for this book is available from the British Library

ISBN 978-0-9926673-0-6

Printed in Great Britain

CONTENTS

ABOUT THE AUTHOR

Dr Keith Kahn-Harris is a London-based sociologist. He is the editor of the *Jewish Journal of Sociology* and has edited the *Jewish Quarterly*. He is co-author (with Ben Gidley) of *Turbulent Times: The British Jewish Community Today* (Continuum 2010) and *Judaism: All That Matters* (Hodder Education 2012). He has also published articles and reviews in many different publications, including *Guardian Comment Is Free, The Independent, New Statesman and Society, Times Literary Supplement, The Forward, Jewish Chronicle, Haaretz and Jerusalem* Post. He has held teaching posts at Birkbeck College, Open University, Goldsmiths College, the School of Oriental and African Studies and Leo Baeck College. Since the mid-1990s he has conducted research for Jewish organisations including the Board Of Deputies, the Jewish Leadership Council, UJIA, Jewish Continuity, Rene Cassin and the Jewish Agency. From 2008 to 2011 he organised dinners and dialogue groups intended to bring together Jews on different sides of the Israel debate. His website is kahn-harris.org

LIST OF ABBREVIATIONS

AIPAC: American Israel Public Affairs Committee

BDS: Boycott, Divestment and Sanctions

BICOM: British Israel Communications and Research Network

EUMC: European Union Monitoring Centre on Racism and Xenophobia

IJV: Independent Jewish Voices

JDG: Jewish Dialogue Group

JLC: Jewish Leadership Council

JCPA: Jewish Council for Public Affairs

JVP: Jewish Voice for Peace

JNF: Jewish National Fund

NGO: Non-Governmental Organisation

ZF: Zionist Federation

FOREWORD BY CLIVE LAWTON

I don't suppose I'm giving away any secrets when I say that the Jews are a fractious lot. All through Jewish history, Jews have squabbled and argued over just about everything that might come to hand and even at times of grave national crisis, we've managed to maintain a fairly vigorous level of intra-communal argy-bargy.

Ask any non-Jews invited to a mainly Jewish populated diner party and they will tell you of their surprise at the intensity – and pleasure – of the arguments carried on across the table. While good English manners tell us to change the subject as soon as anyone looks like they might be feeling a bit involved in the topic, Jews only then start to warm to the event.

This argumentative trait is almost a national characteristic. Jews talk – a lot – and, if that can become an argument about something, all well and good. Non-Jewish teachers, taking their first job in a Jewish school, invariably comment on the comparative absence of physical violence or the threat of it, but instead the noticeable level of talk all the time. No Jewish child will comfortably take 'because I said so' and as for the advice that children should be seen, but not heard...!

So arguing is what we're brought up to and no shame in that. Indeed, the most classical form of Jewish learning – chevruta – the arguing out of text meaning in pairs is predicated on vigorous, take-no-prisoners argument – demands a greater respect for the topic than the *amour propre* of your adversary in the teasing out of 'truth'.

But however determined and challenging one intends to be, this always demands what in sport is called 'playing the ball, not the man'. You're supposed to go for the point of the game, not simply trying to injure or debilitate your opponent. The rabbis tell us in the Talmud that there are two types of argument, those for the sake of Heaven, and those not. The first, they say, will survive; the second not. What distinguishes them? The first are ego-based, devoted to winning rather than seeking out clarity and insight. The first assume that the opponents are arguing in order to understand things better. A successful argument will be when both sides understand better, when things have moved forward a bit, when, as a minimum, both sides understand *each other* a bit better, even if not the topic. Those not for the sake of Heaven simply try to silence the opposition by whatever means come to hand.

And, understandably, it's this feature of current discussion about Israel and its future and possibilities that bothers Kahn-Harris and has given rise to this book.

I first came across the phenomenon of the special personal vitriol reserved for discussions about Israel when, for ten years, I was lead columnist for the London Jewish News (in the late 90s and first flowerings of the 21st century). In that role, I was given more or less carte blanche to write on anything that took my fancy each week. If readers found my comments funny, they laughed, and if not, they groaned. If thought-provoking, they thought and if not, presumably, they turned the page. But not when, from time to time, I wrote about Israel. I hope you will believe me when I say that I nearly always wrote only sweetness and light, or if not that, at least utter common sense. But to no avail. Hardly ever did I approach the subject without someone or other deciding that I was a traitor to the Jewish people, an enemy to Israel or – a favourite this – a self-hating Jew.

Hardly ever did anyone attend to the point I was trying to make or approach the issue which had given rise to my comments. The default response seemed always to want to impugn my personal qualities and credentials, despite a fairly strong pre-existing track record in bold advocacy for Israel in a range of hostile and difficult circumstances. It seemed that no-one wanted to listen to any dissenting thoughts at all. With the equivalent of the child with its fingers in its ears singing lah lah lah to prevent hearing at all, the self-appointed advocates for Israel seemed to try to shout down all others. And taken over all, it seems only to have got worse since then.

Kahn-Harris, in this book, attempts to analyse why this has happened and what exactly is going on. If for no others reason, you should read the book for his masterful and thoughtful analysis of the various existing positions of Jews and Israel advocates on Israel. Not only will you almost certainly find yourself there, neatly pinpointed and defined, but you might actually gain some small additional understanding as to why others stand somewhere else. With warm humanity and careful dispassion, Kahn-

Harris tells of his personal attempts to make a difference to the quality of conversation. Though inconclusive and perhaps even unsuccessful, it will prompt many to think harder about how we conduct this critically important field of debate amongst ourselves in the Jewish world. Currently, no other topic so readily allows us to call for the removal or exclusion of this or that one from the roster of the Jewish community – though, of course, we cannot so readily remove them from the Jewish People – and that should, at least, give us pause for thought.

More significantly though, Kahn-Harris projects forwards a little. How might this story play out? It doesn't look good if we carry on like this. This little book might just give us the language, the insights – and the pause – for us to do something a little more sensible, before it's, stupidly, too late.

Clive Lawton, a former high school headteacher, founding Chief Executive of Jewish Continuity, first Chair of the Third World Development charity, Tzedek, and one of the founders of Limmud, is currently Limmud's worldwide senior consultant and scholar-in-residence at the London Jewish Cultural Centre.

FOREWORD BY GABRIELLE RIFKIND

I n 2007, Keith Kahn-Harris asked me to facilitate a group to examine the deep conflicts in the Jewish community over Israel. I did this with a heavy heart, as this is a subject that evokes shrill and toxic debate. The aim of the group was to explore some of the deep tensions, scars and splits that have emerged in the community with regard to its relationship with Israel. The underlying thesis was that these splits were not only painful, but were undermining effective support for the resolution of the Palestine-Israel conflict. There was an 'uncivil war' at work within the Jewish community.

British Jewry has always played a vital role in both the creation of Israel and its support. But, more recently, questions amongst Diaspora Jews about the State of Israel have become fraught with tensions, difficult to talk about and a sensitive subject that sparks intense feelings. The Palestine-Israel conflict evokes deeply polarised emotions within the Jewish community that frequently evade rational discourse and conversations are frequently conducted in the language of platitudes, recycled arguments and polarised thinking. Loyalty is called on at any price and partisan alignment is frequently demanded and anything less than total loyalty runs the risk of being seen as an act of betrayal. Those who express more critical views and a growing sense of urgency around the necessity to forge an agreement with the Palestinians do not sit comfortably with those who see their duty as one of total support for the state of Israel.

Many Diaspora Jews continue to mirror the conflict of identity between the depiction of the downtrodden, servile, frightened and humiliated Diaspora Jew and the proud, self-confident Zionist Jew. The history of the Holocaust reinforces the enormous sense of vulnerability and the deepest sense of insecurity around Jewish identity. For many, the establishment of the state of Israel was the end of a terrible tragedy, as it represented control over the destiny of the Jewish people. It was to become a country of enormous creativity, an economic miracle and a beacon of democracy in a troubled region. Burdened by a uniquely tragic history, it engendered a sense of pride and legitimacy, but simultaneously, it remained a source of conflict for the lack of resolution on the Palestinian conflict. In spite of this growth in self-confidence, Israel was to remain alarmed by the country's perilous geography and it's being surrounded by a sea of instability and hostility and it always has a deep fear that it is only one military defeat away from destruction.

European Jews reflect these insecurities and, in many ways, mirror many of the difficulties of Israeli society. Here politics is often too dangerous to be spoken about because it evokes the deep differences that exist within Israeli society, with huge chasms between the secular and religious communities. These deep political divides are expressed in the geographical boundaries of Israel, with those who are attached to the biblical land as part of their identity and those who wish to go back to the 1967 borders. Discussions about settlements, Jerusalem and the Palestinian conflict seldom lead to reasoned debate in Israel, something that is recreated within the Jewish community in the Diaspora, often igniting useless anger and frustration.

When Keith invited me to facilitate a group within the community, he did this knowing that I was trained as a group analyst and that I had been running groups in Israel. In 2000, I had been invited to set up training workshops for Israeli group analysts who wanted to deepen their understanding of the group process and develop their skills working with people who had deep histories of trauma. Later, as director of the Middle East programme for the Oxford Research Group, we were to create groups with Israelis who were drawn from across the political spectrum, who reflected the political, social and religious differences that were to be found in Israeli society. The aim of these groups was to examine whether they could find a common agenda for ending the conflict with their Palestinian neighbours.

These groups had their challenges, but nothing was to prepare me for the challenge of the group that Keith had asked me to facilitate. He had hoped we would succeed in establishing a forum for the Jewish community to build bridges in which trust could be deepened and a civil discourse on Israel could take place. The aim of such a group would be not to change minds, but to help participants find the capacity to tolerate a range of different views. Keith had hoped that such a group would create a culture, which would drive participants towards civility – communicating in such a way that they expressed concern about the welfare of the other. There would be a dialogue in which group members would take responsibility for their own behaviour and incivility. We would achieve a level of communication in which abusive remarks, anger and incivility would not dominate the group.

My psychotherapy training had encouraged me to seek to try to understand what is happening to all parties wherever there is misunderstanding, tension and conflict. It is not useful to blame one person without understanding the interactions between those involved and being aware of how each side impacts on the other. History, experience, frustrations, real and imagined slights, injustices and outrages influence how we behave and react towards one another. The professional status of the psychotherapist, to some extent, certifies you as neutral, someone committed to understanding and helping with the problems of the individual or the group. You may not always succeed, you may not even truly be heard, but your bona fide credentials are not usually impugned. Even in deeply troubled conflict between a couple, your authority means you are accepted as not, unfairly, taking sides, but when addressing the Israeli conflict, there would seem to be no such thing as this neutrality.

This neutrality was to come under scrutiny, when I was invited to run Keith's group. I had also been having a number of off-the-record meetings, quietly, behind the scenes, with the leadership of Hamas in which I had attempted to talk to senior Israelis about what possibilities there were to open dialogue here. It always evoked a huge amount of emotion as the experience of the suicide bombings at the time meant very few Israelis were in a state of mind to think about this. I'd written articles in the broadsheets about why we have to engage with our enemies and why any end to conflict would, i ultimately, involve bringing them into any peacemaking activity. I imagine some in Keith's group were comfortable with my engagement, but, for others, it was a source of discomfort. The only problem was it was never openly discussed in the group and, on reflection, I should have encouraged discussion and established whether it intruded on my neutrality and, therefore, my legitimacy to run such a group.

There were moments in the group when there was a genuine attempt to move away from left-right alignments in search of a more respectful language and intellectual honesty. Group members expressed an appreciation of having a safe space to talk about their Jewish identity and their relationship with Israel. The commitment to the group was high with a very consistent level of attendance. Group members challenged each other to take responsibility for their own behaviour and to move away from a culture of blame and there was a genuine attempt to exchange ideas in a community-building process. However, some participants displayed immense difficulty in managing the profound differences which were to emerge, trying to convince other participants of the moral rightness of their position. There were coherent and sometimes strong voices in the group calling for calm and clarity, but those who were more fixated in an ideological position often dominated the discussion. And, as Keith perceptively points out earlier in the book, 'Those who criticise uncivil behaviour in others rarely pay attention to their own behaviour.'

There are certain satisfactions in familiar arguments, even if they are deeply contested, and in comfort zones, in rehearsed positions that can become subsumed as part of our identities. To rise above this, demands self-reflection and a serious commitment to want to change how we behave. It is often much easier to repeat the same arguments, rather than engage in the disciplined work of actively exploring how our behaviour affects and often disturbs others and whether our mode of communication is increasing or decreasing the possibility of getting heard. So much of the debate about Israel is heartfelt and is driven by fears and insecurities, but in order for us to be heard and taken seriously, some of the emotion needs to be distilled for a more rational voice to emerge. I applaud Keith for having the courage to examine this vexatious debate in his richly textured book.

Gabrielle Rifkind is a group analyst and specialist in conflict resolution. She is the Director of the Middle East programme at Oxford Research Group, the convener and founder of the Middle East Policy Initiative Forum (MEPIF) and has facilitated a number of Track II roundtables in the Middle East on the Israel-Palestine conflict, as well as on the Iran conflict.

ACKNOWLEDGEMENTS

This book has had a long gestation period. Many people have helped me along the way. I am indebted to The Bridging Trust, who helped to fund the dinners and the writing of this book, supporting my work when no one else would. I'd like to thank Gabrielle Rifkind who took a risk to help us explore what was new territory for both of us and for writing a foreword to this book. Mitch Chanin of the Jewish Dialogue Group and Rebecca Subar encouraged me at an early stage of my work. Jonathan Freedland took time out of his busy schedule to help and encourage me. Jonathan Cummings made some helpful comments on one of the later drafts of the manuscript. Rebekka Helford copy edited an early draft of this book and made some excellent suggestions as to how to improve it. Clive Lawton made some useful comments on the draft and wrote an excellent foreword.

I am grateful to everyone who attended the dialogue group discussed in chapter seven and the dinners discussed in chapter eight (including those who did not find the process valuable). I learned a huge amount from these experiments and I hope you did too.

My children, Kobi and Ella, coped perfectly with their house being turned upside down for our dinner parties. I hope that, as they grow into adulthood in the Jewish community, they will find a more civil atmosphere in discussions about Israel.

It's hard to express how much I owe to my amazing wife, Deborah. Not only did she show considerable fortitude in tolerating this latest twist in what has been a complicated career, she threw herself into helping me ensure that the dinners we hosted were sumptuous. She also read the manuscript of this book carefully, making some important suggestions.

INTRODUCTION

One evening in 2007, I met up in the pub with an influential figure in the British Jewish community. Both of us have a lot in common in our views on Israel and we both identify with the left. However, we differed in our attitudes to pro-Palestinian sections of the Jewish left. The discussion grew increasingly heated as we grappled with how far one should associate with certain left-wing Jewish figures. Eventually, the developing argument turned to our own Jewish identities. I pointed to my own long involvement in Jewish communal life and compared it to my interlocutor's minimal involvement. I accused him of only being interested in Jewish identity in a negative way, as a response to anti-Semitism. I viciously attacked him with the following words:

> You love the Holocaust! It's the only thing you've got. You've got nothing else Jewishly. You fucking love it!

I then stormed off to the toilets in a rage. Very quickly I realised what I had said and regretted my words. I returned and apologised profusely and the discussion began to cool down. However, the damage was done and our relationship has been difficult ever since.

This book is a direct result of that argument back in 2007. Ever since that evening, I've been reflecting on why conversations between Jews can be so difficult. In particular, I've been reflecting on why Israel is such a sensitive topic. In part, this reflection is an act of atonement for my behaviour in 2007. I don't want to be the kind of person who insults people in such vulgar ways, and, to be fair to myself, I very rarely behave like that. But I'm also aware that the issue of Israel and its impact on the Jewish community can spark intense emotions in me.

And I'm not the only one. In the last few years, in my own quest for answers as to why these issues make me so emotional, I've become increasingly aware that this is a more general problem. Open a Jewish newspaper in the Diaspora and you will be confronted by news stories, op. eds. and letters that give vent to incredible levels of anger, fear and sadness directed at other Jews. In my own work and life in the British Jewish community, I constantly encounter otherwise genial people who behave in extraordinary ways to other Jews when the issue of Israel comes up. This situation is getting worse all the time. As Israel itself is enmeshed in internal and external conflicts which, at the very least, are not getting any better, so Israel has become a source of deepening conflict in the Diaspora, both among Jews and between Jews and non-Jews.

In this book, I try to explain how the Jewish people came to be so divided about Israel. I argue that, even if Jews have never been entirely united over Israel, since 2000 these divisions have become more pronounced. The outbreak of the second intifada, the subsequent unravelling of the peace process, the 2006 Lebanon conflict, Operation Cast Lead in 2009, Operation Pillar of Defence in 2012 – all these events have eroded what, in the post-1967 period, was a broad, although not universal, consensus in the Diaspora that Israel should be publicly supported. As a host of new Jewish positions over Israel has emerged, the Diaspora Jewish communal landscape has changed. The emergence of these new positions has led directly to bitter conflict, not just over how and whether Israel should be supported, but over whether Diaspora Jews have the right to criticise Israel at all. This conflict is too often expressed through personal abusiveness, extreme language, attempts to exclude certain Jews from the community and the creation of pariahs.

What the protagonists in this conflict share is a sense that Israel is vitally important to being Jewish. Whether Israel is the culmination of Jewish dreams or the ultimate Jewish nightmare, everyone is at least agreed on its centrality to the modern Jewish condition. This is understandable. The creation of Israel in 1948 was an earth-shattering event in Jewish history, coming soon after the equally earth-shattering events of the Holocaust. But what the current Diaspora conflicts over Israel show is how hard it has been to adjust to this new reality and, in particular, how hard it has been to find a viable way for Diaspora Jews to relate to Israel. The difficulties with dealing with this unprecedented situation, at the same time as Israel is itself constantly changing and constantly involved in violent conflict, are exacerbated by Israel's status as a *cause célèbre* in the wider world. Everyone seems to have an opinion on Israel and, in an age of Internet-based politics, everyone can express their opinion as vehemently as they like.

This book doesn't just describe the current situation and explain how it came about; I also argue that addressing Diaspora Jewish conflict over

Israel should be an urgent communal priority. The situation cannot be left to fester; too many people are hurt, alienated and abused by the conflict. I make the case that, through developing a pragmatic concern for 'Jewish peoplehood', it is possible to formulate strategies to manage the conflict better. In part, this involves changing how Jewish communities exclude and include people with minority views. But it also involves changing the ways Jews communicate with each other about Israel. I argue that Jews should nurture *civility* and *dialogue* as practices and values – practices and values for which there are Jewish precedents.

Throughout this book, I draw extensively on the case study of the UK Jewish community in which I have been closely involved throughout my life. However, this book is designed to be relevant to Diaspora Jews around the world. The divisions and conflicts with which British Jews are grappling appear in most other Diaspora communities, albeit with local characteristics. I make frequent comparisons to the US community in particular. As the largest Diaspora community in the world, developments in American Jewry heavily influence what goes on in the UK and elsewhere. Indeed, many of the worst examples of Jewish conflict over Israel have taken place in the US.

The UK case study is also a highly significant one. The UK Jewish community is exceptionally diverse with a huge range of institutions and a dynamic pool of volunteers and leaders who have grappled with the Israel conflict in many different ways. Yet it is also a small community, with around 300,000 Jews living in a small number of population centres, most of them in London. This small size makes it impossible for any one faction to completely separate itself from the rest of the community. Tight webs of personal ties and geographic closeness means British Jews are constantly confronted with those whose views they might find abhorrent.

The UK also has strong non-Jewish pro-Israel and pro-Palestinian campaigns. Britain's complex geo-political role in the world – as a country that is both attracted to and repelled by both Europe and the US, as a country that tries to 'punch above its weight', as a diverse multicultural nation with a significant Muslim minority and as the administrator of pre-1948 Palestine – makes it deeply invested in what goes on in Israel.

I also draw on the UK case study as it is in the UK Jewish community that I have made a concerted attempt to find a method of managing the conflict among Jews. As I recount in chapter eight, I have tried to make a difference by holding confidential dinners at my home with Jewish leaders and opinion formers on different sides of the Israel divide. I have tried to nurture a more constructive and convivial private conversation that can ameliorate some of the anger in public conversations. While I do not claim that the UK Jewish community has been transformed by my efforts, I do think that the process I have started is a valuable one that can provide inspiration for other Jewish communities.

This is not a book by someone who is a role model for civility or a neutral figure standing imperiously above the fray. Rather, it is a book by a flawed human being and a flawed Jew. I have strong opinions on Israel, leftist opinions that sometimes conflict with those of much of the Jewish community[1]. I have published articles on Israel and on the Jewish community and am far from disinterested. I am tangled up in the conflict I describe.

But it is also a book by someone who is striving to be a better person, to contain my occasional outbursts of anger, to be more civil and to listen closely and respectfully to those with whom I disagree. This is also a book by someone who is deeply committed to Jewish community, to Jewish peoplehood and to the necessity and inevitability of being part of a Jewish world that contains Jews who see being Jewish differently to me. This commitment will hopefully counter-balance my more ideological side.

Ultimately, as this book will argue, any improvement in Diaspora Jewish conflicts over Israel has to come from within, from Jews who want things to improve. That requires Jews to struggle, as I continue to do, with the contradictory emotions that both divide and unite Jews. Again, I am not about to set myself up as a role model, but I do think that if more Jews would do as I have done and grapple with their own feelings about Israel and other Jews, if more Jews worked on the way they behave towards other Jews with whom they disagree – then maybe, just maybe, things will improve.

***

This book is intended for a number of audiences. British Jews, particularly those who are involved in some way in debates on Israel, are at the 'core' of the book's audience. *Uncivil War* tries to make an intervention into how British Jews behave towards each other when the question of Israel is raised, and in how the British Jewish community and its institutions are organised with regard to divisions over Israel. The book also discusses extensively the way divisions over Israel impact on Jewish communities across the world, particularly in the United States. Although each Jewish community has its own characteristics, the arguments I make in *Uncivil War* can be applied across the Jewish world. This book is also intended for those who are not Jewish and are involved in the issue of Israel-Palestine. Hopefully, it will raise awareness of the manifold ways in which the Israel-Palestine conflict reverberates far outside the region itself. Finally, *Uncivil War* will be of interest to anyone who is part of a community divided by conflict and who seeks a broader perspective on how intra-communal conflict works and how it can be addressed.

Stylistically, this book is something of a hybrid. It contains scholarly analysis, makes policy recommendations and recounts personal stories. I write both as a sociologist and as a committed member of the British Jewish community. The first five chapters of the book are the ones that draw most extensively on my scholarly experience. Chapter one explains the background to Jewish conflict over Israel, discussing the history of Jewish political and religious divisions and the impact that Zionism and the birth of the state of Israel in 1948 have had on the Jewish world. Chapter two details the various Jewish positions on Israel that have emerged since 2000 in the UK and elsewhere in the Diaspora. Chapter three goes on to show how and why those who hold to these positions have come into conflict with one another. In chapter four, I discuss the 'symptoms' of the conflict, the varied ways in which Jewish conflicts over Israel are expressed, often abusively. Chapter five explains why Diaspora Jewish conflict over Israel needs to be ameliorated and managed, making the case through drawing on and reframing concepts of Jewish peoplehood.

In Chapters six to eight, in which I discuss how civility and dialogue can help manage the conflict over Israel, I am well aware that, although I do draw on specialist literature, I am outside my comfort zone and I am not an expert in these matters. However, as I will argue , if there is to be any hope of managing the Israel conflict in Jewish communities, members of Jewish communities have to take some responsibility rather than relying on specialists in conflict resolution. In this book, I have done what I can, drawing on my existing expertise and expanding it into related fields. In chapter six, I discuss the concepts of civility and dialogue, and how they might be mobilised to help manage the Israel conflict. Chapter seven reports on and explains the lessons of an 'experiment' in dialogue in the Jewish community that I conducted in 2008. In Chapter eight, I discuss a series of confidential dinners with Jewish leaders that I ran between 2009 and 2011, going on to show how hospitality and food can be powerful ways of nurturing civil dialogue. Finally, the conclusion to the book makes a call for action to manage the conflict over Israel in the Jewish community, outlining a series of recommendations.

NOTES

1 - For the record, I situate myself somewhere between the 'Jewish radical' and 'Pro-Israel, Pro-Peace' positions described in chapter two.

CHAPTER ONE:
THE BACKGROUND TO THE PROBLEM

The foundation of the State of Israel in 1948 was one of the most revolutionary acts in Jewish history. The achievement of Jewish sovereignty, after a gap of millennia, created a radically new set of possibilities for Jewish existence. A self-defined Jewish state, born into a world of nation states, confronted Jews with difficult challenges: How should Jews exercise state power? What is the responsibility of Diaspora Jews to Israeli Jews and vice versa? What should the position of non-Jewish minorities be in a majority Jewish state? How should Israel relate to traditional Judaism? What kind of Jewish culture should be built in a Jewish state?

These questions were initially confronted, and continue to be confronted, in a permanent state of war. There has never been a period when Israel has been at peace with all of its neighbours. It is a tribute to Israel and the Zionist project that difficult questions about the nature of Judaism have been addressed openly and with vigour throughout Israel's history. That is not to say that there has ever been any kind of consensus within Israel and within the Zionist movement over what kind of state Israel should be. Indeed, the state of Israel was born out of a divided Jewish world and a divided Zionist movement.

A BRIEF OVERVIEW OF JEWISH DIVISIONS

Zionism was just one response to the 'Jewish question' raised in the post-emancipation period. From the late eighteenth century onwards, Jews in many parts of Europe and in the New World were confronted with the opportunities and dilemmas that stemmed from the freedom to take a full part as citizens in the life of the nations in which they resided. Some Jews responded by assimilating as fully as possible, some by keeping Judaism a private matter of belief, some by creating forms of Judaism that would be more consonant with Christian religion, others by re-creating a self-imposed ghetto of stringent Jewish practice. By the start of the twentieth century, a wide variety of Jewish responses to modernity had emerged in Jewish communities across the world. Jewish religious practice alone was divided into a variety of sects, including Reform, Conservative, Modern Orthodox and Haredi (ultra-orthodox) Judaisms.

While the scale and diversity of these differences were unprecedented in the modern world, the Jewish people have never been homogeneous. Jewish practice has always differed ethnically and culturally, with *Ashkenazi* (Jews with German/Eastern European origins), *Mizrachi* (Middle Easterm) and *Sephardi* (Spanish/Portuguese) Judaisms themselves containing considerable diversity. The biblical prophets raged against what they saw as deviations from correct and ethical Jewish practice and were often shunned for their pains. Some Jewish groups, such as the Karaites, Samaritans and – above all – the early Christians, developed into separate sects that in some cases left Judaism far behind. Others, such as the Pharisees and Sadducees, were absorbed back into Judaism or faded out of the historical record entirely. The development of sects and factions was, at times, accompanied by bitter disputes and accusations of heresy, as was the case with the followers of the false messiah Shabbatai Zvi in the seventeenth century. However, Jewish divisions did not always lead to irreparable schisms. For example, in the eighteenth and nineteenth centuries, the *Hassidic* movement, which emphasised mystical and spiritual practice, was bitterly opposed by the *Mitnagdim* (opponents) who emphasised study and a more austere form of Jewish practice, but the distinction between them gradually faded over time, ultimately becoming no more than a source of periodic tension and a difference of emphasis within contemporary ultra-orthodox Judaism.

The ability of Judaism to retain a sense of overarching unity has, historically speaking, been more significant than any tendency towards schism. But in the modern world it has become more and more difficult for unity to be upheld, in part because it has become almost impossible to shun potential schismatics. In the pre-modern era, a controversial figure, such as the seventeenth century Dutch philosopher Baruch Spinoza, could be declared a heretic and excluded from Jewish communal life. In contrast, in western modernity, freedom of religious expression enables different Jewish groups to entrench themselves institutionally. If a Jew is labelled heretical by one set of Jews, it is relatively easy to find another set of Jews among whom one might be accepted.

Today, gloomy accounts of the religious chasms dividing Jews abound.[2] As is often noted, the non-recognition by orthodox authorities of the halachic status of some non-orthodox Jews, particularly in Israel, is a pressing and divisive issue. Yet, for the time being at least, the centre appears to be holding – just about – inasmuch as ties remain holding together all those who identify as Jewish. Israel, the Jewish state, is one such tie.

If religious differences between Jews have created lasting divisions, political divisions have the potential to create even deeper fissures within the Jewish people. Jews have always been politically engaged in some fashion; even in the ghettos there were Jewish representatives who attempted to negotiate with authorities. What is distinctive about the modern era, however, is the possibility that Jews have to engage as full and equal partners in an emancipated public sphere and to develop secular Jewish political movements.

Within western democracies, the dominant trend among communal leaders, such as the nineteenth century Anglo-Jewish gentry in Britain, was to embrace the possibilities of liberal citizenship and full participation in civic life. In this 'Jewish liberal compromise', Jews could be Jews in private, but would be proud British citizens in the public sphere.[3] The self-defined role of communal grandees, right up until well into the post-war period and even to some extent today, was to provide exemplary models of public engagement and private Jewish propriety. At the same time, other Jewish movements embraced very different models of political activism. Communism and socialism were popular among many Jews in western democracies and in Eastern European autocracies. They understood the liberation of Jews from anti-Semitic oppression as part of the wider cause of emancipation from class-based oppression. No consensus existed as to how and whether Jewish identity would persist in a communist or socialist society. For some, as in Soviet communism, Jewish distinctiveness would, preferably, disappear in the transition to communism. For others, the socialist *Bund*, for example, a proudly secular Jewish culture would form an autonomous part of a future, heterogeneous, socialist society.

Zionism, as it emerged in the late nineteenth century, both challenged and reflected these radical Jewish currents. Although socialism was highly influential in many strains of pre-state and post-state Zionism, the achievement of a Jewish sovereignty had a fundamental priority. This emphasis on sovereignty also meant that Zionism represented a departure from the ways in which the Jewish attachment to the biblical land of Israel had long been expressed. Although early Zionism did include some pragmatic voices regarding where sovereignty should be exercised and also included others (like Ahad Ha'am) whose primary concern was cultural rather than political sovereignty, Zionism rapidly became a nationalist movement along the lines of other nationalist movements worldwide. Its main pre-1948 strains, Labour and Revisionist Zionism, shared a belief that only in a sovereign Jewish state could the Jewish people survive and thrive.

At the start of the twentieth century, visions for the Jewish future abounded, ranging from total assimilation to total withdrawal from non-Jewish society. There was no particular reason to imagine that Zionism would necessarily be any more successful than the rest, given the small Jewish population in Ottoman and then British mandate Palestine. The various political Jewish movements contended with each other openly and often bitterly.

THE BIRTH OF ISRAEL AND THE VICTORY OF ZIONISM

Even if, in the immediate post-war period, support for Zionism was greatly boosted in the wake of the Holocaust, there was still no Jewish consensus at the time the state of Israel was declared in 1948. The small but highly motivated *Yishuv* (the pre-1948 Jewish community) in mandate Palestine secured Jewish sovereignty in the face of not only widespread global Jewish resistance to the Zionist project, but also bitter divisions within the Zionist camp itself. These divisions within Zionism engendered subsequent divisions in the post-1948 state of Israel. The Labour-Revisionist divide, exacerbated by Revisionist resentment at Labour hegemony throughout the emerging Israeli society, was the source of angry debates and struggles. The immigration of large numbers of *Mizrachi* Jews to Israel in the 1950s eventually produced a substantial political camp that was resentful at the patronising and sometimes racist attitudes of Ashkenazi elites. The 1977 electoral 'revolution', which resulted in a Likud-led government assuming power for the first time, was a reflection of Israel's inability to maintain a consensus in the face of growing diversity. Religious-secular tensions have also come to dominate Israeli political life, with fundamental conflicts over religious status remaining unresolved. Then, of course, there are differences over the settlements and the peace process, the most pressing issue in recent Israeli politics. To add to all this intra-Jewish disagreement, non-Jewish minorities in Israel often fundamentally dissent from the entire project of Jewish statehood.

Israel is, therefore, a country in which profound disagreements exist over nearly every aspect of society and within which different communities live utterly distinct lives in close proximity. Divisions in Israeli society are more or less contained within a robust democratic framework. At times, violence has threatened to engulf Israeli society, but, as with the resistance by some settlers to the 2005 pullout from Gaza, isolated acts of conflict have not yet resulted in a wider conflagration.

The heterogeneity of Israeli approaches to the future of Israel stands in contrast to the status of Israel within Diaspora communities. In the post-1948 period, particularly since 1967, Zionism and Israel have become a source of consensus – perhaps *the* source of consensus – within most Diaspora Jewish communities. Faced with the actual existence of Israel, the question of whether there should be a Jewish state in principle was superseded by very practical questions as to how to respond to this new reality. With the influx of *Mizrachi* and other Jews and multiple threats to the new state's existence, the question of the legitimacy or otherwise of Zionism changed to a question of how to defend a vulnerable and growing Jewish population in its ancestral homeland. Zionism lost many of its ideological competitors; Bundism, the socialist movement that campaigned for Jewish autonomy and self-expression within the Diaspora, was decimated in the Holocaust and rendered all but irrelevant by the uncongenial atmosphere for Jewish autonomy in Eastern Europe. Communism rapidly lost appeal amongst the increasingly upwardly mobile western Jews, amid incontrovertible evidence of post-1948 Soviet anti-Semitism. Genteel, liberal assimilationism was also superseded in the UK and elsewhere by the emergence of a new generation of leaders who did not believe in quietism.

For the first few decades of its existence, Zionism placed a very heavy focus on *aliyah* (immigration to Israel), but it became clear very rapidly that the increasingly comfortable western Jewish populations were not going to disappear any time soon. If Diaspora Jews were not all going to actually live in Israel, many Zionists felt that the very least they could do was to support it unconditionally. Israel increasingly came to take on a leadership position within world Jewry, for example assuming the mantle of defenders of those who died in the Holocaust with the founding of the *Yad Vashem* Holocaust memorial in 1953 and the trial and execution of Adolf Eichmann in 1961-62. Jews came to look towards Israel as a source of pride and Jewish hopes. Often, this may have been a kind of vicarious support – admiration for the brave pioneers without actually wanting to join them – but it was strongly felt nonetheless.

The Israeli victory in the Six Day War of 1967 solidified Israel's centrality to the Jewish world. The intensely felt fears for Israel's survival that preceded the war and the unexpectedly rapid and overwhelming nature of the Israeli victory evoked intense feelings. A whole generation of Diaspora Jewish leaders can date their involvement in Jewish communal life to 1967.[4] Even if the 1973 Yom Kippur War may have dented dreams of Israel's newfound invulnerability, Israel in the post-67 period came to be seen as the guarantor of a bright and sovereign Jewish future.

Amidst the intensity of emotions that the events of 1967 evoked, anti--Zionism was pushed to the margins of the community: to sections of the Haredi community and the secular left. Support for and loyalty to Israel became a taken-for-granted feature of almost all Jewish communal ins-titutions. The argument that Jews should not undermine Israel through public criticism became mainstream. The institutional infrastructure of western Jewish communities was transformed to reflect the centrality of Israel. Raising money for Israel, through organisations such as the Jewish National Fund – whose blue box was a fixture in countless Jewish houses – and a plethora of 'Friends' of Israeli institutions, universities and hospi-tals, became a major communal priority. Israel came to provide a major focus for Jewish education and for efforts to strengthen Jewish identity. In the UK, in particular, Zionist youth movements and Israel tours became a major part of the lives of Jewish young people. Support for Israel also be-came a Jewish political priority, with the growing strength and importance of lobbying groups, such as the American Israel Public Affairs Committee (AIPAC, founded in 1963, but expanded rapidly in the 1970s) and the de-fence of Israel taking a central role in UK umbrella institutions, such as the

Board of Deputies of British Jews. The public campaigns for Soviet Jewry and against far-right anti-Semitism, which emerged in the 1970s, reflected the importance of Israel in bolstering communal self-confidence.

It would be wrong, though, to argue that, post-1967, all Diaspora communities were always entirely united behind Israel. The different ideologies of the Zionist youth movements and the continued existence of Diaspora branches of Israeli political parties did provide some diversity, even if such organisations were principally focused on supporting a particular faction in Israel, rather than public campaigning in the Diaspora. In the 1980s, with the invasion of Lebanon, the further growth of the settlements and the outbreak of the first intifada, the liberal-left began showing increasing signs of concern about the direction Israel was taking. The foundation of the US branch of Peace Now in 1981 and the UK branch in 1987 signalled the existence of dissenting Zionist voices. In the 1980s, UK Chief Rabbi Jakobovits's outspoken criticism of the settlements may not have eroded the fundamentally supportive position of Anglo-Jewry with regard to Israel, but it did, to an extent, legitimise Diaspora Zionist criticism of Israel.

The consensus that the Jewish community should publicly support Israel remained strong despite the emergence of these signs of disquiet. One sign of the strength of this consensus was the reaction to the Oslo process in the mid-1990s, in which Israel would give back land in the West Bank and Gaza for the eventual establishment of a Palestinian state. While much of religious Zionism in Israel and elsewhere was opposed to the 'land for peace' formula, often passionately so, there was little public campaigning against Oslo amongst UK orthodoxy, although there was more in the US. The principle that Israel should be supported extended from left to right. In the 1990s, as the 'land for peace' and the 'two state solution' became mainstream in Israel, the nature of the pro-Israel consensus changed. The newly optimistic outlook for Israel's security coincided with the globalisation and liberalism of the Israeli economy. From being a pioneer society under constant threat of war, 1990s Israel seemed to be developing into a confident western democracy on the brink of peace with its neighbours and the Palestinians.

At the same time, though, there were also signs in the 1990s that all might not be well. The assassination of Yitzhak Rabin in 1995 drew attention to the vehemence of the opposition to territorial compromise on the Israeli right. Rabin's death was a warning that divisions over the future of Israel were not only bitterly felt, but also had potentially lethal consequences. In the short term though, the assassination of Rabin helped to solidify opinion, in the Diaspora at least, behind the new two-state consensus. Even though the Netanyahu government of 1996-99 was highly sceptical about the two state solution, the limited withdrawals from the West Bank, which were conducted by the administration, further strengthened the consensus: if a Likud-led government could withdraw from territory, then the idea must be mainstream.

THE BREAKDOWN OF THE ISRAEL CONSENSUS

The gradual collapse of the Israel consensus in the Diaspora post 2000 revealed the cracks that had been papered over during the relative optimism of the 1990s. The second intifada, which lasted from September 2000 to roughly 2005, was interpreted in widely different ways in the Diaspora. For some on the right, renewed Palestinian terror was proof that they were never serious about peace and that concessions would simply be seen as weakness and an encouragement to further violence. For some on the left, the two-state solution was a good idea that had been subverted by Israeli unwillingness to evacuate settlements. For those further left, the two-state solution was flawed, in principle, for accepting Palestinian dispossession within the green line.

But for those in the middle of the Diaspora Jewish political spectrum, the outbreak of the second intifada was intensely traumatic. Particularly in the UK, where most British Jews had visited Israel and knew the country well, the constant suicide bombings, which Israel faced in the first few years of the decade, were excruciating to watch. Israel's previous wars had killed far more people, but deaths were largely confined to the battlefield, usually out of sight of camera crews. In the second intifada, civilian deaths were dramatic, widely covered by the news media and took place amid the vibrant street life so beloved by Diaspora visitors to Israel. The March 27, 2002 bombing of a Passover Seder at the Park Hotel Netanya, in which 30 died, was the deadliest terrorist attack of the intifada; the symbolic importance of attacking a Jewish religious celebration could not have been clearer. The 9/11 and 7/7 attacks also brought the threat of Islamist terror to the wider world, to countries with significant Jewish populations. The insecure atmosphere in Israel was easily shared by an insecure Diaspora.

The trauma of the second intifada was further exacerbated by an upsurge in anti-Semitic incidents in Europe. Figures kept by the Community Security Trust in the UK show pronounced 'spikes' in the number of anti-Semitic incidents during times of particularly intense conflict in Israel-Palestine (for example, 2009 – the year of Operation Cast Lead – showed a 69% increase in anti-Semitic incidents compared to 2008).[5] At the same time, concerns began to be raised at the beginning of the 2000s that a 'new anti-Semitism' was emerging.[6] This new anti-Semitism was exhibited in anti-Israel and anti-Zionist discourse that drew on classic anti-Semitic tropes, singling out Israel for disproportionate criticism and delegitimising the very idea of Jewish self-determination. Impassioned anti-Israel demonstrations at the September 2001 UN World Conference Against Racism in Durban, South Africa, convinced some Jews that this new form of anti-Semitism was on the march and was cloaking itself in anti-racist language. The increased public prominence of pro-Palestinian campaigning in the 2000s raised insecurities and anxieties about anti-Semitism among Jewish supporters of Israel.

But this insecurity and anxiety often went along with concern about and ambivalence towards Israel's actions. The election of an Ariel Sharon-led government in February 2001 played a part in this ambivalence. A controversial and blunt politician who was found indirectly responsible for the massacres in the Sabra and Shatila refugee camps in Lebanon in 1982, Sharon was a difficult figure for many Diaspora Jews to identify with. On top of this, the Israeli response to the second intifada, which included near full-scale war in the occupied territories, inevitably resulted in many civilian Palestinian casualties. It was much easier to identify with Israelis fighting on a battlefield than on the streets of Jenin, facing what was clearly a much less well-armed enemy. The ubiquity of the mass media, bolstered by the increasing importance of the Internet, meant that it was hard to avoid confronting the consequences of Israeli actions. The symbolism of the conflict frequently made Israel look like an overbearing aggressor.

The most important harbingers of division in the Jewish community were the 2006 Lebanon War against Hezbollah and Operation Cast Lead against the Hamas regime in Gaza in 2009. Both conflicts, particularly the Lebanon War, resembled conventional warfare much more closely than the Israeli response to the second intifada. Further, the rocket attacks against northern Israel in 2006 and the Negev in 2009 provided multiple examples of Israeli suffering with which Jews could sympathise and identify. Nonetheless, the heavy civilian casualties in Lebanon and Gaza – once again given ample coverage in the media – and the much less restrained use of force compared with the response to the second intifada were upsetting for many Jews to watch.

By 2009, the optimism that had attended the signing of the Oslo Accords had all but disappeared. There was no two-state solution and no Palestinian state. The success of Hamas in the 2006 Palestinian elections and their subsequent takeover of Gaza put a seemingly uncompromisingly anti-Jewish Islamism on Israel's doorstep. Many supporters of Israel blamed the lack of a peace deal on Palestinian intransigence. Conversely, those who had yearned for the evacuation of the settlements were disappointed by the limited West Bank withdrawals, the expansion of existing settlements and the routing of the separation barrier inside the green line. Increasing numbers of self-defined supporters of Israel felt that Israel was not willing to make the necessary sacrifices for peace.

Whereas the right and left of the spectrum found vindication of their views in this situation, for those Jews in the centre, the situation was much more depressing and bewildering. Given the repeated media images of overwhelming Israeli force directed at lightly armed combatants and unarmed civilians, it would take a highly robust and uncompromising view of the conflict to remain staunchly pro-Israel in these circumstances.

BRITISH JEWS AND ISRAEL IN THE NEW MILLENNIUM

A 2004 study of 'moderately engaged' British Jews by Steven M. Cohen and myself – based on interviews conducted at the height of the second intifada – revealed a common trilogy of opinions: I love Israel, I am concerned with some of its actions, I am also suspicious of what the media tells me.[7] A 2010 survey by the Institute for Jewish Policy Research (JPR)[8] also revealed considerable complexity in British Jewish attitudes to Israel. On the one hand, British Jews were overwhelmingly connected to and supportive of Israel: 82% believed Israel plays a 'central' or 'important but not central' role in their Jewish identities, 90% believed that Israel is the 'ancestral homeland' of the Jewish people, 95% had visited Israel and 77% believed that Jews have 'a special responsibility to support Israel'. Most British Jews were 'dovishly' inclined: 67% supported giving up territory for peace with the Palestinians, 74% opposed the expansion of settlements in the West Bank and 78% supported a two-state solution to the conflict. At the same time, 72% saw the separation barrier as 'vital for Israel's security' and 72% saw Operation Cast Lead as 'a legitimate act of self-defence' – all of which suggests a dovishness that goes hand in hand with strong support for Israeli actions. British Jews are more divided on other issues: while 55% see Israel as 'an occupying power in the West Bank', 52% agree that Israel has little or no choice in the military action it takes and 59% feel that 'Israel holds *less* responsibility for the recent failure of the peace process than its neighbours'. On the contentious question of Diaspora criticism of Israel, 35% thought that Jews should 'always' feel free to criticise Israel in the media and around a quarter said this was 'never' justified; 53% said that Jews in Britain have the 'right to judge Israel even though they do not live there'. More religious respondents and those with lower levels of educational attainment tended towards hawkishness.

The JPR report presents a picture of a mainstream majority in the Jewish community for whom a broadly dovish vision of Israel's future goes along with cautious support for Israeli actions. The report also demonstrates that there are significant groups to the right and left of this mainstream and that there is little consensus on the question of the legitimacy of public Jewish criticism of Israel.

Surveys of US Jews show a lower level, but still substantial, attachment to Israel, together with a slightly more hawkish stance on Israel's security issues compared to the UK. A 2010 survey[9] showed that 63% felt 'very much' or 'somewhat' connected to Israel and 75% agreed that caring about Israel is an important part of their Jewish identities. 46% favoured dismantling some or all West Bank settlements and 29% supported sharing Jerusalem in some way. Such findings are similar to ones found in surveys over the last twenty five years, suggesting long-term stability.

In the 2000s, a growing vehemence among Jewish minorities to the left and right coincided with a growing anxiety in the centre. This can be seen in the story of three British Jewish solidarity rallies organised during the decade. The 2002 rally was held in Trafalgar Square to show solidarity with Israel during the second intifada under the slogan 'yes to peace, no to terror'; attracting a crowd of around 40,000, it was relatively uncontroversial in the community. The 2006 solidarity rally during the Lebanon conflict was held in the more private and modest confines of the Jewish Free School in Kenton, London, and attracted a concomitantly modest crowd of around 7,000. The 2009 solidarity rally held during Operation Cast Lead took place in Trafalgar Square and attracted a crowd of up to 15,000. The organisation of the latter rally was complicated by the concerns – mostly privately expressed – of some Jewish organisations about the way Israel was conducting the war. An uncomfortable compromise was struck with a telephone donations number being set up to benefit Israeli and Palestinian hospitals, but even then the Liberal Judaism movement declined to take part. The 2009 rally was also accompanied by counter-demonstrations by Independent Jewish Voices (IJV) and Jews for Justice for Palestinians.

As the 2000s progressed, unquestioningly supportive pro-Israel activity had more and more difficulty in encompassing the majority of the community. Just as the post-1967 period saw an institutional realignment in the Jewish community that reflected the pride and hope invested in Israel, so the post-2000 period saw the development of new institutions that reflected the insecurity and worry generated by Israel.

A major concern of the Israeli government and its supporters in the Diaspora was that Israel was failing to make its case effectively. Palestinian sympathy was growing worldwide, particularly on the left, aided by what Israel supporters viewed as a sympathetic media and the efforts of pro-Palestinian campaigning groups. Israel, therefore, needed to pay greater attention to *hasbara* – literally 'explanation' – and set out its case in ways that would match the perceived sophistication of its enemies. *Hasbara* was an activity in which Diaspora Jews could play an important role, both in bolstering support for Israel within the Jewish community and in explaining Israel's case to non-Jews. Central to *hasbara* is combating what is seen as media bias. US and Israel-based organisations such as Honestreporting, CAMERA, NGO Monitor and StandWithUs provide web-based resources that assist Israel's defenders around the world. In the UK, pro-Israel organisations increasingly embraced the *hasbara* agenda. In particular, the Zionist Federation – a coalition of Zionist groups – has run many training events designed to help supporters of Israel supporters make their case more effectively. New organisations have also been set up, such as BICOM, the Britain Israel Communications and Research Centre which was set up in the early 2000s, to provide media briefings and work towards a more supportive public discourse on Israel in the UK. Just Journalism, active between 2008 and 2012, monitored UK media coverage of Israel and CiFWatch, founded in 2009, monitors anti-Israel bias and anti-Semitism in *the Guardian* newspaper.

It is not just Zionist and pro-Israel organisations that advocate for Israel in the UK Jewish community. Other Jewish communal bodies and representative organisations also see themselves as having a responsibility to defend Israel. The constitution of the Board of Deputies of British Jews, the principle Jewish representative body, obliges it to 'take such appropriate action as lies within its power to advance Israel's security, welfare and standing.' How support for Israel should be articulated by cross-communal bodies such as the Board, however, is a source of increasing disagreement. The Board of Deputies has received periodic criticism that it is not vociferous enough in defending Israel; this criticism became stronger following the election of Vivian Wineman, who had been involved in the UK branch of Peace Now UK in the 1980s, as President in 2009. Criticism that central communal bodies were not supportive enough of Israel increased in 2010 and 2011 as a result of the controversy sparked by comments by Mick Davis, chair of United Jewish Israel Appeal (UJIA) and the board of trustees of the Jewish Leadership Council (JLC). At a public meeting with US author Peter Beinart, Davis asserted the right of Diaspora Jews to criticise Israel since

> the government of Israel... have to recognise that their actions directly impact me as a Jew living in London, the UK...When they do good things, it is good for me, when they do bad things, it's bad for me. And the impact on me is as significant as it is on Jews living in Israel.[10]

Davis was explicitly critical of the path Benjamin Netanyahu's government was following. Davis's comments, which he re-affirmed in a speech at the Herzliya conference in Israel in February 2011, attracted heavy criticism. The chairs of the Zionist Federation and the Jewish National Fund in the UK argued that Diaspora Jews should not criticise Israel publicly, while international Jewish figures, such as Abraham Foxman of the US Anti-Defamation League and the Israeli-Australian commentator Isi Liebler, were also strongly critical. At the same time, other figures, including UK religious leaders, such as Rabbi Tony Bayfield, President of the Movement for Reform Judaism, and even the Israeli politician, Tzipi Livni, publicly defended Davis's comments.

The concern caused by Davis's comments was only heightened as a result of a trip to Israel, planned by the JLC in early 2011, which was scheduled to visit Ramallah to consult with Palestinian leaders. The outcry from some quarters was so strong that the Palestinian leg of the trip was cancelled. Partly as a result of this, the Jewish National Fund pulled out of the JLC in February 2011. As Vivian Wineman was the Chair of the JLC's Council in addition to the Board, the controversy also spilled over to the latter organisation, with a proposal to call for a two-state solution voted down by the Deputies in January 2011.

At the same time, organisations, such as the Board of Deputies and JLC, have also faced criticism for being *too* supportive of Israel and not reflecting the diversity of views within the Jewish community. This criticism has been voiced particularly strongly by Jews for Justice for Palestinians and Independent Jewish Voices (IJV), organisations set up in the 2000s to provide a space for Jews critical of Israel (and, at times, of Zionism, too). IJV was founded to send a clear message that Jewish representative bodies did not represent the section of Jewish opinion that was critical of Israel. As their founding declaration said in February 2007:[11]

> We come together in the belief that the broad spectrum of opinion among the Jewish population of this country is not reflected by those institutions which claim authority to represent the Jewish community as a whole. We further believe that individuals and groups within all communities should feel free to express their views on any issue of public concern without incurring accusations of disloyalty.

IJV was subject to bitter denunciation from the mainstream community, including from some left Zionists. Part of the anger directed at them stemmed from the perception that their signatories were secular Jews, marginal to the community, standing on the sidelines and attacking it. Yet if the picture of a mainstream community opposed by a secular leftist fringe was ever accurate, by the late 2000s it was certainly not. The right of Diaspora Jews to criticise Israel publicly was increasingly asserted by Zionists embedded in Jewish communal activity. In the US, the self-defined 'pro-Israel, pro-peace' organisation J Street was founded in 2008 and grew rapidly into a well-resourced lobby group with strong grassroots support. In 2011, a UK-based pro-Israel, pro-peace group, Yachad, was launched, with the intention of creating a grassroots movement in favour of a two-state solution.

Particularly since Operation Cast Lead in 2009, there have been moves within some central Jewish organisations to open a space for measured criticism of Israel. Mick Davis's words in 2010 did not emerge in a vacuum. UJIA had for some years acknowledged the need for the development of safe spaces within which Jews, particularly young Jews, could talk through their concerns regarding Israel. The New Israel Fund, which raises money for progressive causes in Israel, has organised events for young people to speak freely about Israel. Then there was the increasingly significant emergence of organisations and projects predicated on pluralism. The pluralist conference and educational charity Limmud has become hugely influential in developing new generations of leaders for the Jewish community and Limmud conferences feature speakers who espouse a wide range of views on Israel.

There is no doubt then that the British Jewish community has become more diverse in its views on Israel and that there is an increasing willingness to articulate these views publicly. That is not to say, however, that the Jewish community has necessarily become more ideologically pluralist, as, despite the diversity, there are still substantial sections of the community that argue against public criticism of Israel. The growing diversity of views over Israel is increasingly a source of turmoil in the Jewish community – a struggle over what the Jewish community and Jewishness itself should be. The next chapter looks at the consequences of the increasing diversity of views on Israel in the Jewish community. As we shall see, fragmentation has deepened as Jews have taken up a variety of often-antagonistic positions.

NOTES

2 - See for example: Freedman, S. (2000). Jew vs. Jew: The Struggle for the Soul of American Jewry. New York, NY: Touchstone

3 - Kahn-Harris, K., & Gidley, B. (2010). Turbulent Times: The British Jewish Community Today. London, UK: Continuum, pp. 16-17.

4 - For the UK example, see: Kahn-Harris, K., & Gidley, B. (2010). Turbulent times: The British Jewish Community Today. London, UK: Continuum, pp. 35-36.

5 - Community Security Trust. (2010). Antisemitic Incidents Report 2009 Retrieved from: http://www.humansecuritygateway.com/documents/CST_ AntisemiticIncidentsReport2009.pdf

6 - See for example: Iganski, P., & Kosmin, B. (2003). The New Antisemitism? Debating Judeophobia in 21st-Century Britain. London, UK: Profile.

7 - Cohen, S. M., & Kahn-Harris, K. (2004). Beyond belonging: The Jewish identities of moderately engaged British Jews. London, UK: UJIA/Profile.

8 - Graham, D., & Boyd, J. (2010, July). Committed, concerned and conciliatory: The attitudes of Jews in Britain towards Israel. London, UK: Institute for Jewish Policy Research.

9 - Sasson, T., Phillips, B., Kadushin, C., Saxe, L. (2010 August) Still Connected: American Jewish Attitudes about Israel. Waltham, MA: Maurice and Marilyn Cohen Center for Modern Jewish Studies, Brandeis University

10 - Rocker, S. (2010, November 18). Shock Over Senior UK Jewish Leader's Bibi Criticism. The Jewish Chronicle, p. 18.

11 - Independent Jewish Voices. (n.d.). Declaration. Retrieved May 29, 2013 from: http://ijv.org.uk/declaration/

CHAPTER TWO:
DIVISION

The Jewish communal landscape that has emerged post-2000 is a diverse and complicated one. In this chapter, I outline the main features of this new communal landscape by identifying the main positions taken on Israel within the British Jewish community.[12] The positions are not rigidly fixed – individuals move between them and organisations often contain proponents of a number of them. These positions can also be found in the US and in other Diaspora communities, although their relative popularity and strength vary from country to country.

To summarise, I will identify and discuss the following positions:

- Public Supporters

- Pro-Israel Pluralists

- The Pro-Israel, Pro-Peace Left

- Jewish Radicals

- The Anti-Zionist Left

- The Decent Left

- The Neo-Conservative Right

- The Jewish Religious Right

- The Haredi Community

- Authoritarian Zionists

- Private Engagers

- Zionist Youth Movements

- The Apathetic

- Non-Jewish supporters

PUBLIC SUPPORTERS

Public supporters are the inheritors of the post-1967 tradition of unquestioning Diaspora support for Israel. For public supporters, Israel should always be defended publicly and never publicly criticised. Jews should act as ambassadors for Israel.[13] Public supporters often argue that, if Jews do not live in Israel, they do not have the right to intervene in its politics, particularly over security issues. Further, the wider public discourse is so hostile to Israel, they believe, that to criticise Israel publicly is to give ammunition to Israel's enemies.

The public supporter position was, until relatively recently, the position of the vast majority of Jewish community institutions and, probably, the majority of British Jews. While it retains substantial backing, it is no longer uncontested. Consequentially, those institutions and individuals who hold to the public supporter position are showing signs of retrenchment and even anger, particularly at the pro-Israel pluralist position we will discuss next. The sight of former public supporters criticising Israel publicly is difficult for many public supporters to watch.

In the UK, the Jewish National Fund (JNF) and the Zionist Federation (ZF) have come to be the principal exponents of the public supporter position. The JNF's withdrawal from the Jewish Leadership Council (JLC) in March 2011 and its refusal to join the coalition of organisations that set up the UK Task Force on Issues Facing Arab Citizens of Israel in 2010 stemmed from disapproval of the space being opened up by such organisations for a more critical engagement with Israel. The position of the ZF is paradoxical in that it is an umbrella body with affiliated organisations representing a range of opinions on Israel. It has, at times, allowed space for more critical positions on Israel and, ultimately, joined the UK Task Force. However, in recent years the organisation has placed a major emphasis on advocating for Israel and *hasbara* training in order to give its activists the tools to defend the line of the Israeli government publicly. Further, most of its lay and professional spokesmen have been vociferous in their advocacy of the public supporter position. In February 2013, the Zionist Federation's vote against the application of the 'pro-Israel, pro-peace' organisation Yachad (whose views are discussed later in this chapter), offered evidence of the organisation's increasing inability to reconcile its public supporter tendencies with its ostensible Zionist pluralism.[14]

The argument was not that Yachad was not Zionist, but rather that they were not vociferous enough in defending Israel publicly, which for public supporters is an essential component of Diaspora Zionism.

The public supporter position is so focused on support for whichever Israeli government is in power that, given the growing strength of the Israeli right, it is inevitable that the position is often viewed as right-wing. But there is no reason to think that, should Israel, for example, elect a government that evacuated all or most of the settlements, most public supporters would not support it. The voting down of a Board of Deputies motion in January 2011 to support a two-state solution formally – an action instigated by prominent public supporters – is an example of how public supporters may appear right-wing, but their major motivation is, in fact, to resist any public calls for Israel to do anything. While public supporters often appear right-wing in the moment, their true political inclinations are often obscure. The overwhelming commitment of public supporters is to the survival and safety of the Jewish state. This commitment is allied with a fear that Israel's survival and safety is gravely threatened at the moment and that this threat is tied into a growing threat of anti-Semitism. The role of the Diaspora, then, is to assist in the process of defending Israel by defending the political choices of its people. Political choices are 'outsourced' to the Israeli political system so that what appears to be the political activity of Diaspora public supporters is, in fact, a kind of anti-politics.

Some public supporters do concede that certain kinds of Diaspora public criticism of Israel are, in principle, legitimate. While criticism of Israel's security choices and military actions is unacceptable, criticisms of other aspects of Israeli society may be allowable.[15] Publicly expressed opposition to orthodox control of conversion and marriage is rarely met with the accusation that it undermines Israel's security.

There are tensions within the public supporter position as to the best ways to demonstrate support for Israel. Traditionally, fundraising for Israeli causes, exemplified by the JNF's 'blue box', was the standard way of supporting Israel. Israeli charities still have substantial fundraising arms in the Diaspora, including 'Friends Of' many Israeli institutions. However, this kind of support, while tangible, is 'quiet' and occurs mostly in private – here, public support is expressed simply through a lack of public criticism. Given the perceived need to be seen to defend Israel, public supporters have become much more proactive in recent years. This can be done positively, through such activities as circulating 'good news' stories about Israel (such as Israeli assistance after the 2010 Haiti earthquake). For others, though, public support for Israel requires an aggressive effort to challenge media bias and anti-Israel criticism through organisations such as StandWithUs.

A hardcore of UK public supporters are extremely vigorous in attending hostile public meetings and mounting counter-demonstrations, entering Internet comment threads and publicly challenging pro-Palestinian activists and refuting their claims. There have, at times, been concerns that their vociferousness may be counter-productive, alienating potential supporters; a claim robustly that they robustly counter.[16] Increasingly, public supporters have become frustrated with what they see as Jewish establishment inaction and politeness.[17] They have begun to work through organisations, such as the British Israel Public Affairs Committee and Campaign for Truth, to offer the robust defence of Israel that they seek.

It is possible then that the more quietist, establishment versions of the public supporter position may split off from its more grassroots and activist forms. It is also possible that the latter, in particular, will drift towards a much closer embrace of right-wing politics. Given that the most prominent non-Jewish supporters of Israel are often on the right, particularly among Christian supporters of Israel, it is probably inevitable that the public supporter position may drift from being anti-political towards a more open form of right-wing politics. If Israel continues to have right-wing governments in the indefinite future, the public supporters position may 'forget' that it has supported more dovish governments in the past.

This more political form of the public supporter position is, probably, the only one that is viable in the long-term. One of the effects of new technology and the Internet has been to erode any clear distinction between public and private space. The public nature of social media, in particular, means that it is more and more difficult to find a truly private space in which to express criticism of Israel. It is difficult to be supportive in public and critical in private, as used to be possible, now that the private sphere has been so eroded. For this reason, it is more likely that, in the future, the vast majority of public supporters will be genuinely supportive of Israel's actions – in private and in public – and that the once privately ambivalent will continue to desert this position.

PRO-ISRAEL PLURALISTS

If public supporters represented and, to some extent, still represent the traditional post-1967 mainstream of the Jewish community, pro-Israel pluralists are rapidly becoming the contemporary mainstream. The pro-Israel pluralist position does not differ from the public supporter position to the extent that both are motivated by an unabashed Zionism and commitment to the future of Israel. Indeed, the political views of people who hold to both positions may be identical. The difference lies in a willingness to tolerate the public expression of views that may be critical of Israel and to share one's own private concerns publicly.

The pro-Israel pluralist position has emerged in the last couple of decades in part out of a pragmatic recognition that there are considerable numbers of Diaspora Jews who, while they love and support Israel, are concerned by some of Israel's actions. These often young, liberal Jews have grown up taking the existence of Israel for granted within a multicultural British society where it is no longer expected that members of minority communities will keep their opinions to themselves. Further, since the 1990s, some Israeli leaders have argued that, given Israel's growing maturity and wealth, unconditional support and fundraising is no longer necessary or appropriate. For example, the 1997 document *Brit Am*, produced by Avraham Burg while he was chairman of the Jewish Agency, argued for a 'new Zionism' built on a mutually sustaining partnership between Israel and Diaspora communities.[18]

The pro-Israel pluralist position is, therefore, based on a sense that to discourage discussion of Israel within Diaspora Jewish communities would be anachronistic, ineffective and potentially harmful to the future of those communities. The growth and success of Limmud in nurturing a dynamic new generation of leaders within a pluralist environment demonstrates that, for many Jewish young people, diversity (on Israel and other issues) is a source of vitality and not a threat. Leaders within organisations such as UJIA and the JLC, such as Mick Davis (discussed in the previous chapter), are concerned that the public supporter position is no longer tenable given this new reality.

Although pro-Israel pluralists may sometimes be accused of undermining support for Israel, it is important to recognise that the pluralism they seek is of a limited kind. There is no suggestion that the centrality of Israel in Diaspora Jewish communities, institutions and education should be challenged, nor is there a suggestion that Zionism and the existence of the Jewish state are negotiable. Advocating Boycotts, Divestment and Sanctions (BDS) against Israel is also strictly taboo.

To some extent, the pro-Israel pluralist position seeks to widen the boundaries of Jewish communal discussion of Israel in order to make those boundaries clearer and to police them more effectively. The Tel Aviv-based Reut Institute's widely influential 2010 report *Building a Political Firewall against the Assault on Israel's Legitimacy: London as a Case Study* exemplifies this approach. The report contended that Israel was facing an unprecedented global assault on its legitimacy as a Jewish, democratic state. Faced with this, the Jewish community needs to create a broader coalition against 'delegitimization', including liberals critical of Israeli policies. Critical liberals need to be engaged to prevent them from falling into the arms of the 'delegitimizers':

> Jewish support for Israel has been taken for granted for many years. The prominent roles Jews play in organizations bitterly critical of, or even delegitimizing, Israel have changed this assumption. Many of them have been alienated by Jewish institutions and communities that expected them to sign a blank check of support for Israel, thus, pushing them into the welcoming arms of the delegitimizers. Furthermore, in many communities, Israel has become such a polarizing issue that Jewish communal leadership and Rabbis often refrain from bringing it up. These approaches need to be changed, liberal Jews must be substantively engaged, and their liberal values should not be framed as anti-Israel, even if critical of its policies. (p. 91)

At the same time, while liberal critics need to be engaged, 'delegitimizers' need to be vigorously marginalised:

...delegitimizers operate uninterrupted and their initiatives are often practically unopposed. A central objective is to change this situation by forcing them to 'play defense.' This means systematically exposing information about delegitimizers, their activities, and the organizations that they operate out of. The goal is to eventually frame them, depending on their agendas, as anti-peace, anti-Semitic, dishonest purveyors of double standards. (p. 92)

Pro-Israel pluralism is both implacable in its opposition to 'delegitimization' and relatively flexible in offering a supportive space for difficult Jewish community discussions about Israel. The balance between these two commitments is fragile as one can easily undermine the other. The 2011 'We Believe in Israel' conference in London, which was designed to create a 'big tent' encompassing the whole pro-Israel community, demonstrated the difficulties involved. Some speakers tried to encourage delegates to defend Israel unambiguously, others offered guarded critiques of Israeli policies, while still others tried to encourage a conversation in which ambivalence about Israel could be shared. The kind of 'big tent' events that pro-Israel pluralists have encouraged may, at times, seem little different to old-style public supporter events. The Closer to Israel parade held on 2 June 2013 in central London managed to include more critical Zionist groups, such as Yachad (see below), but the unambiguous celebration of Israel, together with the prominent role that the Israeli ambassador played in it, meant that, from the outside, it may well have looked like a display of support for Israel 'right or wrong'.

The pro-Israel pluralist position is, in some ways, as shy of 'politics' as public supporters are. While some figures, such as Mick Davis, have explicitly criticised the Israeli government, the main policy goal of pro-Israel pluralism is to open up spaces in the Jewish community within which Jewish supporters of Israel can share their concerns about certain aspects of Israel. The need for 'safe' spaces was recognised in the UK in 2004 by the UJIA-sponsored report *Beyond Belonging*. In the US, San Francisco Bay Area's Jewish Community Relations Council's 'Project Reconnections' was initiated in the mid-2000s and aimed to create:

...a forum for the Jewish community to build bridges of connection, deepen trust and understanding, and to have civil discourse on Israel and emerging controversial issues.[19]

The pro-Israel pluralist position has even reached the heart of the Israeli Zionist establishment. The Jewish Agency's Makom project,[20] in partnership with North American Jewish Communities, seeks to encourage a Diaspora 'engagement' with Israel consisting of 'hugging and wrestling' – a love that acknowledges ambivalence. It is this underlying love that, for pro-Israel pluralists, legitimates measured criticism of Israel.

The backing, by prominent Jewish leaders, of the pro-Israel pluralism position means that, for all its encouragement of pluralistic conversation, it may be closely identified with 'top-down' policy-making by a small elite. It certainly seems as though Jewish leaders are some of the most enthusiastic advocates of this position. For example, a European survey of Jewish leaders found that 85% agreed that 'Jewish communities should provide opportunities for members to share different opinions and points of view on Israel and its policies'.[21]

THE PRO-ISRAEL, PRO-PEACE LEFT

The 'pro-Israel, pro-peace left' combines open criticism of Israeli policy on the occupied territories with strong proclamations of love for Israel and Zionism. The launch of the US lobbying group J Street in 2009 consolidated and publicised this emerging Diaspora Zionist liberal-left position. This position draws on a long history of left-wing Israeli Zionism, committed to both a Jewish and a democratic state, particularly the Zionism of Peace Now. The central issue defining this position is the necessity of a two-state solution based on withdrawal from post-1967 settlements. The concern is that, without a two-state solution, Israel will, essentially, have to choose between a Jewish state that would not be democratic and a democratic state that would not be a Jewish state. Although the two-state solution is now so mainstream that it has come to be supported even by Benjamin Netanyahu,[22] there are huge differences between visions of what a Palestinian state could look like and on what territory it could be built. For the pro-Israel, pro-peace position, only a contiguous Palestinian territory could work as a state and this would involve substantial settlement evacuation. Given that even now, over

40 years since the Six Day War, the settlements are still growing, the pro-Israel, pro-peace left is concerned that, if there is no withdrawal soon, a viable two-state solution will become impossible. Thus, there is a considerable urgency to the pro-Israel, pro-peace position.

This urgency helps to explain why the pro-Israel, pro-peace position is beginning to engage Jewish communal leaders who have never, until now, criticised Israel publicly. In the UK, one landmark move in this direction occurred with the publication of a letter to the *Observer* newspaper on 11 January 2009, during Operation Cast Lead.[23] The letter, addressed to 'the government of Israel', was signed by a number of prominent liberal, but mainstream Jewish community figures, including Baroness Rabbi Julia Neuberger, Rabbi Tony Bayfield (then head of the Movement for Reform Judaism), Danny Rich (chief executive of Liberal Judaism) and the historian David Cesarani. The signatories described themselves as 'profound and passionate supporters of Israel', who 'look upon the increasing loss of life on both sides of the Gaza conflict with horror.' While 'Israel had a right to respond and we support the Israeli government's decision to make stopping the rocket attacks an urgent priority... we believe that only negotiations can secure long-term security for Israel and the region.' They were, therefore, concerned 'that rather than bringing security to Israel, a continued military offensive could strengthen extremists, destabilise the region and exacerbate tensions inside Israel with its one million Arab citizens.' Accordingly, the letter stated:

> We stand alongside the people of Israel and urge the government of Israel and the Palestinian people, with the assistance of the international community, to negotiate:
>
> • An immediate and permanent ceasefire entailing an end to all rocket attacks and the complete and permanent lifting of the blockade of Gaza.
>
> • International monitoring of the ceasefire agreement, including measures to ensure the security of the borders between Israel and Gaza as well as the prevention of weapons smuggling into Gaza.

While the letter's recommendations were far from radical, it, nonetheless, represented a significant public statement from those who saw themselves as supporters of Israel. The letter was the result of and a stimulus to numerous private conversations among Jewish activists as to how to best express their concern about the direction Israel was taking.

Amid this atmosphere of concern, persistent rumours began to circulate in 2009 that a UK version of J Street was being developed. It took until April 2011 for the organisation, Yachad, to be fully launched. Under the broad statement 'Yachad is pro-Israel, pro-peace', the new organisation declared:[24]

- Israel's best hope for safety and security lies in a comprehensive peace with its neighbours. That means a two-state solution: Israel and Palestine.

- Time is running out and the two-state solution is in peril

- Now is the moment for diaspora Jews to play their part and do all they can in the search for peace.

While Yachad's principles are very close to J Street's, there is a crucial difference between the two organisations. Whereas J Street combines the building of a mass movement with political lobbying — competing with other pro-Israel lobbying groups, such as AIPAC — Yachad sees itself as a 'grassroots' organisation. In its short life, the organisation has concentrated on holding education sessions and tours of the West Bank. If Yachad is politically engaged, it is principally engaged in the politics of the UK Jewish community, for example, organising a public meeting with Board of Deputies President Vivian Wineman to discuss the 2011 vote to reject a call for a two-state solution.

Above all, Yachad is keen to emphasise its love of Israel, as it states in its 'statement of core principles':

We are Jews who love Israel, who stand with Israel, whose lives are bound up with Israel. We believe in its right not just to exist, but to flourish. We stand against those who defame it.

This emphasis on love of Israel derives in part from an insistence that the pro-Israel, pro-peace position should be viewed as part of the mainstream Jewish community. Many of its leading individuals have backgrounds in

Zionist youth movements and the director, Hannah Weisfeld, is a former education director for Habonim Dror. In some respects, Yachad may provide a kind of continuation of the work of the more progressive Zionist youth movements for an older, but still youthful, age group. Whether or not the pro-Israel, pro-peace position is, in fact, one that is held more strongly among younger Jews, it is often understood as such. The validity of Peter Beinart's oft-quoted argument in his *New York Review of Books* article from May 2010,[25] which suggested that the American Jewish community was 'losing' its young people through its uncritical support for Israel, has been strongly debated,[26] but it has helped to tie in the question of support for Israel with the question of youth. It is possible then that Yahad may exclude older generations of activists and those who, while they share the group's ultimate vision, wish for a more direct form of political engagement with Israel.

The pro-Israel, pro-peace position and the pro-Israel pluralist position are often elided as both of them place a heavy emphasis on opening up a more open discussion about Israel within Diaspora Jewish communities. Yet the pluralism that the pro-Israel, pro-peace position envisages is more thoroughgoing. For example, the J Street conference has given a platform to those who are further to its left, including groups that support BDS, such as Jewish Voice for Peace (while J Street itself does not support BDS).[27]

JEWISH RADICALS

The Jewish radical position shares with the pro-Israel, pro-peace position a commitment to opposing the occupation. However, while the pro--Israel, pro-peace left is concerned to demonstrate its Zionist, pro-Israel credentials, Jewish radicals do not feel bound in the same way. This is not because the Jewish radical position is necessarily anti-Zionist, although some who cleave to this position certainly are. Rather, opposing the occupation is such an urgent priority that the niceties of reassuring other Jews of one's devotion to Israel are deemed less relevant. This approach characterised the formation of Independent Jewish Voices (IJV) in February 2007. Whereas Yachad has taken great pains to formulate its position in terms that self-defined lovers of Israel might recognise, IJV emphasised its distance from mainstream Jewish communal organisations. To the extent that Yachad's desire to reassure has required them to soft-pedal politics, IJV's 'liberated' approach has greater political and campaigning possibilities. At the same time, this approach also alienates a considerable proportion of mainstream Jewish opinion.

The Jewish radical position also involves a much broader critique of Israel than the pro-Israel, pro-peace left. Particularly during the Netanyahu administration, Jewish radicals have warned that Israel is moving in a totalitarian and racist direction, both in the territories and in Israel proper, for example, with proposals for 'loyalty oaths' for Israel's Palestinian citizens gaining serious high-level political support.

The ideological positions motivating Jewish radicals vary considerably. The position encompasses those who define themselves as Zionists, post-Zionists, anti-Zionists and – probably the majority – those for whom such questions are less relevant than the imperative to resist Israel's current trajectory. One of the key differences in the Diaspora between Jewish radicals and the out-and-out anti-Zionist left (discussed below) is the connections the former have with Israelis. Indeed, it is frequently the Israeli left that provides the inspiration for Jewish radicals, through organisations such as Physicians for Human Rights, Machsom Watch and Women in Black. Another area of division between the Jewish radicals and Jewish anti-Zionists is over the question of BDS, calls for which have become a mainstream part of pro-Palestinian activism. Jewish radicals may reject cultural and academic boycotts, but embrace boycotts of settlement products and selective divestment from Israeli companies. The latter is the official position of both Jewish Voice for Peace in the US and Jews for Justice for Palestinians in the UK. While supporters of Israel may not distinguish between partial and total BDS, the failure to embrace total BDS is one factor that pushes Jewish radicals closer to the Israeli left rather than the pro-Palestinian movement.

Another reason why Jewish radicals are ambivalent about BDS is that, for all their marginality, they want to hold on to the possibility of influencing other Jews who might be frightened by BDS. As David Landy argues in his study of Jewish opposition to Israel in the UK:

> ...those who reject boycott think it important to contest *collective* Jewishness and prioritise the Jewish community in the field of activism. A Jewish community that does

not support Israel is seen as an important element in the fight for Palestinian liberation. Many of the anti-boycott people were somewhat dismissive of 'non-Jewish Jews' disconnected from and not interested in the community, not because they were worse people, but because they were not deemed to be as effective in the struggle for Palestinian rights.[28]

So while Jewish radicals have often been shunned by the pro-Israel Jewish community, they still frame their activism in Jewish terms. They are not simply the Jewish branch of the pro-Palestinian movement as the anti-Zionist Jewish left sometimes is.

The organisations Jews for Justice for Palestinians and IJV often uphold a Jewish radical position, but Jews for Justice for Palestinians, in particular, is split between Jewish radicals who support, at most, a boycott of set-tlement products and fully-fledged pro-BDS anti-Zionism.[29] The Jewish radical position is, therefore, often viewed with deep mistrust from the centre and right of the community as being simply a staging post on the way to outright anti-Zionism. Further, the lack of desire to reassure the community, in the way that Yachad has sought to do, has meant that Jewish radicalism has drawn disproportionate support from the margins of the community (although perhaps not to the extent its detractors of-ten claim). It is possible, though, that if Israel continues in a right-wing political direction and if the pro-Israel, pro-peace left in this country con-tinues to downplay political engagement, the Jewish radical position will continue to grow. The future of the Jewish radical position depends, in part, on who defines pluralism in the community. If the pro-Israel plura-list position dominates, Jewish radicals are likely to remain outside the 'big tent'. However, if the pro-Israel, pro-peace position dominates, it is likely that room could be made for at least some Jewish radicals.

THE ANTI-ZIONIST LEFT

It is unlikely that room will be made for anti-Zionist Jews within the mainstream Jewish community in the foreseeable future. While there is a long tradition of Jewish anti-Zionism, in the post-1967 period Jewish anti-Zionism came to be largely confined to sections of the secular left and the

Haredi community. While the secular Jewish left has never been entirely anti-Zionist, nor is it today, anti-Zionism has helped to entrench the marginality of some secular leftists from much of the Jewish community. Post-1967, anti-Zionism has become taboo in the mainstream community and, even within other sections of the Jewish left, it is strongly contested.

Anti-Zionism is often understood in the Jewish community as a form of anti-Semitism in that it denies the Jewish people the sovereignty granted to other peoples. The 2005 definition of anti-Semitism by the European Union Monitoring Centre on Racism and Xenophobia (EUMC), designed to be a tool for classifying hate crime incidents, includes the following as a possible manifestation of anti-Semitism: 'Denying the Jewish people the right to self-determination, e.g. by claiming that the existence of a state of Israel is a racist endeavour.' While the EUMC definition was only designed to facilitate the classification of hate crimes in EU countries, it has been taken by some campaigners to be a definition of anti-Semitism in all cases: one that equates anti-Zionism with anti-Semitism in all circumstances.

Questions of anti-Zionism are, therefore, closely related to questions of anti-Semitism. Even those who would not go so far as to say that anti-Zionism is equivalent in all cases to anti-Semitism are quick to point out anti-Semitic themes in anti-Zionist discourse, as Anthony Julius does in his *Trials of the Diaspora: A History of Anti-Semitism in England*.[30] Anti-Zionist Jews are frequently accused of providing an alibi against accusations of anti-Semitism within the pro-Palestinian movement. The anti-Zionist position (and often the Jewish radical position, too) is generally accompanied by a refusal to equate criticism of Israel and Zionism with anti-Semitism. Jews are often at the forefront of the pro-Palestinian movement's attempts to deny anti-Semitism, as, for example, the successful vote in May 2011 by the University and College Union to repudiate the EUMC definition in discussions of anti-Semitism and Israel. There have been, though, some attempts to combine an anti-Zionist position with a recognition of anti-Semitism. For example, the slogan of the website New Jewish Resistance[31] is 'Fighting Zionism and Anti-Semitism, defending Pan-Semitic Unity' and the 2007 pamphlet[32] *The Past Didn't Go Anywhere: Making Resistance to Antisemitism Part of all our Movements* demonstrates an equal commitment to opposing anti-Semitism and Israel. Nonetheless, anti-Zionism remains strongly associated with a refusal to confuse criticism of Israel/Zionism with anti-Semitism and Jewish opposition to anti-Zionism is, concomitantly, strongly associated with opposition to anti-Semitism.

But anti-Zionism is not as simple a phenomenon as it is sometimes made out to be. First, it is important to distinguish between what one might call pragmatic anti-Zionism and its more ideological forms. In the former category are those who have come to the conclusion that only by rejecting Zionism and its legacy can peace come to the region. Some of those who advocate a 'one-state solution', in which a Jewish state is abandoned in favour of one that encompasses both Palestinians and Israelis, do so because they feel that a two-state solution is no longer achievable. This group includes some who may, at one stage, have been Zionists. The historian Tony Judt, who died in 2010, was once a left-wing Zionist, but, over time, came to see Zionism as unsustainable and in 2003 came out publicly advocating a bi-national state.[33] It may be that this category of anti-Zionist will grow the longer a two-state solution is unachieved, as those despairing at Israel's current direction come to see a one-state solution as the only possible future. This category also includes those who are sometimes known as 'post-Zionists', who, while they may have some historical sympathy with Zionism, feel it is a movement whose time has passed.

The more ideological category of anti-Zionists consists of those who believe not only that Zionism is invalid today, but that it was never valid in the first place. Historically, the socialist argument against Zionism was, broadly, that it represented a form of particularist chauvinism that subverted the possibility of solidarity among the international proletariat. The UK's Jewish Socialist Group, founded in 1974, was part of this socialist, anti-Zionist movement, finding inspiration from the pre-war non-Zionist, socialist and Bundist movements.

There is a tension within left anti-Zionism between a universalist, anti-nationalist argument – in which nation states are always problematic – and an anti-imperialist argument, in which the nationalism of non-western peoples is supported against 'imperialist' nationalism. As the 'new left' became more prominent in the 1960s, so anti-Zionism increasingly became expressed in anti-imperialist terms. Israel represented a form of western capitalist colonialism that displaced and oppressed indigenous people. In the last couple of decades, as socialism has lost ground as an ideology, pro-Palestinian activism has become a self-contained left-wing cause in its own right, taking inspiration from the successful anti-Apartheid struggle in South Africa. Since 2000, pro-Palestinian activism has become a virtually mainstream cause among leftists, gaining support from activism against the Iraq War and the war on terror. Jewish anti-Zionism has, therefore, been pushed into becoming part of the growing pro-Palestinian movement. This means that Jewish anti-Zionism has a bigger profile than ever before.

The increasing focus on Palestinians within Jewish anti-Zionism is exemplified by the first paragraph of the charter of the International Jewish Anti-Zionist Network (IJAN):

> We are an international network of Jews who are uncompromisingly committed to struggles for human emancipation, of which the liberation of the Palestinian people and land is an indispensable part. Our commitment is to the dismantling of Israeli apartheid, the return of Palestinian refugees, and the ending of the Israeli colonization of historic Palestine.[34]

While IJAN affirms a broader struggle for 'human emancipation' and against racism, the cause of Palestinian liberation takes centre stage in this struggle.

The anti-Zionist left position differs from the Jewish radical position in its largely negative view of the possibilities of Israeli activism and its lack of desire to work within the Jewish community. Whereas Jewish radicals seek out Israeli organisations with whom to work and generally take a cautious approach to BDS, the anti-Zionist left focus their work on supporting pro-Palestinian activists; given that a call for BDS is the mainstream position among most pro-Palestinian groups, they support that call wholeheartedly. While some organisations, such as IJAN and Jews for Boycotting Israeli Goods, fall firmly into the anti-Zionist left camp, other organisations fall within both camps. Some of the ambiguity and tension between the anti-Zionist left and Jewish radicals can be found in the Jews for Justice for Palestinians' slogan: 'Two Peoples, One Future'. On the one hand, the recognition that Israelis/Jews constitute a 'people' as well as do the Palestinians allows for strong connections to be forged with the Israeli left and could also imply a two-state solution.

On the other hand, the 'one future' could also hint at an anti-Zionist one-state solution.

The anti-Zionist left's embrace of the Palestinian movement, the one-state solution and BDS, ensures that the position will be deeply threatening to many within the Jewish community. Given Israel's central place in contemporary Jewish identity and Jewish communal institutions, to reject Israel entirely is to automatically marginalise oneself. The strong sense of persecution and marginality that those within this group feel contributes to a particular kind of Jewish identity. Jewish anti-Zionists often talk of a kind of 'reclaiming' of Jewish identity from Zionism. Mike Marqusee, in his book *If I Am Not for Myself: Journey of an Anti-Zionist Jew*, states:

> I find in anti-Zionism emancipation both as a Jew and as a human being, and any consequent diminution in my Jewishness is strictly in the eye of the beholder.[35]

There are, indeed, considerable resources on which anti-Zionists can draw in reconstructing Jewish identity. Not only is there a long secular anti-Zionist Jewish political tradition, there are also Jewish religious thinkers who have challenged fundamental aspects of political Zionism, such as Martin Buber, Yeshayahu Leibowitz and Daniel Boyarin. More broadly, there is the universalist strain in Jewish thinking that Marqusee invokes in the title of his book.

All that said, the majority of the anti-Zionist left do appear to be secular, with limited involvement in Jewish communal practice and limited knowledge of even those sources that could support their position. The criticism is often made of the anti-Zionist left and also of Jewish radicals that they are simply 'using' their Jewishness in a cynical attempt to legitimate their positions. In the blogosphere, they are sometimes dismissed as 'AsaJews', prefixing their statements with 'as a Jew...' or as ASHamed Jews (a fictional organisation in Howard Jacobson's satirical novel *The Finkler Question)*. However, the same criticism is not made of secular Jews who are pro-Israel. In any case, when Israel speaks in the name of world Jewry, it is simply inevitable that some will seek to counter this move. The *a priori* dismissal of anti-Zionist Jewish identity is premature in that being a Jew certainly means a great deal to many who hold this position. The process through which witnessing the suffering of the Palestinians, carried out in their name, provokes anti-Zionist Jews to 'activate' their Jewish identity is not necessarily that different to or any less valid than any other self-discovery of Jewish identity.

THE DECENT LEFT

The post-2000 period has seen another in a long sequence of schisms within the left. Just as the 1956 Soviet invasion of Hungary divided the left, the war on terror and the second intifada sparked similarly divergent responses. Support for the Palestinian cause and rejection of what is seen as American imperialism in the Middle East has created at least a certain synergy – and, in some cases, common cause being made – with Islamic radicalism. Against this tendency, a section of the left sees in Islamism a modern-day form of fascism, anti-Semitic to the core, and views opposition to Islamism as being among the best traditions of the left. This section of the left has, therefore, been highly critical of trends within Palestinian society, particularly the rise of Hamas, and has been equally critical of pro-Palestinian campaigning that overlooks or condones these developments. More broadly, this section of the left is generally supportive of the principles behind (if not always the execution of) the Iraq and Afghanistan Wars, opposition to Iran and its proxies and the war on terror, in general.

Those who hold to this position have sometimes called themselves the 'decent left'. The term was coined in a 2002 article, by the US philosopher Michael Waltzer, in the magazine *Dissent* which reflected on the US left's reaction to the 9/11 attacks:[36]

> The radical failure of the left's response to the events of last fall raises a disturbing question: can there be a decent left in a superpower? Or more accurately, in the only superpower? Maybe the guilt produced by living in such a country and enjoying its privileges makes it impossible to sustain a decent (intelligent, responsible, morally nuanced) politics. Maybe festering resentment, ingrown anger, and self-hate are the inevitable result of the long years spent in fruitless opposition to the global reach of American power. Certainly, all those emotions were plain to see in

the left's reaction to September 11, in the failure to register the horror of the attack or to acknowledge the human pain it caused, in the Schadenfreude of so many of the first responses, the barely concealed glee that the imperial state had finally gotten what it deserved.

Jews, such as Waltzer, have been prominent in the development of the decent left (as they also have in the 'indecent' left). This is, in part, because tolerance of anti-Semitism in the pro-Palestinian left is seen as one of the main symptoms of what needs to be opposed. In the UK, Jews such as David Aaronovitch and Shalom Lappin were prominent in the 2006 document the 'Euston Manifesto',[37] which articulated a set of principles for the UK decent left. Among the articles of the manifesto was a firm commitment to a two-state solution:

> We recognize the right of both the Israeli and the Palestinian peoples to self-determination within the framework of a two-state solution. There can be no reasonable resolution of the Israeli-Palestinian conflict that subordinates or eliminates the legitimate rights and interests of one of the sides to the dispute.

This went alongside an equally strong commitment to opposing tyranny and anti-Semitism:

> We decline to make excuses for, to indulgently "understand", reactionary regimes and movements for which democracy is a hated enemy — regimes that oppress their own peoples and movements that aspire to do so. We draw a firm line between ourselves and those left-liberal voices today quick to offer an apologetic explanation for such political forces.

> The recent resurgence of another, very old form of racism, anti-Semitism, is not yet properly acknowledged in left and liberal circles. Some exploit the legitimate grievances of the Palestinian people under occupation by Israel, and conceal prejudice against the Jewish people behind the formula of "anti-Zionism". We oppose this type of racism too, as should go without saying.

Another organisation that echoes the decent left position is Engage, which was founded in 2005, initially to counter campaigns to boycott Israel within the Association of University Teachers, subsequently developing into a broader resource for fighting anti-Semitism on the left. Engage does not see itself as campaigning on Israeli/Palestinian issues:[38]

> Engage is a single issue campaign. It focuses on one issue, antisemitism, and is therefore concerned also about the demonization of Israel, and of Jews who don't think of themselves as anti-Zionists. We believe that a new commonsense is emerging that holds Israel to be a central and fundamental evil in the world. We disagree with this notion and we think that it is dangerous. The danger is that this kind of thinking may well lead to, and license, the emergence of a movement that is racist against Jews in general.

Moreover, Engage does not see itself as pro-Israel, or even as necessarily Zionist:

> Engage is a left wing campaign. We "support" neither Israel nor Palestine; we support a cosmopolitan or internationalist politics that supports those who fight for peace and against racism within both nations... Engage comes out of a socialist tradition that maintains a sceptical view of nationalism. We do not see nationalism as necessarily racist or evil, but neither is it our own tradition; we are not nationalists.

That said, their position seems to have a lot in common with that of the Jewish radicals:

> We support those who campaign for Palestinian rights and we believe that what we have to say would strengthen, not weakens, their campaigns. We also support the Israeli peace movement, weak and disorientated as it may be. We believe that the demonization of Israel weakens the Israeli peace movement and pushes Israelis who are for peace into the arms of the Israeli right.

One of the defining features of the decent left is that, while Jews are prominent in it, it does not see itself as an inherently Jewish position, as Engage claims:

> We do not speak "as Jews" but as socialists, liberals, trade unionists or academics. A number of the people centrally involved in Engage are not Jewish.

Yet the decent left does play a major role within the Jewish community and takes on a distinct form within it. It is at the forefront of opposition to BDS, particularly the academic boycott, and is supported by and interacts with other Jewish organisations in doing so. Its analysis has proved influential among Jewish opinion formers and is reflected in statements about anti-Semitism by the Community Security Trust, among other organisations.

While the decent left may, at times, be critical of Israel, its political activism is only sporadically directed towards critiques of Israeli politics. Rather, the commitment to fight anti-Semitism and to resist leftist support for Islamism trumps other commitments. For this reason, the decent left can, at times, make common cause with neo-conservatives (discussed subsequently) and public supporters in opposing BDS, anti-Semitism and Islamism, but it almost never makes common cause with the pro-Palestinian movement. This often leads the decent left to be lumped in with neo-conservatives, when their views are very different in many respects. The divide between the decent left and Jewish radicals and the anti-Zionist left – and sometimes even the pro-Israel, pro-peace left – is, therefore, profound, even though on paper they agree on many points.

THE NEO-CONSERVATIVE RIGHT

Just as the pro-Israel pluralist and pro-Israel, pro-peace positions are frequently confused, so, too, are the public supporter and neo-conservative positions. Neo-conservatism is a term that is frequently used in a lazy fashion to label any right-wing perspective on Israel. Neo-conservatism was, initially, an ideology developed by a small group of American intellectuals, such as Irving Kristol and Norman Podhorertz in the 1970s. Many were liberals disillusioned with anti-Americanism and anti-imperialism and with the social upheavals that began in the 1960s.

59

Neo-conservatism's central principle is a robust defence of the US model of capitalism and democracy, together with a commitment to extend this model to non-western societies. With regard to Israel, neo-conservatism sees the Jewish state as an essential outpost of US-style democracy in a region dominated by anti-democratic Islamism. The defence of Israel, therefore, represents the frontline of a wider battle for democracy and western civilisation. Neo-conservatism became particularly influential following the election of George W. Bush in 2000.

The neo-conservative right has generally acknowledged the principle of the two-state solution, as Netanyahu did in his June 2009 Bar Ilan University speech. However, it places the responsibility for the continued failure to achieve a two-state solution on the Palestinians, with their embrace of terror and Islamism. It also partly blames multinational institutions, such as the UN, and international collusion with the Palestinians for the Palestinians' failure to embrace peace. The Palestinians are argued to have repeatedly responded to offers of peace with violence and with genocidal, anti-Semitic rhetoric. The response to the 2005 Gaza pullout, with the election of Hamas and continued rocket attacks against southern Israel, demonstrated to neo-conservatives that evacuating settlements will not bring peace. That the neo-conservative right does not see settlements as an obstacle to peace does not mean that they will not ever countenance withdrawal from any territory captured in 1967, nor that they are permanently ideologically committed to them whatever the circumstances. However, in the current circumstances, they would perceive the evacuation of territory as a sign of weakness that offers still more opportunity for Palestinian violence.

American Jews have been central to the development of neo-conservatism, with the journal *Commentary*, initially founded by the American Jewish Committee in 1945, reflecting the journey to the right in the 1970s and 1980s of its editor, Norman Podoretz. Jewish advisors and office holders in the George W Bush administration, such as Paul Wolfowitz, had a strong influence over the turn towards a neo-conservative foreign policy following the 9/11 attacks. In the 2000s, neo-conservatism became the principle form that right-wing Diaspora support for Israel came to take. Neo-conservatism moved the right-wing Jewish pro-Israel argument away from insular nationalism and towards an attempt to ally Israel's interests with US/western interests

– to defend Israel was to defend western civilisation. In the process, the revisionist Zionism of Jabotinsky, Shamir and Begin, which at one time provided the mainstream of the Zionist right, was replaced by a neo-conservative right-wing Zionist mainstream. This journey was aided by Israeli politicians such as Benjamin Netanyahu and Natan Sharansky who have made common cause with neo-conservatism.

The neo-conservative right is particularly strong in America, where most of its major ideologues are based. Its influence can be seen in Jewish organisations such as AIPAC and the Zionist Organization of America, which, while they are far from homogeneously neo-conservative, frequently base their advocacy for Israel on a neo-conservative emphasis on the common interests between America and Israel. Neo-conservatism is less well-established in Britain and has yet to find an institutional home within the Jewish community. However, a frequent – if independently-minded – proponent of neo-conservatism in the UK is Melanie Phillips, who writes regularly for the *Jewish Chronicle* and appears frequently at Jewish community events. Organisations sympathetic to neo-conservatism, such as the Henry Jackson Society, often work with Jewish organisations and are vocal in their support for Israel.

One of the reasons that the neo-conservative right is often confused with the public supporter position is that Israel's government has been right-wing dominated since March 2009. The views of Netanyahu are particularly congenial to neo-conservatism. For this reason, neo-conservatism often simply appears as unconditional support for Israel and public supporters may 'borrow' its rhetoric. Yet unlike the public supporter position, the neo-conservative position would not, should Israel turn in a leftward direction, turn in this direction. Indeed, neo-conservatives do criticise Israel, generally for its inability to communicate its case effectively. Further, they also criticise mainstream Jewish organisations when they fail to demonstrate a robust enough defence of Israel. That isn't to say that the neo-conservative right takes a pluralist position on Israel within the Jewish community, far from it, as they are often bitterly critical of the Diaspora left and even of the quietism of some public supporters. Rather, the neo-conservative right is less interested in achieving communal consensus than it is in propagating its views. As such, the neo-conservative right is a kind of mirror-image of Jewish radicals and the anti-Zionist left.

THE JEWISH RELIGIOUS RIGHT

The neo-conservative position is also frequently confused with the religious right position. In the US, neo-conservatism is closely allied with the US Christian right as, for example, in the Emergency Committee for Israel, founded in 2010 by neo-conservative Jew, William Kristol, and Christian conservative, Gary Bauer. Similarly, in Jewish debates over Israel, the neo-conservative position and the religious right position often appear to be identical. Both see the defence of Israel as a struggle for civilisation itself. Both see the evacuation of settlements as a dangerous form of surrender to Islamic and Arab militancy. Both positions are prominently represented within the current Israeli governing coalition.

Part of the difference in the two positions relates to their distinctive views on the settlements and the Jewish presence in the West Bank (and previously, Gaza). For the neo-conservatives, the large-scale evacuation of the settlements is to be resisted, but some territorial concessions are feasible as is, in theory at least, some kind of Palestinian state. For the religious right, settlement of Judea and Samaria is a religious duty and to give up land would be, at best, a dereliction of religious duty and, at worst, an act of heresy. It is perfectly possible and, indeed, quite common for neo-conservatives to have an entirely secular outlook and, indeed, revisionist Zionism was, historically, a secular movement. Neo-conservatism, while it sees the defence of Israel as ideologically vital, is based as much as anything on an evaluation of Israel's security needs in what is seen to be a hostile world. Although the religious right may couch its arguments in terms of Israel's security, ideologically, the needs of security take second place behind a religious commitment to the land of Israel.

The Jewish religious right is almost exclusively orthodox. By naming this position as the religious right, I am aware that there are a host of other Jewish religious positions regarding Israel, both on the right and left. There are both Zionist and non-Zionist forms of progressive Jewish theology. There are also orthodox Zionisms that allow for territorial compromise and some that are positively dovish (such as Rabbi Michael Melchior's *Meimad* movement in Israel). But in most places in the Diaspora, other religious Zionisms tend to become subsumed into other positions. Aside from Haredi anti-Zionism (discussed later), the only religious position on Israel that stands largely on its own terms is the kind of uncompromising religious right position I have described.

At the same time, though, in the UK, the religious right position has a low public profile. Full-blooded statements that the West Bank should be Jewish-run in perpetuity are rare in the non-Haredi Jewish press and rarer still in the mass media. Yet right-wing orthodoxy is far from marginal in the UK and right-wing orthodox rabbis are common in the United Synagogue, the largest mainstream religious movement in the UK. In the UK, though, the religious right is largely quietist, focused on its own community and not seeking to persuade outside it. The Oslo Accords and the Gaza pullout, both bitterly opposed by the religious right, were not accompanied by significant demonstrations by the religious right in the UK. Religious Zionist organisations, such as Mizrachi UK, have little involvement in the public defence of Israel and in Jewish communal debates. Indeed, those on the religious right have sometimes complained of being excluded from mainstream communal events.[39]

The situation is different in the US, where the religious right is much more politically visible and influential. The strength of the Christian right in the US provides a congenial environment in which religious support for Israel can be expressed. The US Jewish religious right do, on occasions, hold public demonstrations against Israeli policies (for example, in New York in 2005 against the Gaza disengagement).[40]

AUTHORITARIAN ZIONISTS

On the right of the Jewish world, some have embraced what is essentially a totalitarian position. At its most extreme, this view holds that Israel should annex the territories, expel both its non-Jewish residents and the non-Jewish citizens of Israel within the green line and be run as a theocracy or a totalitarian state. This position is most closely associated with Rabbi Meir Kahane, founder of the Jewish Defense League in the US and the Kach party in Israel. His legacy is continued by US groups, such as the American Jewish Task Force. Unlike in the US, in the UK Jewish totalitarianism has failed to obtain much traction, at least publicly. Tiny numbers of UK Jews have supported UK fascist political parties and there is a Jewish division of the English Defence League. Few UK Jews have been vocal in support of authoritarian secular forms of contemporary Israeli politics, such as Avigdor Lieberman's Yisrael Beiteinu faction (previously a party, now a part of Likud).

THE HAREDI COMMUNITY

In the UK and elsewhere, the fast-expanding Haredi (ultra-orthodox) community, by and large, lives separately from the wider Jewish community. Haredi Jews hold to a number of positions on Israel, ranging from religious Zionism to forms of anti-Zionism that reject the principle of a pre-messianic Jewish state. While differences over Israel in the Haredi community largely play out within that community and do not touch the wider community at all, there are exceptions. The Lubavitch movement, through its outreach work and its provision of rabbis to centrist orthodox communities, is closely connected to the non-Haredi community. Lubavitch holds to a right-wing position on Israel as with other aspects of its theology and practice, but tends not to emphasise this in its work with non-orthodox Jews. At the other end of the spectrum, the anti-Zionist Neturei Karta sect takes a very public anti-Israel position, often appearing at pro-Palestinian demonstrations. Their willingness to make common cause with non-Jews – including Muslim anti-Zionists, even to the point of some of them attending a 2006 Holocaust denial conference in Tehran – makes them pariahs in the rest of the Jewish community, including even among other anti-Zionist Haredi groups. Haredi groups in the Diaspora from across the spectrum have also, on occasions, demonstrated against the Israeli government on other issues, as in June 2013 when 20,000 gathered in New York to protest against plans to draft Haredim into the Israeli army.

PRIVATE ENGAGERS

Some Jewish leaders and organisations who maintain a public supporter position in public, take a much more actively engaged position in private. Due to their financial support for Israeli institutions and pro-Israel causes a small number of influential communal philanthropists and grandees have access to Israeli political and policy-making circles. Some use this access to quietly push a dovish line, whereas others may use it to support right-wing Israeli causes. With little public fanfare, Israeli political parties on all sides of the spectrum have a long history of soliciting foreign donations. Diaspora philanthropy, whether directed at Israeli political parties, at NGOs or at other projects, can represent a *de facto* engagement with Israel that can be *more* effective than any public position on Israel. For example, the US philanthropist Irving Moskowitz has been an important figure in funding settlement expansion in East Jerusalem.

A different form of private engagement can be found in the work of the Conservative, Labour and Liberal Democrat Friends of Israel. They are not specifically Jewish organisations and, indeed, part of their *raison d'être* is to buttress non-Jewish political support for Israel, but, in practice, many of their staff and active supporters are Jewish. These groups tend to avoid the limelight, concentrating on developing links between parliamentarians and Israel, particularly through arranging visits to the country. Their 'position' on Israel is rarely articulated extensively in public forums beyond expressing support for the Jewish state and the two-state solution.[41] Given their closeness to the UK political establishment and their concomitant access to Israeli politicians, they have a potential influence in Anglo-Israeli relations.

Another private engager organisation, the British Israel Communication and Research Centre (BICOM) has, since its founding in the mid-2000s, worked quietly to create a 'supportive environment for Israel' in UK politics and media. However, its organisation of the May 2011 'We Believe in Israel' conference suggests that it may be moving towards a more public stance, located somewhere between the public supporter and pro-Israel pluralist positions.

ZIONIST YOUTH MOVEMENTS

The various Zionist youth movements provide one of the most important ways in which Jewish youth become engaged with Zionism and Israel. The summer tours, year courses and youth clubs that they run are designed to create love for and knowledge of Israel and to promote immigration to Israel. Through their development of peer leadership, they also provide a common route into leadership within the wider Jewish community.

The youth movements also have distinctive ideologies, ranging from the moderate religious Zionism of Bnei Akiva to the socialist Zionism of Habonim, and some connect with Israel-based youth movements.

It might be expected that the ideologies of the youth movements could produce ideological divisions over Israel within the wider UK Jewish community. However, while some of their ideologies do offer an implicit critique of Israeli Government policies – the more liberal movements against the settlements, for example – it is rare for them to promote political engagement with Israel within the UK. In practice, most of the time, the youth movements hold a *de facto* public supporter position. There are a number of reasons for this. The strong emphasis on *aliyah* to Israel does not offer an obvious role for Diaspora critiques of Israel. The youth movements, for all their varied ideological stances, work within a Jewish Agency-supported structure centred on leadership training in Jerusalem. Movements may also be tacitly discouraged from political engagement in the UK by the institutions that support them and by charity law which places strict limits on political work.[42] For these reasons, the divisions between Jewish youth movements do not, in the main, feed into divisions in the wider UK Jewish community.

THE APATHETIC

Not all Jews are invested in Israel. Some Jews do not hold to any particular position on Israel, either defining their Jewishness completely without reference to Israel or being apathetic about Jewishness in general. Some supporters of Israel have expressed concern that Jewish apathy regarding Israel is a growing problem. While the apathetic do not necessarily contribute to Jewish communal divisions regarding Israel, it is important to recognise their presence, not least in order to appreciate that not all Jews are invested in the arguments discussed in this book.

NON-JEWISH SUPPORTERS

Israel receives strong support from some non-Jews. Christian supporters of Israel, some of whom define themselves as Christian Zionists, are particularly strong in the US, but are organised in the UK as well. Christian

Friends of Israel have developed contacts with Jewish pro-Israel groups, appearing on platforms on Jewish-organised events.[43] Non-Jewish activists have become closely involved in pro-Israel activism in the Jewish community. Chas Newkey Burden, for example, who writes the blog Oy Va Goy,[44] has spoken at Jewish events and become involved in pro-Israel organisations. Self-defined philo-Semites, such as Paul Johnson and Julie Burchill, have been strong defenders of Israel in the public realm.

These non-Jewish supporters are part of the Jewish communal conversation. They bolster the organisations with which they work and the positions they support, thereby complicating the 'Jewish' nature of the positions we are discussing. Further, while they support Israel and Jews, they do so without any responsibility or accountability to the Jewish community. They, therefore, may be less reticent to criticise Jews who do not share their opinions and be less concerned about the diversity in the Jewish community.

Non-Jewish supporters tend to be on the centre or the right of the spectrum regarding Israel. There does not appear to be a non-Jewish equivalent of Jewish radicalism or the anti-Zionist left – non-Jews are subsumed within the broader pro-Palestinian movement – although there are projects promoted by Jewish radicals in which Israelis and Palestinians collaborate. There are non-Jews aligned with the decent left, such as former *Jewish Chronicle* political editor Martin Bright and former MP Dennis MacShane. The pro-Israel, pro-peace left does have non-Jewish support, including within interfaith organisations such as One Voice, but the particular focus on demonstrating love of Israel that defines the pro-Israel, pro-peace left has no real non-Jewish equivalent.

THE GLOBAL JEWISH SITUATION

The increasing fragmentation over the issue of Israel seen in the UK Jewish community since 2000 is part of a wider trend in the Jewish world. Many of the developments in the UK either mirrored or were directly engendered by developments in the US, Israel and elsewhere. Developments in *hasbara* were led by Israeli and US organisations. J Street directly influenced the formation of Yachad. Jews for Justice for

Palestinians was inspired by organisations, such as Jewish Voice for Peace in the US and various Israel-based NGOs and campaigning organisations. Similar organisations have been founded in France, Australia and other countries. The work of high profile Jewish opinion-formers, such as Peter Beinart and Alan Dershowitz in the US, attracts comment and criticism across the Jewish world.

While Jewish communal maps with regard to Israel are changing across the world, the exact nature of these maps varies from community to community. There is little constituency for the authoritarian populism of Avigdor Lieberman in the UK, but his position is more popular in the former Soviet Union. The religious right is stronger in the US than in any other Jewish community outside Israel. The US Jewish community is much more able and willing to engage in political lobbying than any other Jewish community. In smaller Jewish communities, such as in Scandinavia and parts of Europe, there is less diversity and a stronger continuing commitment to the public supporter position. This is partly because there are not enough people to sustain the diversity one sees elsewhere and partly because of a sense that communities are less vulnerable when they stay united.

Broadly speaking, the communal maps of Jewish communities in English-speaking Jewish communities appear to be more fragmented than elsewhere in the Diaspora. Yet while communal maps may differ, the challenge of how to relate to Israel in Diaspora Jewish communities remains difficult and urgent.

***

The existence of different positions on Israel within Diaspora Jewish communities does not, in and of itself, guarantee that there will be conflict between those who hold to those positions. Yet conflict is what we have at the moment. The next chapter will explain how division has led to conflict.

NOTES

12 - After completing this chapter, I was made aware of the similarities between my approach and the practice of 'conflict mapping' within conflict resolution work.

13 - The Jewish Free School runs a competition called 'The Ambassador' – modelled on an Israeli TV show of the same name - in which students compete to be the most effective ambassadors for Israel.

14 - Dysch, M. (2013, February 28). Zionist turns on Zionist in 'anti-Israel' attack. The Jewish Chronicle. Retrieved May 29, 2013 from http://www.thejc.com/news/uk-news/102862/zionist-turns-zionist-anti-israel-attack;Shaviv, M. (2013, March 9). Left-wing Zionist group's rejection ignites UK debate. The Times of Israel. Retrieved May 29, 2013 from http://www.timesofisrael.com/left-wing-zionist-groups-rejection-ignites-uk-debate/

15 - See, for example: Berger, P. (2011, March 31). Interview: Daniel Dilker. The Jewish Chronicle. Retrieved May 29, 2013 from http://www.thejc.com/news/world-news/47270/interview-daniel-diker

16 - See for example: Hoffman, J. (2011, April 21). We are helping not hindering Ahava [Web log post]. The Jewish Chronicle. Retrieved May 29, 2013 from http://www.thejc.com/blogs/jonathan-hoffman/we-are-helping-not-hindering-ahava

17 - Dysch, M. (2012, April 19). 'You don't defend Israel properly'. The Jewish Chronicle. Retrieved May 29, 2013 from http://www.thejc.com/news/uk-news/66600/you-dont-defend-israel-properly

18 - Burg, A. (1997, December). Brit Am, Covenant of the People: The Zionist Element Draft Outline of the Policy of the Zionist Movement. Paper presented to the 33rd Zionist Congress Jerusalem, Israel.

19 - Jewish Community Relations Council of San Francisco, Marin, Sonoma, Alameda and Contra Costa Counties. (n.d.). Project Reconnections. Retrieved May 29, 2013 from http://www.jcrc.org/ycd_projectreconnect.htm

20 - http://www.jafi.org.il/JewishAgency/English/Jewish+Education/Strategic+Partnerships/Makom

21 - Kosmin, B. A. (2012, April). Second Survey of European Jewish Leaders and Opinion Formers. Oxford, UK: JDC International Centre for Community Development.

22 - In his 14 June 2009 speech at Bar Ilan University he laid out a vision of a two-state solution in which a Palestinian state would be demilitarised, Jerusalem would be undivided and various other caveats.

23 - Israel, we support you - but hear our plea. (2009, January 10). Retrieved May 29, 2013 from http://www.guardian.co.uk/world/2009/jan/11/gaza-israelandthepalestinians

24 - Countdown to Yachad. (n.d.). About us. Retrieved May 1, 2013 http://www.countdo-wntoyachad.org.uk/about-us#

25 - Beinart, P. (2010, May 12). The failure of the American Jewish establishment. New York Review of Books. Retrieved May 29, 2013 from http://www.nybooks.com/articles/archives/2010/jun/10/failure-american-jewish-establishment/?pagination=false.

26 - Cohen, S. M., & Kelman, A. Y. (Eds.) (2010). Special Issue: Are Israel and Young American Jews Growing Apart: Debating the Distancing Hypothesis. Contemporary Jewry, 30(2-3), 141-319.

27 - Plitnick, M. (2011, March 2). See? We can talk about BDS [Web log post]. Retrieved May 29, 2013 from http://mitchellplitnick.com/2011/03/02/see-we-can-talk-about-bds/

28 - Landy, D. (2011). Jewish Identity and Palestinian Rights: Diaspora Jewish Opposition to Israel. London, UK: Zed Books, pp. 156-157.

29 - A 2009 Jews for Justice for Palestinians member survey revealed substantial percentages both for and against different kinds of boycotts. See Symons, L. (2009, July 30). Divestment tops the Jews for Justice survey. The Jewish Chronicle. Retrieved May 29, 2013 from http://www.thejc.com/news/uk-news/divestment-tops-jews-justice-survey

30 - Julius, A. (2010). Trials of the Diaspora: A History of Anti-Semitism in England. Oxford, UK: Oxford University Press.

31 - http://newjewishresistance.com/

32 - Rosenblum, A. (2007). The Past didn't go anywhere: Making Resistance to Antisemitism Part of all our Movements. Retrieved May 29, 2013 from http://www.pinteleyid.com/past/

33 - Judt, T. (2003, October 23). Israel: The Alternative. New York Review of Books. Retrieved from http://www.nybooks.com/articles/archives/2003/oct/23/israel-the-alternative/?pagination=false

34 - International Jewish Anti-Zionist Network. (n.d). Charter of the International Jewish anti-Zionist Network. Retrieved June 16, 2001 from http://www.ijsn.net/about_us/charter/

35 - Marqusee, M. (2008). If I am not for myself: Journey of an Anti-Zionist Jew. London, UK: Verso, p. 289.

36 - Waltzer, M. (2002, Spring). Can There Be A Decent Left? Dissent.

37 - The Euston Manifesto for a renewal of progressive politics. (n.d.). Retrieved May 29, 2013 from http://eustonmanifesto.org/the-euston-manifesto/

38 - Engage – The anti-racist campaign against antisemitism. (n.d.). About Engage. Retrieved June 16, 2011 from http://engageonline.wordpress.com/about-engage/

39 - See for example: Rocker, S. (2011, November 24). Big Tent 'ban' not a ban, but a balance. The Jewish Chronicle. Retrieved May 29, 2013 from http://www.thejc.com/news/uk-news/58947/big-tent-ban-not-a-ban-a-balance

40 - Popper, N. (2005, June 10) Protest Against Gaza Plan Falls Short of Expectations The Forward. Retrieved from :

http://forward.com/articles/3639/protest-against-gaza-plan-falls-short-of--expectati/#ixzz2WgIb1iFL

41 - In 2011 Labour Friends of Israel re-launched themselves as a more campaigning--focused organisation, pursuing a two-state solution. It is possible then that the organisation may move towards the pro-Israel, pro-peace position.

42 - As when in 2004 the UJIA withdrew support from the right-wing Zionist movement Beitar as a consequence of its public campaigning work which endangered both organisations' charitable status.

43 - For example, a representative of Christian Friends of Israel co-chaired the Zionist Federation's January 2010 'Lobby Day' in the Houses of Parliament.

44 - http://www.oyvagoy.com/

CHAPTER THREE:
FROM DIVISION TO CONFLICT

It is perfectly possible for individuals and groups to simply accept that other individuals and groups hold different opinions and put forward their own opinions without rancour. Yet this is far from the case at the moment. Rather, divisions on Israel lead to active antagonism between supporters of different positions. That doesn't mean that every supporter of every position is in direct conflict with supporters of every other position. Not every individual or organisation attacks those with opposing views. Instead, a diverse collection of conflicts exists between organisations and individuals.

Many of the most intractable conflicts occur between those whose views are relatively close together ideologically. This is the case with the conflict between public supporters and pro-Israel pluralists. Until very recently, the public supporter position dominated the UK Jewish community. The fragmentation of this position over the question of just how much one can criticise Israel has led to conflict between organisations and individuals previously close to each other. The criticism of Mick Davis, chair of the UJIA, by the chairs of the Zionist Federation and the JNF has opened up fissures between organisations whose previous relationship was largely complementary. A similar conflict between previously close friends takes place between the decent left on one side and Jewish radicals and anti-Zionist Jews on the other.

There are, of course, positions in opposition to which otherwise conflictual groups tend to unite. Opposition to the 'delegitimization' of Israel unites everyone from the pro-Israel, pro-peace left to the neo-conservative right. In general, the capacity to form temporary coalitions of this kind is stronger to the centre and the right than it is on the left.

Differences over Israel do not always map exactly onto other kinds of differences. Many who would take a public supporter or even neo-conservative position on Israel may be strongly and publicly critical over, for example, the Israeli orthodox right's control over conversion. Neither does the spectrum of opinion over Israel equate to a left-right split on other issues. Many public supporters may support leftist positions on UK political issues and, conversely, there are plenty of pro-Israel, pro-peace supporters on the right of the UK political spectrum.

The positions taken on Israel within the UK Jewish community are constantly in flux. Once taboo issues can rapidly become mainstream and vice versa. Anti-Zionism was once a commonly held, respectable position in Anglo-Jewry. Calls for pluralism on Israel were, until very recently, largely confined to the left. As recently as 2007, the IJV declaration – the substance of which, if not the language used in it, is in some respects not too far away from the pro-Israel pluralist position – ignited a firestorm of outrage in the community. Realignment is an ever-present possibility. The public supporter position becomes temporarily more popular during times of war in Israel. Those who, during quieter times, express guarded criticism of Israel may put aside these criticisms in favour of solidarity. Such was the case in November 2012 when, during Operation Pillar of Defence, a letter to the Israeli ambassador in London, signed by UK Jewish leaders, declared:

> At this difficult and challenging time for the State of Israel and its citizens we wanted to send you an important message of support and solidarity from leaders and key institutions of the UK Jewish community. These sentiments prevail across all sections of our community, reflecting the national consensus within Israel itself.[45]

The signatories included many heads of organisations, who had, individually and collectively, backed the pro-Israel pluralist and pro-Israel, pro-peace positions. Yet, during quieter times, the public supporter position has been eroding, to the extent that it has threatened to disappear into that of the neo-conservatives on the one hand and of the pro-Israel pluralists on the other. It is also possible that the pro-Israel, pro-peace position will, over time, unify with the pro-Israel pluralist position. It is similarly possible that Jewish radicals and the anti-Zionist left will unify over time. The current heterogeneity of positions on Israel may prove to be a transitional stage on the way to a much more polarised community.

The fluid nature of the current situation may be related to emerging generational differences over Israel. Those who came to maturity in different eras – pre-1948, pre-1967, pre-first intifada, pre-second intifada, post-second intifada – developed their opinions in response to a variety of conditions in Israel. Those who have only known Israel as a regional superpower in conflict with the Palestinians may not be able to identify with those who knew Israel as a developing country, struggling for independence in the shadow of the Holocaust. It is also likely that those who have grown up in the more publicly self-assertive Jewish community of the 1990s and 2000s may find exhortations to avoid public criticism of Israel anachronistic. The plurality of options now available within the Jewish community for those seeking alternative forms of Jewish expression contrasts with the situation for previous generations, who faced a stark choice between communal conformity or secular marginality. This allows Jews critical of Israel to remain communally engaged in a way that previous generations might not have been able to manage and challenges both the traditionally secular and marginal Jewish left as well as the more conservative mainstream.

There are contradictory tendencies are at work in Jewish communal conflicts over Israel – forces that accentuate conflict and forces that ameliorate it. Anglo-Jewry is far from Balkanised with regard to Israel. The different positions I have described are held by overlapping constituencies within a community of less than 300,000. It is, in part, the social proximity between those who cleave to different views on Israel that accounts for much of the fractiousness that accompanies debates on the subject. This can be seen with regard to the Haredi community. The existence of anti-Zionist views in many sections of the Haredi community attracts much less comment and dispute than anti-Zionist views held by secular Jews. This is because, with the exception of the Neturei Karta, most Haredi anti-Zionist groups (such as Satmar) do not articulate their views in public in the Diaspora and there is little contact between Haredi Jews of this kind and the non-Haredi Jewish community. In contrast, the non-Haredi anti-Zionist left is socially closer to the mainstream of the Jewish community and they articulate their views publicly, in competition with other Jewish leaders.

The lack of Balkanisation can also be attributed to a still strong desire for community. Jewish representative bodies, particularly the Board of Deputies and the JLC, are subject to continual criticism for the line they take on Israel. Caught between the desire to represent Anglo-Jewry and a desire to defend Israel, such organisations face an effectively impossible task. Yet such representative bodies still exist and Jews and Jewish organisations holding a wide range of positions on Israel still engage with them.

For the time being, at least, organisations and leaders who take very different positions on Israel are still able to cooperate on some level. The 15 May 2011 'We Believe in Israel' event was supported by organisations as various as JNF, the New Israel Fund, the Israeli Embassy, UJIA, BICOM, the Zionist Federation and the Board of Deputies. The coalition that supports the UK Task Force on Issues Facing Arab Citizens of Israel includes the Board of Deputies, the New Israel Fund, the Pears Foundation, the UK Friends of the Abraham Fund Initiatives, UJIA and the Zionist Federation. The 2 June 2013 Close to Israel parade in London also included Yachad and the New Israel Fund as well as other Zionist groups.

One of the reasons why the drive for communal cooperation is still relatively strong, despite the widening gaps between communal positions on Israel, is that many Jewish organisations themselves represent a diversity of views on Israel. UJIA, for example, may be moving towards a pro-Israel pluralist position on Israel, but it, nonetheless, relies on fundraising from a broad coalition of supporters. Jews for Justice for Palestinians is often condemned as an anti-Zionist organisation, but its signatories include supporters of a range of positions, including even the decent left.

Conflict over Israel in the UK Jewish community is not, therefore, a simple product of the plurality of different positions and organisations in the Jewish community, nor is conflict entirely unrestrained by the forces of pluralism and community. To understand why and how conflict occurs in the community, we have to appreciate the deeper reasons why so much emotion is invested in Israel.

THE ROOTS OF THE CONFLICT – THE HOPE AND DESPAIR OF ISRAEL

The establishment of the state of Israel was, in some respects, a very mundane event. The achievement of Jewish sovereignty was a matter of building sewage systems, post offices and town halls. This version of Zionism, as a mundane process of state-building, is reflected in the

Hebrew poet Bialik's famous quote that 'We will be a normal state when we have the first Hebrew prostitute, the first Hebrew thief and the first Hebrew policeman.'[46] But, of course, Zionism has always had another strain which is much more idealistic and is encapsulated in this paragraph in the declaration of independence:

> The State of Israel will be open for Jewish immigration and for the Ingathering of the Exiles; it will foster the development of the country for the benefit of all its inhabitants; it will be based on freedom, justice and peace as envisaged by the prophets of Israel; it will ensure complete equality of social and political rights to all its inhabitants irrespective of religion, race or sex; it will guarantee freedom of religion, conscience, language, education and culture; it will safeguard the Holy Places of all religions and it will be faithful to the principles of the Charter of the United Nations.

This idealism is also evident in the common use of the term *aliyah* (ascent) for Jewish immigration to Israel and in the use of terms such as 'redemption of the land' to describe Jewish settlement. For religious Zionists, this idealism takes on a mystical dimension, as the Jewish return to Israel, the in-gathering of exiles (*Kibbutz Galuyot*), is frequently seen as a precursor to the messianic age.

The hopes placed in Zionism and Israel are profound. They touch on Jews' deepest desires, identities, traumas and fears. Scholars have shown how, particularly in the pre-state period, the condition of Diaspora was associated with physical and metaphysical weakness, in a largely unconscious internalisation of anti-Semitic accusations that Jewish men were somehow feminised and somehow not fully human.[47] The proud, strong, suntanned *sabra* (Israeli-born Jew), a soldier, farmer and man of action, presented an irresistible image of strength to a Jewish people recovering from the disaster of the Shoah. Even if Diaspora Jews did not plan to move to Israel, they could still take pride and hope from the development of Israel and the new Zionist man. The huge popularity in the Diaspora of Leon Uris's 1958 book *Exodus* and the subsequent film version, together with other fictional images of resilient Zionists, exemplified the dreams and fantasies invested in Israel.[48] Daring Israeli actions, such as the abduction of Adolf Eichmann and the raid on Entebbe, thrilled much of the Diaspora.

Pride in Israeli strength has often gone hand in hand with fears over Israel's weakness. Its small size and location in what is sometimes described as a 'bad neighbourhood' make Israel seem vulnerable. Its military victories, particularly the Six Day War, have sometimes been understood as 'miracles', rather than as the result of the superiority of its armed forces.

The centrality of Israel in Jewish emotional life has been reflected in the organisation of Jewish communal life. Post-1948 and, particularly, post-1967, support for Israel became a consensual rallying point for Jewish communities which were ever more divided religiously. Diaspora communities invested in Israel emotionally, financially and institutionally, through fundraising, education and, particularly, through tours of the country. Israel is a place of 'peak experiences', of intense teenage and young adult tours, in which growth and sexual exploration take place in an emotionally heightened atmosphere.

The possibility of greater numbers of Jews turning against Israel, therefore, stimulates concerns, not just that this development may weaken Israel, but also that it may weaken Jewish communal infrastructure. The erosion of consensus on Israel can feel like the erosion of Jewish community itself. The centrality of Israel in the Jewish community has, to some extent, left it hostage to fortune. At times, the intense investment in Israel can backfire. Some of those who were most passionately Zionist in their youth and attended organised Israel programmes become disillusioned when they find that the reality of Israel cannot match their expectations.[49] The corollary of pro-Israel hope can be anti-Israel disappointment – both involve the same level of emotional investment, with polar opposite results.

As the Oslo process began to come apart in the 2000s, so supporters of Israel had to adjust to a return to a situation in which Israel faced continual conflict. This process was traumatic for many, particularly those who had invested heavily in the idea of the two-state solution. Although for much of the country's history, support for Israel meant living with constant warfare, in the pre-Oslo days there was a certain phlegmatic acceptance of hostility to Israel. Post-Oslo, it has been difficult to accept a return to that hostility. Those who blame Palestinian intransigence or Israeli naïveté for the failure of Oslo are frequently more bitter and angry at their opponents than they would have been pre-Oslo.

For most of Israel's history and pre-history, support for Israel meant accepting that significant sections of the world (mostly in the Middle East, Africa and the Soviet bloc) were strongly opposed to either the actions or the very existence of the Jewish state. Post-2000, the perceived return to this pariah status is hard for many to accept. The situation is compounded by the perception that countries previously supportive of Israel, such as the UK, are becoming increasingly critical. Again, there can be no return to earlier generations' acceptance of Israel's lonely status in the world. 'Delegitimization' is thus felt as an unprecedented threat, even if that is not the case historically speaking. The fact that Israel was formed in much less supportive circumstances than those prevailing today provides no comfort.

If Israel faced opposition from other nation states for much of its history, in recent years, Israel and Zionism face criticism from a much more broad-based movement than ever before. Israel now faces a global movement that is similar to, though perhaps not yet as big as, the anti-apartheid movement of the 1980s. The Palestinians, largely invisible and ignored pre-1967, now have passionate supporters around the globe. Israel also faces intensive scrutiny from globalised media outlets and internet-based campaigners. Leaving aside the question of whether Israel's actions in Operation Cast Lead in Gaza between December 2008 and January 2009 were proportional or justified, it is certainly true that Israel has conducted similar operations at other points in its history with much less comment.

In his book, *Israel Versus Utopia,* author Joel Schalit argues that 'the Middle East has become a metaphor for the world.'[50] Middle Eastern politics is so thoroughly enmeshed in the politics of the US, the UK and many other countries that the region has become a kind of cypher for peoples' hopes and fears. The complaint is sometimes made that those who criticise Israel, particularly those who advocate boycotts, divestment and sanctions, are singling out Israel in ways that are disproportionate, particularly when compared to the lack of attention they may pay to states guilty of far worse crimes. While this complaint may sometimes be accurate, it is once again the corollary of the kind of support for Israel that treats the defence of the country as of paramount importance. In this respect, all sides in the conflict have much in common.

THE ROOTS OF THE CONFLICT – A NEW ERA IN JEWISH HISTORY

Divisions over Israel turn into outright conflict in part because of the emotions and hopes invested in Israel. Another reason for the conflict is that it takes place during a particular time in Jewish history in which a number of factors conspire to make it qualitatively different from other Jewish conflicts in history.

One such factor is the forgetting of the pre-1948 Jewish political tradition. As I argued in chapter one, before 1948 and even for a while afterwards, Zionism was only one of a number of Jewish responses to modernity. Different Jewish political approaches contended fiercely for support. The Zionist movement itself was riven with political factions. The post-independence state of Israel has built on this Jewish political tradition in a highly heterogeneous democracy. In contrast, in the Diaspora, the political tradition has largely ossified. As communism and socialism declined rapidly and Zionism became a point of consensus, so Diaspora communities became unused to living within a plurality of Jewish political visions. The emergence of heterogeneous positions on Israel in the last few years can, therefore, feel unprecedented. Lack of awareness of the previous diversity in Jewish political visions and the fact that Israel was born in the face of these makes today's more modest diversity seem like a novel threat to some.

The communal consensus over Israel marginalised non-Zionist Jews and leftist critics of Israel. This may have caused resentment among those who were marginalised, but marginality was accepted to the extent that the mainstream of the community was condemned as irredeemably conservative. Today, those who espouse once marginal positions are much less willing to stay on the margins. The 2007 IJV declaration did not simply criticise the mainstream, it put forward an alternative vision of what a democratised Jewish community could look like. In the US, Jewish Voice for Peace (JVP), whose advocacy of BDS of settlement produce has made it a pariah in many pro-Israel quarters, has sought a seat at the Jewish communal table, seeking, for example, membership in some of the Jewish Hillel student centres on university campuses.[51]

The youth wing of JVP's 'Young Jewish Declaration', issued in 2013, concluded with the words:

> We will not stop. We exist. We are young Jews, and we get to decide what that means.[52]

New technology has multiplied outlets for diverse forms of Jewish expression and has increased the potential reach of previously marginal voices. Against the backdrop of a western world in which diversity and multiculturalism are valued (albeit not unanimously), it is inevitable that the same demands for recognition that undermined homogeneous visions of western societies will also be made within minority communities. In short, it is now virtually impossible for consensus to be enforced in the Jewish community.

Related to the decay of communal consensus on Israel is the decay of communal consensus on anti-Semitism. The post-2000 rise in criticism of Israel has been accompanied by a rise in accusations of anti-Semitism. The evidence for this lies in two areas – a rise in anti-Semitic attacks on Jews and the emergence of a 'new anti-Semitism' that attacks Jews under the cover of anti-Zionism and criticism of Israel. The first area is measurable and, therefore, relatively uncontroversial. However, the existence of the new anti-Semitism is bitterly disputed by significant numbers of Jews. This controversy over anti-Semitism is a comparatively new phenomenon in Jewish history. Anti-Semitism used to be relatively easy to identify partly because most anti-Semites would not deny that they hated Jews. Jews, of course, disagreed profoundly over what caused anti-Semitism and how to combat it, but one could not deny that anti-Semitism existed and was a problem.

The Holocaust provided the most vivid example of what anti-Semitism could lead to, but it also lies at the root of current controversies over the identification of anti-Semitism. Post-Holocaust, only small numbers of neo-Nazis advocated open 'classic' anti-Semitism as it became increasingly taboo, at least in western societies. In communist countries, anti-Semitism was cloaked in anti-Zionism, as in the 1968 purge of Jews in Poland. With anti-Semitism increasingly expressed in coded language, disputes emerged over how to crack the code. At the same time, with Holocaust Remembrance Day now commemorated in many European countries and Holocaust museums in many countries, remembrance of the Holocaust has become an increasingly important part of Jewish identity in recent decades, enabling a renewed sensitivity to anti-Semitism. As multiculturalism became an acceptable and even dominant ideology in most western countries, Jews have felt increasingly empowered to oppose anti-Semitism publicly.

The result of these developments has been that anti-Semitism has become a highly sensitive and emotive topic. Those accused of it are often incensed by the accusation and their denials stoke further anger in the accuser. Jews who dispute definitions of anti-Semitism are sometimes viewed as treacherous and dangerous.

Jews have not yet developed strategies to cope with this new era in Jewish history. Few will accept the loss of communal consensus over Israel and anti-Semitism, which leads some to resort to increasingly shrill (and futile) attempts to isolate and pathologise those responsible. Concomitantly, those who have contributed to the breakdown in consensus find it difficult to accept the hatred to which they are subject.

THE ROOTS OF THE CONFLICT – POLITICS IN THE AGE OF THE INTERNET

Jewish conflicts over Israel are also taking place within a fast-changing world. Renewed Jewish political conflict is not simply a return to the pre-1948 situation; it is happening in a context very different from the pre-state era. The eclipse of communism, the rise of religious fundamentalism and the decline in membership of British political parties are just some of the factors that have shaped the politics of the world in which we live today. But of paramount importance for the issues discussed in this book is the impact of the Internet and modern communications technologies.

One of the key factors in producing the overwhelming global interest in Israel discussed in the previous section is the ubiquity of mass media. Israel's wars from 1967 onwards were covered extensively in the foreign media. Israel is close to Europe, has good travel connections, is small in size and has a free press, all of which make it much more accessible to journalists and TV crews than other conflict zones. Israel's conflicts are also exceptionally 'telegenic' in that they provide striking images and stories – from suicide bombings of pavement cafes to children throwing stones at tanks. The growth of 24-hour news and the ease of communication brought by satellite technology have only exacerbated Israel's ubiquity on the world stage.

The Internet has intensified the omnipresence of Israel. It is now relatively easy for anyone with an opinion to share it online. On the web, tiny minorities are able to make a disproportionate impact; a website representing one person's view can look the same as one representing the view of thousands. Political organising becomes much easier as isolated individuals can find each other more easily. The Internet, therefore, ensures that minority voices, which in prior eras were easier to ignore, can now make their presence felt. In the case of the Jewish community, the Internet has bolstered the organisational capacity of the right and left, rendering the distinction between mainstream and margins much more complicated. It is almost impossible now for anyone to claim to speak for all Jews, as evidence of dissent is easy to find. It is also extremely difficult to judge from the Internet whether a minority opinion is held by a small number of people or by many.

The popularity of comment threads on web publications also means that opinions are subject to direct contestation. Publications, such as *Guardian Comment Is Free*, Israeli publications, such as the *Jerusalem Post* and *Haaretz* and Jewish communal publications, such as the *Jewish Chronicle*, are filled with fierce debates over Israel. Commenters from around the world are able to jump in to discussions anonymously, with little need for restraint. Moderators of comment threads often find it hard to keep up with the volume of opinions and moderation criteria themselves become the subject of controversy.[53]

While the Internet can be a source of liberation and connection, all too often it creates heat with little light. The cacophony of opinions, together with the sheer flood of available information, can exacerbate conflict and make engagement with the views of others difficult. In the case of debates about Israel, protagonists face one of the most controversial and intensely discussed issues on the Internet. The proliferation of sites of contestation magnifies the scope of the conflict, making a kind of paranoia a real possibility.

***

In the next chapter, I will look at the 'symptoms' of the conflict. The emotional intensity of the conflict and the high stakes for which its protagonists play yield certain pathological ways of behaving. As we shall see, bitterness, anger and outright hatred are all too common.

NOTES

45 - Jewish Leadership Council. (2012, November 15). Conflict with Hamas: Communal Leaders Express Solidarity with Israel. Retrieved May 29, 2013 from http://www.thejlc. org/2012/11/conflict-with-hamas-communal-leaders-express-solidarity-with-israel/

46 - Despite extensive enquiries, I have been unable to find a source for this quote, which appears unreferenced in various forms (sometimes attributed to David Ben Gurion) in many places on the internet. It may be that it is apocryphal, but it, nonetheless, encapsulates an important strain within Zionism.

47 - See for example: Boyarin, D. (1997). Unheroic Conduct: The Rise of Heterosexuality and the Invention of the Jewish Man. Berkeley, CA: University of California Press.

48 - See Breines, P. (1990). Tough Jews: Political Fantasies and the Moral Dilemma of American Jewry. New York, NY: Basic Books.

49 - See for example: Benedikt, A. (2011, June 14). Life after Zionist summer camp [Web log post]. Retrieved May 29, 2013 from http://www.theawl.com/2011/06/life--after-zionist-summer-camp

50 - Schalit, Joel. Israel Vs Utopia. New York: Akashic Books, 2009.

51 - Beckerman, G. (2011, April 13). JVP, harsh critic of Israel, seeks a seat at the communal table. The Forward. Retrieved May 29, 2013 from http://www.forward.com/articles/137016/#ixzz1LNdUEKDL

52 - Young Jewish Declaration. (n.d.). Retrieved June 7, 2013 http://www.youngjewish-proud.org/about/

53 - For example, a main aim of the blog CiF Watch – http://cifwatch.com/ – is to contest moderation standards on Comment Is Free.

CHAPTER FOUR:
SYMPTOMS OF THE CONFLICT

C onflicts over Israel in Diaspora Jewish communities are often expressed through insults, anger and bitterness. The symptoms of the conflict I discuss in this chapter are not manifestations of a vigorous and healthy debate, but rather of a failure to deal with conflicting opinions in a way that is healthy for its participants and for the Jewish community as a whole. They are also predicated on a common tacit assumption – that simply expressing disagreement is not enough. Too often, disagreement is expressed through a ferocity that betrays a lack of confidence in the power of argument on its own.

A major difficulty in writing this chapter has been how to do so without excessive finger pointing. Given the small size of the UK and other Diaspora Jewish communities and the sensitivity of the issues discussed, singling out particular individuals for their behaviour can be viewed as an aggressive act in and of itself. Moreover, given that this book aims to communicate with Jews across the divide, putting certain Jews 'in the dock' could automatically close down any sympathy with my arguments from some readers. Although many of the examples I discuss are a matter of public record and cannot be anonymised, in a small number of cases I have chosen not to provide references.

I would stress that the symptoms of the conflict I discuss in this chapter are not confined to advocates of one particular position on Israel. Such is the emotional intensity of the Israel conflict that many of us are 'guilty' at times of resorting to unpleasant behaviour. As I showed in the introduction, this includes myself. My hope is that the acknowledgement of my own bad behaviour, with which I opened this book, will help me – and others – to empathise with those whose behaviour I single out. As I shall argue later in this book, bad behaviour in debates within the Jewish community needs to be combated through a common process of taking responsibility for one's actions and discourse.

ABUSE AND INSULTS

The heightened emotion that permeates Jewish conflicts over Israel finds its most direct expression in abuse and insults directed at those with different views. As with my own behaviour in 2007, sometimes this abusiveness occurs face-to-face in arguments peppered with insults. Much of this occurs privately, unrecorded. In the dinner and dialogue sessions I hosted between 2009 and 2011 (discussed in chapter eight), many Jewish leaders and opinion formers recounted incidents in which they had been attacked verbally.

Sometimes, though, such behaviour occurs in public or semi-public settings. On March 15 2011, Jonathan Hoffman, then a vice-president of the Zionist Federation and a Deputy on the Board of Deputies, recounted an incident the occurred at the previous day's meeting of the International Division of the Board on his blog:[54]

> ...the Chair (Paul Edlin) accused me of being offensive to him and others ('some of your exchanges of emails have been very vexating and upsetting'). One Deputy was so incensed at this unsubstantiated and unprompted slur that he walked out in protest. Another Deputy protested in the meeting at this attempt to smear and humiliate me. I then walked out but returned after a couple of minutes. As I entered the room I said to the Chair 'one more time and you've had it' meaning 'abuse me without ground and in public one more time and I will take it further and go public' - at which point I was thrown out by the Chair. Mine was a perfectly justified response to bullying and the abuse of power.

Whoever was actually at fault in the meeting is irrelevant. What is relevant is that a meeting that was, in part, concerned with Israel, degenerated into angry accusations and counter-accusations of abusive behaviour. Public meetings on Israel, within and outside the Jewish community, are frequently disrupted by such incidents in which those on different sides express their views in ways that others find insulting. Again, who is at fault on particular occasions is less important than the participants' sense that they are being abused and insulted.

The Internet makes it easy for anyone to publicise their views and it is, similarly, easy to 'talk back'. On March 23 2011, I wrote a tweet that expressed frustration with that day's bus bombing in Jerusalem, suggesting that it would strengthen the Israeli right. Shortly after, I received an e-mail from a right-wing Israeli acquaintance who accused me of arguing that Israeli rightists are happy after bus bombings. She continued:

> You are an evil, evil person and G-d is really going to get you one day. You make me sick. Your asinine, moronic, putrid way of thinking is the precise reason why I have nothing to do with you... You arrogant little fuck who knows nothing of real life. How dare you.

Those who publish their opinions on Israel in the press or online frequently receive hate mail. For example, in May 2011 Jeffrey Goldberg, national correspondent for *The Atlantic* in the US, reported that he had recently received an upsurge in hate mail:[55]

> The hate mail has come in a flood. Usually, my hate mail is from Nazis and Hamas sympathizers, decrying my bloodthirsty, neoconnish tendencies. Now the hate mail is coming from the right.

Goldberg quoted some choice examples, some of them highly obscene, such as:

> You are a tired whore who spends your days sucking obamer dick [sic].

Hate mail is not confined to those occupying one particular place on the political spectrum. Some writers, such as Jeffrey Goldberg, report receiving hate mail from both the right and the left. Other pro-Israel writers report receiving mail and comments that are anti-Semitic in tone. For example, in September 2010, the pro-Israel blog CiFWatch reported receiving a torrent of crude and abusive anti-Semitic comments and cartoons when one of their posts was linked to on a 9/11 conspiracy site.[56]

Internet comment threads that deal with Israel can become battlegrounds in which people from different sides attack and abuse each other. While some sites have comment moderation policies, knowing where and how to draw the line can be difficult when faced with floods of comments. Popular comment sites almost always fill up with angry and abusive comments whenever Israel is discussed. While writing the first draft of this chapter, I checked the latest article on Israel in *Guardian Comment Is Free* – a very popular comment site – and found a total of 413 comments.[57] A substantial minority was deleted by moderators, but there were still many milder, though still vituperative, comments. To take one at random:

> That's twice you have selectively quoted to misrepresent me and twice you have had the nerve while pulling stunts like that to accuse me of dishonesty. Once could be carelessness but twice looks like it's deliberate.

> To start throwing charges of dishonesty about you should at least have the courtesy to understand the meaning of the word and to ask whether you yourself live up to the standards you seek in others.

Such comments are a symptom of a conflict permeated with insults, abuse and accusations of lies and dishonesty. Of course, such language is not confined to conflicts over Israel. 'Trolls', those who deliberately try to disrupt and cause arguments on Internet comment threads, can appear on even the most innocuous topics. More broadly, some have argued that the tone of contemporary public debates is permeated with bitterness, fury and sarcasm.[58] What marks out conflict over Israel is partly the intensity and inevitability with which communication degenerates and partly the fact that this kind of communication is not simply confined to anonymous exchanges online – it has real consequences for Jews and Jewish communities.

AD HOMINEM ATTACKS

A related symptom of the conflict is the *ad hominem* (literally 'to the person') attack. That is, attacking a person's argument by attacking the person. One common kind of *ad hominem* attack is to question the Jewish credentials of other Jews. This kind of attack is most commonly (but, as well shall see, not exclusively) made on Jewish leftist critics of Israel. The groupings that I called the anti-Zionist left and Jewish radicals in chapter two contain a high proportion of secular Jews who are otherwise uninvolved in Jewish communal activities. The accusation is often made that such Jews 'use' their Jewishness in a cynical fashion in order to attack Israel and absolve pro-Palestinian activism from accusations of anti-Semitism. On one comment site, a Jewish pro-Israel blogger challenged his Jewish opponents as follows:

To the Jewish Israel bashers:

Please confirm the following:

1. Examples of active participation in synagogue services over the last six months
2. The number of mezuzot in your home
3. Fluency in reading/speaking Hebrew
4. Participation in rabbinical shiurim in the past six months
5. Positions held within the Jewish community
6. Extent of *kashrut* observance
7. Examples of active support for Israel in the past six months
8. Frequency of synagogue attendance

Setting rhetorical tests like these to Jewish critics of Israel is a common tactic. The assumption is that 'Jewish Israel bashers' could not pass such tests. This disparagement of the Jewish identity of critics of Israel is not only insulting, it is also empirically dubious. Not only is the Jewish left a much more diverse group than is often thought, but to suggest that they are only interested in their Jewish identity in order to criticise Israel makes assumptions about the complexities of Jewish identity which are almost never grounded in any significant knowledge of the Jews accused. Further, there are also secular Jews involved in pro-Israel activism and they are never accused of 'using' their Jewish identities in a similar way.

Probably the best-known *ad hominem* attack is of being a 'self-hating Jew'. The self-hating Jew has internalised anti-Semitism and projects it back out at other Jews in an effort to be acceptable to anti-Semites. Historically speaking, it is widely acknowledged that, in the post-enlightenment period, some Jews did view other Jews in ways that reflected anti-Semitic stereotypes and sought to distance themselves from other Jews accordingly.[59] The desire by Jews to be acceptable to non-Jewish society in the pre-World War II period almost inevitably meant seeing other kinds of Jews – generally 'eastern' and orthodox –

91

as unacceptable. Ironically, historical studies have also shown that the use of anti-Semitic stereotypes was endemic within sections of the early Zionist youth movement. Zionism sought to create a tough, healthy and productive 'new Jew' in contrast to the weak and parasitic *shtetl* Jew.[60]

Those who apply the concept of self-hatred to today's Jews emphasise historical continuity. One Jewish signatory to a 2006 advert criticising Israel's conduct in the war in Lebanon received an unsolicited letter from a well-known Jewish academic:[61]

> In every generation there are Jews who internalise the dislike of Jews in the society surrounding them, and become fearful. They try to appease the non-Jews and save themselves from the fate they fear awaits them by distancing themselves from other Jews' attitudes. As an example one need only go back to the end of the 19th century when the poor Jews began to arrive in the UK from Eastern Europe and the well-established British Jews went to great lengths to differentiate themselves from the newer immigrants, followed by rejection of Zionism and willingness to accept limits on immigration early in the 20th century. History is repeating itself. You need to have some insight into the psychology that drives the fearful to do this. On the contrary, now is the time to stand up for the morality and historical continuity represented by Israel and to show some courage.
>
> It is particularly ironic that you should do this close to the anniversary marked yesterday, when terrorists, who share some of the outlook expressed in the Times ad, killed so many of our fellow citizens. Where is your condemnation of that? Where is the concern of Jews for 'Justice' for the victims of Darfur, Pakistan, Tibet, women in the Arab world etc? Where is your compassion for Gilad Shalit and his family, an innocent life requiring protection by his state? This blindness towards any alleged injustice except where it involves Israel shows the mindset for what it is. It is moreover an easy path to – spend £10000 on an ad and that is all you have to do. Why not spend the money on a better cause? Shame on you,

The author of this letter did not know the recipient personally. Despite this, the author makes multiple assumptions about the recipient's motivations and opinions, none of which he/she was in a position to know anything about. Even assuming that the concept of Jewish self-hatred is valid in principle, the only way it could ever be correctly applied to particular Jews would be when the accuser had substantial knowledge of the biography, opinions and psychology of those that they accuse. Certainly, the writer of the letter had no such knowledge, and, generally speaking, neither do most people who use the term self-hatred to attack other Jews.

The self-hating Jew is usually assumed to be a secular Jew who has turned his/her back on Jewish communal life. At the end of the forward to his collection of essays *The Wicked Son: Anti-Semitism, Self-Hatred, and the Jews,* David Mamet paints a portrait of this kind of self-hating Jew as the 'wicked son' in the Passover Haggadah who distances himself from the community:

> To the wicked son, who asks, 'What does all this mean to *you*?' To the Jews who, in the sixties, envied the Black Power Movement; who, in the nineties, envied the Palestinians; who weep at *Exodus* but jeer at the Israel Defense Forces; who nod when Tevye praises tradition but fidget through the seder; who might take their curiosity to a dogfight, to a bordello or an opium den but find ludicrous the notion of a visit to the synagogue; whose favourite Jew is Anne Frank and whose second-favourite does not exist; who are humble in their desire to learn about Kwanzaa and proud of their ignorance of Tu bi'Shvat; who dread endogamy more than incest; who bow the head reverently at a baptism and have never attended a *bris* [circumcision] – to you, who find your religion and your race repulsive, your ignorance of history a satisfaction, here is a book from your brother.[62]

Mamet implies that there is a standard that a 'real' Jew must meet in order to have the right to claim a Jewish identity, a standard based on Jewish knowledge, communal involvement and support for Israel. Ironically, the setting of a standard for Jewishness contradicts traditional halachic definitions of Jewishness, based on descent, rather than beliefs or behaviour.

Even though the concept of Jewish self-hatred does have a serious intellectual pedigree, it has morphed into a kind of all-purpose insult for left-wing Jewish critics of Israel. Amongst the hate mail received by Jeffrey Goldberg was the following:

> you're just another liberal asshole, or a self-loathing Jew.

> Probably both.

> What a dick!

One variation of the concept of the self-hating Jew is that of the 'AsAJew'.[63] The AsAJew has little connection to Judaism or to the Jewish community other than speaking out against other Jews and the Jewish state, always prefacing his/her statements with 'as a Jew I...' By speaking as a Jew, the AsAJew, like the self-hating Jew, uses his/her Jewish background cynically. Moreover, it is argued, they indemnify non-Jews from accusations of anti-Semitism. For example, in the 2011 debate within the University and College Union regarding whether to retain the EUMC definition of anti-Semitism, those who rejected the definition were accused of using the support of AsAJews as a way of deflecting attention from their own anti-Semitism.[64]

To an extent, the critique of AsAJews is fair in that crude affirmations of one's Jewishness can create a lazy identity politics in which 'speaking as' something becomes its own justification. However, unless the critique of AsAJews is applied equally to *all* similar forms of crude Jewish identity politics, then it is hypocritical. The Engage project, which was discussed in chapter two and fights leftist anti-Semitism, has been an important pioneer of the AsAJew concept and does not define itself as speaking from a Jewish position. Yet while Engage itself may not be hypocritical, it does not critique pro-Israel Jews who speak as Jews. Indeed, supporters of Israel frequently speak as Jews or as Israelis, a tactic that is as eminently open to critique just as leftist AsAJews are.

In any case, even though the AsAJew accusation does draw attention to some important issues in Jewish identity politics, it is all too frequently used simply as a term of abuse with little precision. To take a random example, a comment on a *Jewish Chronicle* blog post that mentioned the left-of-centre *Guardian* journalist Jonathan Freedland, said as follows:

> ...do me a favour Freedland, as a Grauniad[65] asaJew, you
> simply have no credibility.

Freedland, who also has a column in the *Jewish Chronicle*, is deeply
involved in Jewish communal life and the accusation that he speaks
cynically as a Jew – if, indeed, it is applicable to anyone – is certainly not
applicable to him. The brevity and sarcasm inherent in the term AsAJew
makes it all too easy to wield it as a weapon.

The same is true of the concept of the 'ASHamed Jew', which appears in
Howard Jacobson's 2010 Booker prize-winning novel *The Finkler Question.*
The eponymous Finkler, a prominent UK secular Jewish intellectual and
media figure, announces on *Desert Island Discs* that, while he is Jewish
'on the matter of Palestine I am profoundly ashamed.' His declaration
attracts considerable support and soon a group of other secular Jewish
intellectuals is meeting regularly under the name 'ASHamed Jews'.
Jacobson's comic novel is highly effective in satirising the pretensions of
leftist Jewish intellectuals, but the boundary between satire and political
critique is a blurred one. Jacobson himself is a prominent critic of the
kind of Jews he satirises in the novel. As he argued in a 2010 article in
the *Jewish Chronicle*:[66]

> When it comes to Jewish anti-Zionists, their Jew-hatred is
> barely disguised, not in what they say about Israel but in
> the contempt they show for the motives and feelings of
> fellow-Jews who do not think as they do.

> ...let's call the thing that drives us by its proper name. Hiding
> behind Israel is a cowardly way for a Jew to express his anti-
> Jewishness. That half the time he is battling his psychic
> daddy and not his psychic homeland I don't doubt, though
> I accept that, in political discourse, we have to pretend that
> what we are talking about is what we are taking about.

Like the AsAJew, the ASHamed Jew and the 'Finkler' have become
prominent figures in blog posts and comment threads. Satire and critique
become debased as simple abuse.

Some Jewish critics also accuse the Jewish left of 'treachery' or similar.
This argument was made by Zalmi Unsdoerfer, chair of Likud-Herut UK,

at a public meeting entitled 'Is it okay to be Jewish and criticise Israel?' held on 4 March 2011:[67]

> After 8 wars in 60 years... our enemies know they can't beat us on the battlefield. So now they fight us with delegiti- misation. In the media, academia, unions.... every forum, quango and parlour meeting – they defame and demean the Jewish state. For Jews to assist in this delegitimisation is to expose our position in war. In WW2 there was a warning: 'Loose lips sink ships.' People were careless sometimes. But when it's deliberate... well, that is pure treachery.

Similarly, in an interview with Israeli army radio in January 2010, the prominent US Jewish lawyer and public intellectual Alan Dershowitz strongly attacked Richard Goldstone, author of the UN's report on the 2009 Gaza War:[68]

> The Goldstone Report is a defamation written by an evil, evil man. Goldstone is an evil man. No one should mince words about it. He allowed his Jewishness, the fact that his name is Goldstone, and that he has connections to Israel – he allowed himself to be used to give...a *heksher*, a certification of purity to a defamation.

> It would be as if the Czar, when he wrote the Protocols of the Elders of Zion, he asked a prominent Jew to edit the report and sign the Protocols in order to show that it had credibility.

> Galey Tzahal: Do you hint Prof. Dershowitz that he is a *moser*, someone who betrays his own people?

> D: Absolutely. There is a prayer that is said every day for people like him: *La-malshinim al t'hi tikvah* ('there shall be no hope for the betrayers'). He is a man who uses his language, his words against the Jewish people. I regarded him as a friend. I now regard his as an absolute traitor.

Those who have been accused of being self-hating Jews or similar are emphatic in their rejection of this criticism. Tony Lerman, ex-Director of the Institute for Jewish Policy Research, for example, published a lengthy critique of the concept of Jewish self-hatred in the *Jewish Quarterly* in 2008,[69] stating that:

> ...the concept of 'Jewish self-hatred' is entirely bogus and it serves no other purpose than to marginalise and demonise political opponents.

Lerman argued that the concept of Jewish self-hatred was born out of a specific moment at the turn of the nineteenth/twentieth century and, while it was true that Jewish critics did often rely on anti-Semitic tropes, this was not necessarily evidence of self-hatred:

> Criticising an aspect of one's identity does not automatically imply criticism of that identity per se. The concept is fundamentally weak because it fails to allow that self-criticism can be searching and very deep without becoming self-hatred... Even the use of anti-Semitic rhetoric is no proof of self-hatred. It was common in arguments over Jewish identity in the nineteenth and twentieth century and, as we have already seen, pressed into service for Zionism and for those who opposed it.

In any case, whether or not the concept was valid in the first place, Lerman argues that circumstances have changed:

> ...the dilemma that led to the phenomenon of Jewish self-hatred came to an end with the Holocaust, so there seemed little reason for it to remain current. In most post-Holocaust centres of Jewish life, especially the United States, assimilation, though striven for, was a less anxious process, and Jews were not alone in their quest to integrate.

Lerman, therefore, concludes that:

> The concept of the 'self-hating Jew' strengthens a narrow, ethnocentric view of the Jewish people. It exerts a monopoly over patriotism. It promotes a definition of Jewish identity which relies on the notion of an eternal enemy, and how much more dangerous when that enemy is a fifth column within the group. It plays on real fears of anti-Semitism and at the same time exaggerates the problem by claiming

that critical Jews are 'infected' by it too. And it posits an essentialist notion of Jewish identity.

The Jewish left is often, for good reason, extremely sensitive about accusations of self-hatred or disloyalty. The 2007 IJV declaration included the statement:

> We further believe that individuals and groups within all communities should feel free to express their views on any issue of public concern without incurring accusations of disloyalty.

At the same time, sections of the Jewish left also show a desire not just to reject the concept of Jewish self-hatred, but also to create an alternative conception of the Jewish tradition. The IJV declaration also states:

> We hereby reclaim the tradition of Jewish support for universal freedoms, human rights and social justice.

The prominent UK Jewish radical Brian Klug has attempted, in his work, to articulate a simultaneously Jewish and universalist vision of justice. As he states at the end of the epilogue to his collection *Being Jewish and Doing Justice*:

> ...when Jews around the world speak out about Israel, condemning its breaches of human rights and denouncing policies that are inimical to peace... we are not turning *against* our Jewish identity: we are turning *towards* it. We are seeking to mend its breaking heart by affirming a Judaism of justice. Being Jewish, we are heeding the directive that Moses gave to *am Yisroel*, the people of Israel, who, standing at Sinai, suspended between the house of bondage and the Promised Land, heard the words pointing out a higher road to life, 'Justice, justice shall you pursue' (Deut. 16:20): words that resound down the centuries and, like the blast of the shofar, remind the people who they are.[70]

Such attempts at affirming an alternative conception of Jewish identity do not appease their critics. Indeed, they can actually inflame passions, being read as an attack on other forms of Jewish identity. Although Brian Klug and others do not claim to be offering an essentialist view of Jewish identity, their work can easily be misread as such. Moreover, less subtle Jewish leftists can seem to imply that supporters of Israel have the 'wrong' Jewish identity. The charter of the International Jewish Anti-Zionist Network does seem to suggest that not only is Zionism a perversion of Judaism, but also that Jews must dissociate themselves from Israel in order to be fully ethical beings:[71]

> Zionism is racist. It demands political, legal and economic power for Jews and European people and cultures over in-digenous people and cultures. Zionism is not just racist but anti-Semitic. It endorses the sexist European anti-Semitic imagery of the effeminate and weak 'diaspora Jew' and counters it with a violent and militarist 'new Jew,' one who is a perpetrator rather than a victim of racialized violence.

> Do you wish to dissociate yourself from the Israeli ethnic cleansing of Palestine and the destruction of history, culture and self-governance? Do you believe there is no peace without justice? Do you feel enraged and saddened that the holocaust against Jewish people is being used to perpetrate other atrocities? Then we call on you to join with us in ending Zionist colonialism.

At a lecture at the Palestine Center in Washington DC in April 2010, John Mearscheimer (co-author of a controversial work on the 'Israel lobby') suggested that:

> American Jews who care deeply about Israel can be divided into three broad categories. The first two are what I call 'righteous Jews' and the 'new Afrikaners,' which are clearly definable groups that think about Israel and where it is headed in fundamentally different ways. The third and largest group is comprised of those Jews who care a lot about Israel, but do not have clear-cut views on how to think about Greater Israel and apartheid. Let us call this group the 'great ambivalent middle.'[72]

This bifurcation of Jews into either 'righteous' or 'racist' camps is crude and reproduces a division between good and bad Jews that mirrors the concept of Jewish self-hatred. Any approach to Israel-related conflict that makes unwarranted assumptions about what individual Jews feel and *should* feel is a kind of abuse that rides roughshod over the diversity and complexity of Jewish identity.

Behind many of these personal attacks on people's Jewishness lies an inability or unwillingness to believe that another Jew could genuinely believe something that one finds abhorrent. The accusations and attacks often express a kind of incredulity; to hold certain beliefs while proclaiming oneself Jewish can only be explained as a kind of pathology based on psychologically flawed motivations. To their detractors, abhorrent Jewish identities are only explicable as a perversion, never as the result of sincere, thought-through beliefs. The accusation of Jewish self-hatred, in its cruder formulations at least, verges on being an accusation of mental illness. Indeed, proclaiming one's opponent as being mentally ill or autistic is one of the cruder tactics used in Israel conflicts.[73]

Accusations of dishonesty and bad faith are, therefore, common in Jewish conflicts over Israel and related issues. One example of this is what the academic and co-founder of Engage, David Hirsh, has called the 'Livingstone formulation'.[74] Hirsh quoted then-mayor of London, Ken Livingstone, as saying 'for far too long the accusation of antisemitism has been used against anyone who is critical of the policies of the Israeli government.' Similar assertions to Livingstone's are common, for example in the IJV Declaration:

> The battle against anti-Semitism is vital and is undermined whenever opposition to Israeli government policies is automatically branded as anti-Semitic.

Hirsh sees such statements as automatically branding any accusation of anti-Semitism as having been made in bad faith. At its laziest, as in Livingstone's own formulation quoted earlier, this accusation of bad faith seems to be a blanket one in that 'the accusation of anti-Semitism has been used against *anyone*...' However, the IJV declaration is subtler in attacking only those instances 'whenever' accusations of anti-Semitism are made automatically. In eliding this distinction, those who attack the 'Livingstone formulation' can, themselves, appear to fall into the trap of making blanket accusations of bad faith. At their worst, debates about anti-Semitism and Israel can degenerate into two sides that mirror each other in accusing the other of speaking dishonestly and disingenuously.

USE OF NAZI ANALOGIES

In the decades following the Second World War, the Nazis have become the epitome of evil in much public discourse. This has led to a situation in which comparing one's opponents to Nazis has become an all-too-common rhetorical trope, designed to brand other views as completely beyond the pale. 'Godwin's Law', proposed in the early 1990s by the author Mike Godwin, states that 'As an online discussion grows longer, the probability of a comparison involving Nazis or Hitler approaches one.'[75] While tongue-in-cheek, to an extent, Godwin's law does identify a tendency that is particularly evident in online communication for arguments to spiral out of control to the point where the ultimate recourse of comparison to the Nazis is invoked. The corollary of Godwin's Law is sometimes taken to be that the first to invoke the Nazis automatically 'loses' an argument, or that once the Nazis are invoked the argument is played out.

For Jews, being on the receiving end of Nazi comparisons is understandably highly potent and taken to be not just bad form, but the worst of all insults. In pro-Palestinian campaigning, it is not uncommon for Israel to be compared to Nazi Germany and the sufferings of the Palestinians even compared to the Holocaust. For example, a search in Google Images for the words 'Israel Nazi' reveals many cartoons and placards that, for example, replace the Star of David on the Israeli flag with swastikas, and other examples that play with Nazi and Holocaust imagery to insult Israel. The Nazi comparison is not simply over the top – even if you believe that Israel is oppressing the Palestinians, there is clearly no process of mass extermination going on – it is designed to insult Israel and its Jewish supporters in an excruciating way. Jewish suffering in the Holocaust is either rendered irrelevant by this comparison, or it treats Jews and Israel as having betrayed the victims of the Nazis. Unsurprisingly, therefore, comparing Israel and Jews to Nazis is often seen as *ipso facto* anti-Semitic. The 2005 European Union Monitoring Council on Racism and Xenophobia's (EUMC) working definition of anti-Semitism,[76] for example, states that 'drawing comparisons of contemporary Israeli policy to that of the Nazis' can be a manifestation of anti-Semitism.

Despite the extreme sensitivity of Nazi comparisons, Jews have, at times, used them to attack other Jews. For the most part, this is confined to those with pronounced left and right-wing views. For example, the British communist, Jewish writer Tony Greenstein has, on occasions, compared Israel and Zionism to Nazism.[77] Some Jewish anti-Zionists emphasise what they see as, at best, the commonality of interests or, at worst, the active collaboration between the Nazis and the Zionist movement.[78]

On the Jewish right, one insult sometimes directed at Jewish critics of Israel is that of being a 'kapo' (concentration camp prisoners appointed as supervisors by the Nazis). One brief example of this is the headline of a May 6 2009 blog post in Pamella Geller's right-wing US blog Atlas Shrugged: 'Kapo Emanuel Threatens Israel, Bullies Jews to Pick their Poison as Obama Seeks to Disarm the Tiny Nation.'[79] The Emanuel referred to is Rahm Emanuel, Barak Obama's (Jewish) chief-of-staff from 2009-10. A 14 September 2010 blog post on the blog Israpundit was entitled 'Dhimmi Kapo Jew: ABE FOXMAN Fawning Up To Muslims.'[80] Here, the figure of the kapo is elided with that of non-Muslim 'Dhimmi' in Islamic law. A similar insult is of being a member of the 'Judenrat', the Nazi-appointed Jewish ghetto leaders. Another Israpundit post, on 19 June 2011, attacking the National Jewish Democratic Council, was entitled, 'National Judenrat Democratic Kapos (NJDC) Whitewash Islamization Threat.'[81] The infamous 'Self-Hating and/or Israel-Threatening List',[82] run by a far-right Jewish group, 'names and shames' thousands of Jews who have expressed some criticism of Israel and makes the accusation:

> If anyone still wonders how the Holocaust against European Jewry could have ever happened, all he has to do is observe the behavior of today's 'Judenrat' traitors. They run forth to an anti-Semitic world trying to prove that THEY are the good Jews --- not those arrogant Israelis! The Truth, however, is that these radical, leftist, academic, socialist, 'progressive,' enlightened know-nothings are not even worthy of the name 'Jew.'

In general, most Jewish organisations outside of the far left and far right have tended to avoid Nazi comparisons. However, in less controlled contexts, particularly in the anonymity of the Internet, they remain an ever-present possibility when communication about Israel breaks down.

CREATING BOUNDARIES AND PARIAHS

Jewish conflicts over Israel are essentially conflicts about boundaries and where to draw them; what sorts of views are essential for Jews to hold and what sorts of views should disqualify Jews from consideration as part of the Jewish people and of Jewish communities? In these conflicts, some Jews are seen as unfit to be considered part of the Jewish people. When the Jewish credentials and good faith of opponents are attacked, the implication is that they should be shunned by other Jews.

Some individual Jews have been marked out for particular opprobrium and pariah status. Earlier, we saw how critics accused Richard Goldstone of treachery for his report on the Gaza conflict. In April 2010, threats of demonstrations by the South African Zionist Federation led Goldstone to withdraw his plan to attend his grandson's bar mitzvah in Johannesburg. A compromise was eventually brokered by the South African Board of Deputies whereby Goldstone was able to attend in return for meeting leading South African Jews.

A similarly highly publicised case of exclusion, although not from the Jewish community, occurred in 2011, when another Jewish critic of Israel with considerable notoriety, playwright Tony Kushner, had an offer of an honorary doctorate rescinded by the City University of New York after a member of the board of trustees objected to his, allegedly, anti-Zionist views (the doctorate was eventually granted after a public outcry). In October 2006, historian Tony Judt, who had recently come to advocate a one-state solution to the Israel-Palestine conflict, had a lecture at the New York Polish consulate cancelled after the consul withdrew the use of the venue as a result, at least in part, of telephone calls from a number of American Jewish organisations.

The question as to whether Jewish organisations attempt to 'stifle dissent' over Israel is a highly contentious one. Accusations of muzzling can sometimes veer towards a kind of anti-Semitism that accords too great a measure of power to Jewish organisations. Further, sometimes official disapproval and condemnation are confused with exclusion and censorship. At the same time, those who are accused of muzzling opposing views sometimes accuse their accusers of attempting to muzzle them in turn. Alan Dershowitz, for instance, accused Richard Goldstone of 'politicising' his grandson's bar mitzvah by discrediting the rabbis who opposed him and championing the rabbis who supported him:

> Richard Goldstone should not use his grandson's bar mitzvah to selectively silence rabbis who disagree with his report, while encouraging rabbis who agree with it to use the bar mitzvah as a sword against the report's critics and as a shield against legitimate criticism.[83]

As with the mutual accusations of bad faith over anti-Semitism, accusations and counter-accusations of muzzling can become mirror images of each other. Support for one's own position is frequently downplayed so as to portray oneself as a victim. Those on the left of the Jewish community often downplay their support in non-Jewish circles in order to focus on their lack of support within the narrower confines of the Jewish community. Conversely, those who take a pro-Israel position may downplay the strength and resilience of Jewish and pro-Israel organisations both within and beyond the community. That which results can seem like a bizarre contest to portray oneself as more excluded than the other.

But there is no doubt that, at times, Jewish organisations do attempt to exclude certain Jewish voices. In April 2010, the San Francisco Jewish Community Federation released guidelines as to which organisations it would fund, explicitly excluding 'positions that undermine the legitimacy of the State of Israel'. This was partly a response to repeated controversies over funding of the San Francisco Jewish Film Festival, which had screened a number of pro-Palestinian documentaries and films. In May 2011, Limmud Oz (Australia) announced a ban on presenters who advocate BDS. In October 2011, the Jewish Foundations of North America excluded the Deputy Director of the left-wing group Jewish Voice for Peace from the voting in an online contest to identify 'Jewish heroes'.[84]

The setting of exclusionary red lines by Jewish communal organisations appears to be a growing trend. As I discussed in chapter two, the flipside of the pro-Israel pluralist position is the exclusion of those who 'delegitimize' Israel. The influential Reut report, mentioned in chapter two, argued that while the pro-Israel tent needs to be expanded to include more critical Zionist voices, 'delegitimizers' of Israel need to be uncompromisingly opposed:

Outing, naming and shaming the delegitimizers – As mentioned, delegitimizers operate uninterrupted and their initiatives are often practically unopposed. A central objective is to change this situation by forcing them to 'play defense.' This means systematically exposing information about delegitimizers, their activities, and the organizations that they operate out of. The goal is to eventually frame them, depending on their agendas, as anti-peace, anti-Semitic, dishonest purveyors of double standards.[85]

One of the dangers of this strategy is that, even if Reut and others have more or less clear criteria as to what constitutes a 'delegitimizer', in practice, this legitimates much less focused denunciations. The attempts of organisations, such as Reut, to develop a strategic response to what they consider high-level threats to Israel and the Jewish people cannot be disengaged from the atmosphere of mutual distrust that often prevails at the grassroots.

Jonathan Freedland recalls in his book *Jacob's Gift* an incident in synagogue one Rosh Hashanah:

> British Jewry is a small community and I spotted a familiar face. He came close and beckoned me forward, bending to whisper in my ear. 'I'm amazed you dare show your face in here.' I stiffened. It was only one person and only one comment, but I had just felt the breath of excommunication.

As Freedland recognises, he was not being officially 'excommunicated', but the disapproval and rudeness of one person in the highly charged space of the synagogue can have a major impact (enough to recount the story in a book written several years later).

Formal sanctions and processes of rejection from the Jewish community may be rare, but suggestions that someone be shunned are much more common, and, arguably, they hurt as much as formal excommunication would. In any case, even if formal excommunication is effectively impossible (outside the Haredi world, at least), it is perfectly possible to make life extremely difficult for other Jews by refusing to work or associate with them. Exclusion of this kind tends to happen quietly, so it is difficult to track. I myself once lost funding for a project when someone with whom I was cooperating decided she could not work with me after a public statement I had made on Israel.[86] The IJV-associated collection *A Time to Speak Out* contains a number of anecdotes in which contributors recount the subtle and not-so-subtle ways they have been marginalised or excluded from the community.[87] A 2012 memoire by Tony Lerman provides unambiguous evidence of active attempts to exclude him from some communal settings for his views on Israel and anti-Semitism.[88]

Calls to exclude and marginalise are not only directed at the left from the 'establishment'. They can also be directed at established Jewish leaders by the 'grassroots'. For example, Mick Davis's high profile call for greater pluralism over discussion of Israel, discussed in chapter two, together with his own criticisms of the Netanyahu government, were met with calls for his resignation from an *ad hoc* coalition of pro-Israel campaigners. In March 2011, a petition was circulated calling for Davis's resignation:

> In view of his suggestion that anything short of a Palestinian state amounts to 'apartheid', his accusation that Benjamin Netanyahu lacks courage and his insistence that non-Israelis should have a say in Israeli policy (including security issues, regarding which Israeli parents alone send their sons and daughters to the IDF) the undersigned call on the unelected Mick Davis to resign from the UJIA Chairmanship and declare that they will not donate a penny to UJIA until he goes.

Much of the criticism of Davis focused on his wealth and his unelected position as chair of the JLC and United Jewish Israel Appeal. The Australian-Israeli Isi Liebler, a former chairman of the governing board of the World Jewish Congress and a columnist for the Jerusalem Post argued in November 2010:

> Mick Davis, also known as 'Big Mick', displays characteristics associated with the nouveau riche, akin to the behavior of some of the Russian Jewish oligarchs. His opinions are rarely challenged and he contemptuously rejects the suggestion that holding a communal role in any way precludes him from publicly expressing views which would normally be considered incompatible for anyone occupying such a position.[89]

Such criticisms demonstrate that resentment of communal leaders' positions on Israel is not confined to the left. At the same time, there is a crucial difference between critiques from the left and the right. The right-wing may criticise leaders for the positions they hold, but, generally speaking, they are more intent on replacing them with a leadership more to their liking than they are in criticising hierarchies in the Jewish community *per se*. Although groups like IJV have sometimes been accused of seeking to replace the existing communal leadership with a different one,[90] for the most part, the Jewish left prefers to critique hierarchies rather than replace them. The attempt to exclude some Jews from the Jewish community and the Jewish people is, therefore, primarily a strategy of the right and centre of the Jewish political spectrum.

Of course, part of the reason why the left is not so focused on exclusion is that it simply doesn't have the power to do so. Further, certain elements of the anti-Zionist left position, in particular, while they do not seek to exclude Jews from the Jewish community, do try to marginalise pro-Israel Jews from the wider community. Some strains of BDS attempt to exclude Israelis and supporters of Israel from, at least, the self-defined 'progressive' community and, at most, to completely isolate Israel from the rest of the world. *De facto*, if not always *de jure*, BDS can imply the exclusion of Jews from society, given that the majority of Jews are Zionists to some degree. Further, groups such as the IJAN also imply that progressive-minded Jews need to dissociate themselves from pro-Israel Jews. This attempt at exclusion and marginalisation of Israel and, inevitably, of at least some Diaspora Jews, carries with it frightening anti-Semitic resonances for many Jews.

At the same time, pro-Israel Jews may also call for boycotts. For example, in July 2011, pro-Israel campaigners protested outside a show held at the London Jewish Cultural Centre by the anti-Zionist Jewish comedian Ivor Dembina.[91] Also in July 2011, the opening of the skincare shop 'Lush' in Brent Cross shopping centre – close to areas with large Jewish populations – was accompanied by an informal campaign criticising the shop for promoting a pro-Palestinian song on its website.[92]

As I shall argue in the following chapter, to some extent, the drawing of boundaries is an inevitable part of both politics and community-building. The problem occurs when those boundaries are drawn narrowly and when the drawing of boundaries becomes an end in and of itself. The danger of drawing boundaries is that the practice builds up momentum to the point where it becomes impossible to live with difference at all – and even to live with those who live with difference. One example of this is a tweet sent in December 2010 by the pro-Israel blog CiFWatch that criticised Jeremy Newmark, director of the JLC, for attending the Limmud conference on the grounds that John Ging, head of the United Nations Relief and Works Agency in Gaza, was speaking as well. Newmark was not actually appearing in the same session as Ging and the conference featured around 1,000 different sessions (including many that were strongly pro-Israel). The implication was that any institution that has any kind of contact at all with institutions deemed anti-Israel should be shunned. This is a fairly extreme example of the common phenomenon of attributing 'guilt by association', in which any kind of connection to those who are pariahs, makes one a pariah oneself. The blogosphere is alive with minutely argued posts bent on proving that x is associated with y and, therefore, is the same as y. It creates a logic the end point of which is a kind of political purity, untainted by any kind of association with the despised other. Related to this is the well-known phenomenon of the 'narcissism of minor differences', in which people who have more in common than divides them, nevertheless, focus on their differences to the point where they cannot remain in contact. It is a vice that is found at all points in the political spectrum, but it has, perhaps, been developed to a particularly fine art on the left, which has long been riven with schisms. In my own experience, the most challenging and difficult conversations over Israel occur between the decent left and other left positions. Despite their many shared values, the differences over anti-Semitism and Israel cannot be bridged.

There is a kind of absurdity to some of these conflicts that provides rich material for satirists and comedians. In the film *Life of Brian*, the Monty Python team brilliantly sent up hair-splitting leftist politics with the irreconcilable rift between the Judean People's Front and the People's Front for Judea. Similarly, US comedian Emo Phillips has the following routine:

> I was walking across a bridge one day, and I saw a man standing on the edge, about to jump off. So I ran over and said: 'Stop! Don't do it!' 'Why shouldn't I?' he said. I said, 'Well, there's so much to live for!' He said, 'Like what?' I said, 'Well... are you religious or atheist?' He said, 'Religious.' I said, 'Me,

too! Are you Christian or Buddhist?' He said, 'Christian.' I said, 'Me, too! Are you Catholic or Protestant?' He said, 'Protestant.' I said, 'Me, too! Are you Episcopalian or Baptist?' He said, 'Baptist!' I said, 'Wow! Me, too! Are you Baptist Church of God or Baptist Church of the Lord?' He said, 'Baptist Church of God!' I said, 'Me, too! Are you original Baptist Church of God, or are you reformed Baptist Church of God?' He said, 'Reformed Baptist Church of God!' I said, 'Me, too! Are you reformed Baptist Church of God, reformation of 1879, or reformed Baptist Church of God, reformation of 1915?' He said, 'Reformed Baptist Church of God, reformation of 1915!' I said, 'Die, heretic scum,' and pushed him off.[93]

Yet while easy to satirise, the logic that leads to such absurdities is hard to escape. Part of the problem lies in the fact that, while the desire to create boundaries and pariahs can be found throughout history, the ability to exclude is much weaker today than it ever has been before. Participants in conflicts over Israel are too often caught in an impossible trap; when faced with people who seem to threaten their security and their deepest values, they wish to banish them, yet in the age of the Internet, no one can ever be fully banished. The resulting frustration only increases their rage.

OBSESSION WITH PURITY AND TRUTH

The ultimate result of Jewish conflicts over Israel is all too often the desire to separate from Jews who hold other views. Behind it lies a desire for a kind of 'purity' that marks opponents as somehow unclean. Purity is enshrined in an absolutist attitude to truth that sees one's own position not as one motivated by particular values and judgements, but as the only possible position a person could honestly take. The self-presentation of those who hold particular views on Israel is often that they are simply cyphers for the truth. If one views one's own position as absolute truth, then anyone holding a contrary position can only be doing so out of mendacity, bad faith or perversity.

For these reasons, a common feature of conflicts over Israel is appealing to what are seen to be self-evident truths. One example of this is the use of the 2005 EUMC's working definition of anti-Semitism.[94] With regard to the connection between anti-Semitism and Israel, the definition stated:

> Examples of the ways in which antisemitism manifests itself with regard to the State of Israel taking into account the overall context could include:
>
> • Denying the Jewish people their right to self-determination, e.g., by claiming that the existence of a State of Israel is a racist endeavour.
>
> • Applying double standards by requiring of it a behaviour not expected or demanded of any other democratic nation.
>
> • Using the symbols and images associated with classic antisemitism (e.g., claims of Jews killing Jesus or blood libel) to characterize Israel or Israelis.
>
> • Drawing comparisons of contemporary Israeli policy to that of the Nazis.
>
> • Holding Jews collectively responsible for actions of the state of Israel.

The EUMC definition is the linchpin of some pro-Israel activism strategies.[95] It allows some forms of criticism of Israel and all anti-Zionism to be labelled as anti-Semitic. The EUMC definition is invoked so as to imply that it is not a document made by flawed human beings, but the first and last word on the subject. The EUMC definition thus becomes a constantly cited absolute truth that trumps any possible counter-argument and needs no further explication. One extraordinary example of this can be seen in a comment thread on a blog post from early 2012 on the *Jewish Chronicle* website. The writer of the post had invoked the EUMC definition and I responded in the thread by asking the author to clarify and justify why the definition is so important. He responded:

> A widely accepted definition drawn up by acknowledged experts in the field does not require "justification" any more than the mathematical definition of π (the ratio of a circle's circumference to its diameter) needs "justification"

or any more than the definition of the hypotenuse (the longest side of a right-angled triangle) needs "justification".

The only people who require "justification" of the EUMC Definition are those for whom it's inconvenient. That includes - but is not limited to - all antisemites.

Ironically, Jewish and non-Jewish critics of Israel often share similar assumptions. They agree that the EUMC definition unambiguously defines anti-Zionism as anti-Semitism and that the definition, if it were to be upheld, would be the last word on the subject. Much energy is focused on discrediting or overturning the EUMC definition as its opponents believe that allowing it to stand would prevent effective criticism of Israel. In May 2011, the congress of the University and College Union voted to distance itself from the EUMC definition and to make no use of and dissociate itself from the definition on the grounds:

...that the EUMC definition confuses criticism of Israeli government policy and actions with genuine antisemitism, and is being used to silence debate about Israel and Palestine on campus.

What has largely been missing from debates about the EUMC definition is any recognition that it might be ambiguous in certain respects. One way of understanding the definition is that it only seeks to suggest ways that anti-Semitic hate crimes *can* happen and that the denial of the Jewish right to a state *can* be construed as anti-Semitic. Further, the EUMC could be seen as just one way of defining anti-Semitism; a contribution to a debate, rather than the last word on the subject. Instead, both its supporters and detractors load so much weight on the definition that it becomes a proxy for the entirety of the debate.

Another example of this kind of conflict is over the question as to whether building settlements on lands occupied by Israel in the 1967 War is illegal according to international law. As with the EUMC definition, calling settlements 'illegal settlements' has become an unquestioned trope among their critics. As a response, supporters of Israel devote a great deal of attention to proving that settlement building is not illegal.[96] What this leads to is a plurality of minutely contested legal points that become ever more contested and complex over time. What gets lost is any sense that international law might be unclear on certain points and, further, that international law might be fluid, flawed and open to change. Further, arcane conflicts over the interpretation of international law avoid much deeper questions about the moral legitimacy or otherwise of the settlements.

A similar issue is the use of history as a weapon in the conflict. At stake in historical debates about Israel are fundamental questions about who is ultimately responsible for the current conflict. Given the enormous amount of extant information, huge numbers of events and issues can be subject to contested interpretations. Historians are used almost as weapons in the conflict, with the likes of Ilan Pappe on the left and Efraim Karsch on the right becoming active protagonists. All too often, the work of one particular historian is seen to 'prove' the rightness of one's position. This is a travesty of the process through which history is written. No historian ever has 'the last word' in a historical debate, as scholarship is, by its very nature, an open-ended process.

The absolutist narrowing of the conflict down to points of detail creates so much sound and fury that counter-veiling forces to absolutism become weaker. Little place is left for doubt and nuance amid the constant contestation, rendering communication between protagonists difficult and obscuring possible points of connection between apparently opposing sides.

The obsession with purity and truth constitutes a peculiar kind of fundamentalism. Those who practice it may do so in the service of impeccably liberal concerns. What lies behind this fundamentalism, then, is not necessarily a monolithic, fundamentalist view of the world, but rather a sense that, in this issue, there is no alternative to fundamentalist tactics. In part, this may come about when one's opponent uses fundamentalist tactics and one cannot think of any other way of responding than to do so in kind. Fundamentalist tactics also offer a powerful way of bolstering one's self-confidence within the conflict. To 'outsource' one's arguments to a particular law, definition or writer is to see oneself as simply one node in a powerful web of arguments. There is no need to open oneself up to others, to share one's ambivalence or vulnerability. Fundamentalism guards against the terrible fears and insecurities that the Israel conflict stirs up.

CONFLICT FOR ITS OWN SAKE

The tendency towards absolutism and fundamentalism in debates over Israel both explodes and narrows the conflict. It explodes it as almost everything becomes contested and no quarter can be given on any point. It narrows the conflict down as it erodes discussion of bigger, more crucial issues. Conflict is sparked by often trivial events and protagonists lose sight of the long-term visions they are trying to achieve.

Regardless of position, Israel activism in the Diaspora always risks losing sight of Israel itself. Much of what Israel activists do in the UK is not directly focused on having an effect in Israel. Those who support BDS do so because they believe that this kind of activity can support Palestinians, who have called for a boycott, and because they believe that it will isolate Israel and, in so doing, produce far-reaching change. Yet the campaign to gain support for BDS is itself so challenging that it requires a huge amount of focus, energy and time so that it can become an end in itself. The same is true for some kinds of pro-Israel activism, such as fighting BDS and pro-Palestinian anti-Semitism. Israel itself may recede into the background as conflicts outside Israel grab all the attention.

Conflict and the arguments it spawns can be an intoxicating process. With the ubiquity of online commentary, it is easy to be dragged into constant argument. These days no one can ever really have the 'last word' and so there can never be an end to provocation. Conflict over Israel has become so entrenched and positions so fixed that activism and argument can almost become a ritual, even entertainment. For example, a debate between American writers Peter Beinart and Daniel Gordis in New York in May 2012 was publicised with a boxing-style poster as a 'Heavyweight fight on Zionism'. Demonstrations and other forms of protest can become so predictable that even those sympathetic to the cause can become jaded. One Jewish leftist blogger commented on the seizure of the 'Jewish Boat to Gaza' in September 2010:[97]

> The British catamaran *Irene*, the "Jewish boat to Gaza," was diverted to Ashdod without incident and without capturing world attention as during Israel's boarding of the Turkish *Mavi Marmara*. This was the second boat following the

Marmara to be diverted. Predictions of a media circus failed to bear fruit.

Apparently, the global media is bored of this stunt already. Frankly, I am too. It stinks of pageantry, now that both sides know how the game is played. The boat announces their operating rules, the IDF states its intent to intercept, both sides play nice, and the Gaza blockade goes on. Which is not to say the stunt abjectly failed to raise awareness, nor that the violent prior episode was in any way preferable. (God forbid!)

FUTILITY AND SELF-DEFEATING LOGIC

It is understandable that some of those involved in the conflict over Israel may grow weary of finding themselves in a cycle of similar arguments. In April 2007 the journalist Nick Cohen wrote a column in the *Jewish Chronicle* entitled 'Dialogue with a western leftist' which reproduced the kind of argument he often finds himself involved in.[98] The piece ended as follows:

[Cohen] "...Your trouble is that you are a voyeur. The violence of bearded reactionaries with a Koran in one hand and a Kalashnikov in the other excites you. You prefer their thrilling intransigence to the arguments of boring men in suits in Ramallah, who are willing to compromise for a better life. You need the burning corpses of Palestinians and Jews to bring light to your empty life."

[Detractor] "And your trouble is you are a sly apologist for imperialism. You never condemn Israeli atrocities, but use nit-picking points of detail and clever rhetorical tricks to distract attention from crimes against humanity. You are a neo-con and a zio-Nazi, and I am never going to speak to you again."

[Cohen]"Don't worry, there are millions more like you out there, and I'll be having this conversation for the rest of my life. Send in the next one on your way out."

What is depressing about this column is that Cohen's satire of circular arguments over Israel is not matched by any kind of desire to find a way to break the cycle. His detractor's shrillness is more than matched by his own.

What Cohen has identified – semi-unwittingly – is the self-defeating logic of arguments over Israel. Shrill arguments not only fail to persuade others, they can even do the opposite. This is, of course, not a phenomenon exclusive to conflicts over Israel. Research has shown that, psychologically, there is a tendency for exposure to views contradicting our own to actually reinforce our views.[99] Even if the complexities of convincing people and creating social change are, understandably, too much for most people to totally understand and master (even professional psychologists and public relations consultants cannot overcome them), what *is* surprising is how some individuals involved in conflicts over Israel appear to be totally unaware that the problem even exists.

The frequency with which protagonists in the Israel conflict identify pariahs is evidence that the use of self-defeating strategies is deeply ingrained. It is clear that, in many cases, those who are treated as pariahs and marginalised from the Jewish community or, indeed, from other communities, go on to become more forthright and even extreme in their views. Not only is it all but impossible to silence people, the reverse is often the case. There are well-known examples (which I do not cite here for fear of perpetuating the very process I am condemning) of British Jews – on the right and the left – whose rhetoric and behaviour have become more trenchant as a result of their vilification and exclusion from various communities and spaces. One reason why exclusion and marginalisation rarely produce the desired effect is that it allows those targeted to present themselves as victims, even martyrs. The 'heroic' status accorded to those who have been victimised further stokes the intractability of the conflict.

The result of the self-defeating futility of much debate over Israel is that ostensibly opposing protagonists can become mirror images of each other. Angry, abusive behaviour confronts angry, abusive behaviour, both sides bolstered by a keen sense of being persecuted. Those who criticise the uncivil behaviour of others rarely pay attention to their own behaviour, and those who criticise others for hating them (or for hating themselves) may ignore their own hatred.

ALIENATION AND HURT

Not everyone who is exposed to conflict over Israel ends up following this self-perpetuating spiral. The toxicity of the conflict can simply alienate people to the extent that they retreat into silence. This is not so much because they find their own beliefs under attack (although, of course, they do), but because the conflict *in its entirety* is too exhausting and intimidating to enter. Even those who relish the fight can become exhausted and burned out.[100]

The conflict's virulence is such that it requires considerable fortitude to enter. All too often, the conflict appeals to people's basest instincts and worst behaviour, particularly online. The 'Internet Fuckwad Theory',[101] which states that a normal person confronted with the anonymity of the Internet may undergo a negative personality change, may be an exaggeration, but not by much. 'Difficult' characters – those who are most implacable in their views and most abusive in their language – become disproportionately important in the conflict. Campaigning groups come to rely on such people because more sensitive characters cannot flourish easily in the conflict.

Part of the impetus behind the growth of the pro-Israel pluralist and pro-Israel, pro-peace positions has been the desire to create a 'safe space' for discussion of Israel. While one could criticise the safe space model for keeping potentially subversive views away from the public sphere, it is certainly true that the need and desire exist to find ways in which people can be 'protected' from the worst effects of the conflict. Even those campaigning groups that are more outward facing and that actively participate in the conflict may owe at least some of their support to a simple desire to find a degree of mutual protection.

Despite the partial recognition in some quarters that safe space is needed, there is an increasing danger that the voices most needed in the conflict – nuanced, concerned, civil – may be most at risk of self-exclusion. In the face of the apparent reality that one can only articulate one's views about Israel in ways that are uncompromising and shrill, some are bound to choose silence.

VIOLENCE

The conflict in Israel-Palestine itself is characterised not just by all the same symptoms discussed in this chapter, but also by endemic violence: not just between Israelis and Palestinians, but also between Israelis and between Palestinians. While the assassination of Rabin and violent resistance to withdrawals from the occupied territories have been perpetrated by those on the right, those on the left and even the centre are often accused of, whether inadvertently or deliberately, making violence against Israelis more likely.

So far, in Diaspora Jewish communities there is, thankfully, little sign that the conflict over Israel will erupt into real violence. There have been some scuffles between pro-Israel and pro-Palestinian demonstrators, but these are, so far, rare. At the same time, though, a fear of violence permeates intra-Jewish conflict over Israel in the UK. Those who accuse Jews of colluding with anti-Semitism and those who would destroy Israel are, at some level, expressing genuinely held fears that violence directed at them will follow at some stage. The fears of Jews who criticise Israel are similarly grounded in concerns about Israel's potential for violence and its impact on the Palestinians.

The symptoms of the conflict reflect this spectre of violence, both as a stimulus for fear and as sublimated into aggressive language. Even if it rarely causes physical pain, conflict between Jews over Israel in the UK does create hurt and suffering that is all too real.

***

Many of the symptoms of the conflict discussed in this chapter can also be found in conflicts over other issues. Abortion, for example, particularly in the US, can generate the same kind of behaviour. In the chapters that follow, I will discuss ways of addressing the conflict over Israel in the UK Jewish community. Some of the approaches I discuss could be applied to other conflicts, but others are unique to the Jewish case. Grounding this discussion in the Jewish case offers an opportunity for cautious optimism that the symptoms of the conflict can be ameliorated. As I will argue in the next chapter, it is precisely the Jewishness of the conflict that provides the most powerful case for action.

NOTES

54 - Hoffman, J. (2010, March 15). Statement regarding Board of Deputies international division yesterday [Web log post]. The Jewish Chronicle. Retrieved on May 10, 2010 from http://www.thejc.com/blogs/jonathan-hoffman/statement-regarding-board--deputies-international-division-yesterday

55 - Goldberg, J. (2011, May 23). A cornucopia of hate mail, Obama (and Goldblog) edition. The Atlantic. Retrieved on May 30, 2013 from http://www.theatlantic.com/international/archive/2011/05/a-cornucopia-of-hate-mail-obama-and-goldblog-edition/239253/

56 - CiF Watch under attack! (2010, September 15). Retrieved on May 30, 2013 from http://cifwatch.com/2010/09/15/cif-watch-under-attack/

57 - Strenger, C. (2011, July 12). Israel's boycott ban is down to siege mentality. The Guardian. Retrieved on May 30, 2013 from http://www.guardian.co.uk/commentisfree/2011/jul/12/israel-boycott-ban?commentpage=all#start-of-comments

58 - See, for example: Denby, D. (2009). Snark: A Polemic in Seven Fits. Oxford, UK: Picador.

59 - See for example: Gilman, S. (1990) Jewish self-hatred: Anti-Semitism and the hidden language of the Jews. Baltimore, MD: John Hopkins University Press.

60 - See for example: Boyarin, D. (1997). Unheroic Conduct: The Rise of Heterosexuality and the Invention of the Jewish Man. Berkeley, CA: University of California Press; Dekel, M. (2010). The Universal Jew: Masculinity, Modernity and the Zionist Moment. Evanston, IL: Northwestern University Press.

61 - Used with permission.

62 - Mamet, D. (2009) The Wicked Son: Anti-Semitism, Self-Hatred, and the Jews. New York, NY: Schocken, pp. xi-xii.

63 - See for example: SlingshotKiller. (2011, June 23). 'As a Jew' explained [Web log post]. Retrieved on May 30, 2013 from http://cifwatch.com/2011/06/23/as-a-jew--explained/

64 - Hirsh, D. (2011, June 2). Richard Kuper, 'Asa Jew'... [Web log post]. Retrieved on May 30, 2013 from http://engageonline.wordpress.com/2011/06/02/richard-kuper--asa-jew/

65 - The longstanding nickname of The Guardian newspaper is the Grauniad for its alleged propensity for poor sub-editing.

66 - Jacobson, H. (2010, July 28). Anti-Zionism – facts (and fictions). The Jewish Chro-

nicle. Retrieved on May 30, 2013 from http://www.thejc.com/comment-and-debate/comment/36256/anti-zionism-facts-and-%EF%AC%81ctions

67 - Transcript available at: Unsdoerfer, Z. (2011, March 4). Is it OK to be Jewish and criticise Israel [Web log post]? Retrieved on May 30, 2013 from http://zalmi.blogspot.com/2011/03/is-it-ok-to-be-jewish-and-criticise.html

68 - Silverstein, R. (2010, January 31). Dershowitz calls Goldstone 'Evil,' 'Traitor to Jews;' Shin Bet urges NIF investigation [Web log post]. Retrieved on May 30, 2013 from http://www.richardsilverstein.com/tikun_olam/2010/01/31/dershowitz-calls-goldstone-evil-traitor-to-jews-knesset-to-investigate-nif/

69 - Lerman, A. (2008, Summer). Jewish Self-Hatred: Myth or Reality. The Jewish Quarterly.

70 - Klug, B. (2011). Being Jewish and Doing Justice: Bringing Argument to Life. London, UK: Vallentine Mitchell, p. 368.

71 - International Jewish Anti-Zionist Network. (n.d.). Charter of the International Jewish anti-Zionist Network. Retrieved on June 16, 2001 from http://www.ijsn.net/about_us/charter/

72 - Mearsheimer, J. J. (2010, April 29). The Future of Palestine: Righteous Jews vs. New Afrikaners. Monthly Review. Retrieved on May 30, 2013 from http://mrzine.monthlyreview.org/2010/mearsheimer300410.html

73 - I have decided not to include examples of this here due to the inflammatory and often libellous nature of such accusations.

74 - Hirsch, D. (2007). Anti-Zionism and Antisemitism: Cosmopolitan reflections. New Haven, CT: Yale Initiative for the Interdisciplinary Study of Antisemitism [caps].

75 - Godwin, M. (1994). Meme, counter-meme. Wired. Retrieved on May 30, 2013 from http://www.wired.com/wired/archive/2.10/godwin.if_pr.html [is this OK?]

76 - European Union Monitoring Council on Racism and Xenophobia. (2005). Working definition of Antisemitism. Retrieved on July 7, 2012 from http://fra.europa.eu/fraWebsite/material/pub/AS/AS-WorkingDefinition-draft.pdf

77 - Mikey. (2008, September 16). Alef list posting number 7- Tony Greenstein and the Zionism equals Nazism equation [Web log post]. Retrieved on June 1, 2013 from http://arvsaz.blogspot.co.uk/2008/09/alef-list-posting-number-tony.html

78 - See for example: jews4big. (2013, January 19). Zionism and Antisemitism: Racist political twins – A J-big briefing [Web log post]. Retrieved on June 1, 2013 from http://jews4big.wordpress.com/2013/01/19/zionism-and-antisemitism-racist-political-twins--a-j-big-briefing/

79 - Geller, P. (2009, May 6). Kapo Emanuel threatens Israel, bullies Jews to pick their poison as Obama seeks to disarm the tiny nation [Web log post]. Retrieved on June 1, 2013 from http://atlasshrugs2000.typepad.com/atlas_shrugs/2009/05/kapo-emanuel--threatens-israel-bullies-jews-to-pick-their-poison.html

80 - yamit82. (2010, September 14). Dhimmi Kapo Jew: ABE FOXMAN Fawning Up To Muslims [Web log post]. Retrieved on June 1, 2013 from http://www.israpundit.com/archives/27875

81 - Levinson, B. (2011, June 19). National Judenrat Democratic Kapos (NJDC) white-wash Islamization threat [Web log post]. Retrieved on June 1, 2013 from http://www.israpundit.com/archives/37075

82 - Self-Hating and/or Israel-Threatening LIST. (n.d.). Retrieved on June 1, 2013 from http://www.masada2000.org/shit-list.html

83 - Dershowitz, A. (2010, April 28). It is Goldstone who is politicizing grandson's bar mitzvah [Web log post]. Retrieved on June 1, 2013 from http://www.huffingtonpost.com/alan-dershowitz/it-is-goldstone-who-is-po_b_555390.html

84 - JFNA tosses Israel critic from heroes contest [Web log post]. (2011, October 14). Retrieved on June 1, 2013 from http://ejewishphilanthropy.com/jfna-tosses-israel--critic-from-heroes-contest/

85 - Reut Institute. Building a Political Firewall against the Assault on Israel's Legitimacy: London as a Case Study. Tel Aviva: Reut Institute, November 2010. http://www.reut--institute.org/data/uploads/PDFver/20101219%20London%20Case%20Study.pdf.: 92.

86 - Rosenfelder, R., & Kahn-Harris, K. (2007, September 2). The problem with dialogue. New Jewish Thought. Retrieved on June 1, 2013 http://www.newjewishthought.org/2007/09/the-problem-with-dialogue/

87 - Karpf, A., Klug, B., Rose, J., & Rosenbaum, B. (Eds.) (2008). A time to speak out: Independent Jewish voices on Israel, Zionism and Jewish identity. London, UK: Verso.

88 - Lerman, A. (2012). The Making and Unmaking of a Zionist: A Personal and Political Journey. London, UK: Pluto.

89 - Liebler, I. (2010, November 24). Candidly speaking: The de-Zionization of Anglo Jewry. The Jerusalem Post. Retrieved on June 1, 2013 from http://www.jpost.com/Opinion/Columnists/Candidly-Speaking-The-de-Zionization-of-Anglo-Jewry

90 - That is the implication, for example, of David Hirsh's accusation that the Jewish radical left are the 'new conservatives': Hirsh, D. (2006, August 13). Radical 68ers have become the new conservatives of the Jewish community in Britain [Web log post]. Retrieved on June 1, 2013 from http://www.engageonline.org.uk/blog/article.php?id=578

91 - Rosen, R. (2011, July 21). Ivor Dembina's show no joke for protester. The Jewish Chronicle. Retrieved on June 1, 2013 from http://www.thejc.com/news/uk--news/51991/ivor-dembinas-show-no-joke-protester

92 - Elgot, J. (2011, July 28). Lush: Saudia Arabia gets under our skin. The Jewish Chronicle. Retrieved on June 1, 2013 from http://www.thejc.com/news/uk-news/52353/lush--saudia-arabia-gets-under-our-skin

93 - The wisdom of Emo Phillips. (n.d.). Retrieved on June 1, 2013 from http://cmgm.stanford.edu/~lkozar/EmoPhillips.html

94 - European Union Monitoring Council on Racism and Xenophobia. (2005). Working definition of Antisemitism. Retrieved on July 7, 2012 from http://fra.europa.eu/fraWebsite/material/pub/AS/AS-WorkingDefinition-draft.pdf

95 - See for example: CiF Watch. (n.d.). How we define Antisemitism. Retrieved on June 1, 2013 from http://cifwatch.com/how-we-define-antisemitism/

96 - See for example: Phillips, D. M. (2009, December). The illegal-settlements myth. Commentary. Retrieved on June 1, 2013 from http://www.commentarymagazine.com/article/the-illegal-settlements-myth/

97 - Kung Fu Jew. (2010, September 29). Jewish boat to Ashdod achieves pageantry [Web log post]. Retrieved on June 1, 2013 from http://jewschool.com/2010/09/29/24159/jewish-boat-to-ashdod-achieves-pageantry/

98 - Cohen, N. (2011, April 27). Dialogue with a western leftist. The Jewish Chronicle. Retrieved on June 1, 2013 from http://www.thejc.com/comment-and-debate/columnists/48235/dialogue-a-western-leftist?utm_source=twitterfeed&utm_medium=twitter

99 - McRaney, D. (2011, June 10). The backfire effect [Web log post]. Retrieved on June 1, 2013 from http://www.youarenotsosmart.com/2011/06/10/the-backfire-effect/

100 - Newkey-Burden, C. (2011, July 25). Blogland: Here be dragons. The Jewish Chronicle. Retrieved on June 1, 2013 from http://www.thejc.com/comment-and-debate/comment/52156/blogland-here-be-dragons

101 - Internet fuckwad theory. (2011). Retrieved from Encyclopedia Dramatica on June 1, 2013 from https://encyclopediadramatica.se/Internet_Fuckwad_Theory

CHAPTER FIVE:
THE CASE FOR TREATMENT

The first four chapters of this book have, I hope, demonstrated that, in the last few years, serious divisions have emerged in Diaspora Jewish communities over the question of Israel, that these divisions have given rise to endemic conflict and that this conflict feeds on itself and is often conducted in abusive ways that cause hurt to those involved. In this chapter and the rest of the book, I will develop a strategy for managing this conflict.

THE CASE FOR TREATMENT

But first, a pressing question needs to be addressed before I can begin to outline how the conflict can be managed: *why is any of this a problem?* Conflict between Jews over Israel is, after all, only one of myriad conflicts in the world today. It certainly isn't the worst – no Diaspora Jews are killed by other Jews for their beliefs. If the conflict is rooted in powerful emotions and real political/ideological/religious differences and is, therefore, inevitable, why not simply live with it? The greater Israeli-Palestinian conflict must surely be the primary conflict to address? Why does it matter so much what happens among Jews in the Diaspora? My case for treatment rests on four principle justifications:

> 1. *The situation is unlikely to improve dramatically any time soon – and may well get worse.*

The conflict over Israel in the Diaspora is, of course, affected by developments in Israel itself. There are few signs that political conflict within Israel, between Israel and the Palestinians and between Israel and neighbouring countries is going to improve any time soon. The continuing lack of a permanent Israeli-Palestinian settlement is pushing Jews in different directions as to the best way forward. It is, therefore, reasonable to expect that differences over Israel are likely to increase, at least in the short to medium term. Even if some kind of Israeli-Palestinian accord is reached, it is likely to divide opinions.

2. 'Victory' is impossible.

One of the defining features in recent Jewish conflict over Israel is that, while the old public supporter position has eroded, no other position has come to dominate the field. Rather, a plurality of positions has emerged, most of which have substantial support, institutional grounding and a strong public profile. It is hard to envisage a time when one position will dominate as it did in the past – there can be no 'victory'. While one position can dominate a particular institution, in the community as a whole, there is no way to completely erase or marginalise any particular position. That does not, of course, mean that individuals cannot be persuaded by others. The situation is likely to remain fluid. However, the self-defeating tactics and strategies discussed in the previous chapter ensure that not only is ultimate victory endlessly deferred, but, also, that those who attempt to destroy opponents' arguments or credibility, risk actually strengthening them.

3. Potential alienation of more ambivalent, quieter voices.

Given the heightened emotions inherent in this issue, it can be hard for Jews to take a position without becoming entangled in conflict. Even 'quieter' forms of engagement can become difficult. It is hard to attend a pro-Israel public meeting or demonstration without running the gauntlet of loud protestors. It is hard to sign a petition criticising Israel without risking public exposure of one's views to potentially hostile voices in the community. The conflict also works against more ambivalent voices. Such is the vehemence on all sides that it is difficult to find a public space in which it is safe to say 'I'm not sure' or 'I'm confused'.

In fairness, the pro-Israel pluralist and pro-Israel, pro-peace positions were born out of a desire to create a 'safe space' for these ambivalent voices to be heard. However, even here the opprobrium that such positions receive can make entering this space difficult. In any case, the strict 'red lines' around the pro-Israel pluralist position mean that it is very difficult to express doubts about Zionism and Israel as a Jewish state. It is similarly difficult for those who might have some sympathy with the settlements to find a safe space to talk through their own feelings and concerns.

4. Real pain and hurt has been caused.

Conflicts over Israel in the Diaspora cause harm to Jews across the spectrum. The most active protagonists can become wounded and embittered by their experiences. Interacting with some other Jews can become a constant struggle to the point where the mere presence of Jews holding other positions can become upsetting. For those who see Israel as the guarantor of Jewish existence in the world, Jews who reject the Jewish state are undermining one's own personal security. For those who see Israel as morally compromised, Jewish support for Israel undermines Jewish values. It is often upsetting to see so many Jews holding views that one sees as damaging.

THE THREAT TO JEWISH PEOPLEHOOD

This case for treatment is fundamentally pragmatic; the conflict is damaging and it can only get worse. Therefore, the conflict is a problem and *something* needs to be done to help Jews to manage it better. But beyond this pragmatic recognition of the problem, I would argue that the conflict needs to be addressed for more idealistic reasons. The case I want to make is that the conflict over Israel threatens the very possibility of Jewish 'peoplehood' and that Jewish 'peoplehood' is an ideal worth striving for.

Perhaps the best way to appreciate the value of Jewish 'peoplehood' is to describe its opposite. This would be a world in which Jews form a variety of communities and other kinds of groups along ideological, religious, geographic and other lines and those communities and groups actively denounce the legitimacy of others. This is a divided Jewish world, endlessly squabbling about who has the 'right' to call themselves truly Jewish. Jews in this world feel little or no connection to others who call themselves Jews and seek to gain distance from them at every opportunity.

Some would argue that this is the situation in which we find ourselves at the moment! Leaving aside the issue of Israel, religious conflicts mean some Jews deny the Jewishness of others who call themselves Jews. There are few social connections and beliefs in common between, say, Haredi Jews on the one hand and secular Jews on the other. However, I would argue that we have not quite arrived at a situation in which Jews are so irrevocably alienated from each other that it has become impossible to speak of some kind of thread that connects all Jews. The legacy of the Holocaust, the persistence of anti-Semitism and even the mutual need to respond to the existence of the state of Israel do provide a common set of challenges with which Jews struggle.

It is likely though that, given the fragmentation caused in the last couple of centuries by the emergence of a whole range of mutually incompatible forms of Jewishness, adding another source of conflict to the mix could be the 'final straw'. If Israel continues to be a source of conflict at the pace it has in the last couple of decades, then the already fragile bonds tying Jews to each other could be shattered entirely.

Commentators have often highlighted the fragmentation of the Jewish world and conflict between Jews.[102] However, their attention has usually focused on religious divisions, rather than political ones. Religious division alone is of sufficient concern to lead some Jewish leaders and thinkers to feel the need to affirm the ultimate unity of the Jewish people. In his 1993 book *One People?*[103] Jonathan Sacks argued forcefully that Jewish peoplehood is foundational to Judaism:

> The idea of 'one people' is a religious commitment that cannot be given coherence in any other frame of discourse... That idea belongs not to nature, race, or politics, but to covenant. (213)

He further argued that:

> The fragmentation of peoplehood, brought about by modernity, cannot simply be acceded to without deep conflict with inescapable Jewish values. (86)

Sacks saw Israel as a point of unity within a Jewish people divided by religion:

> Today's Jewry is both uncompromisingly divided and unprecedentedly united: divided by religious difference, but united by a powerful sense - reinforced by the Holocaust and the State of Israel - of a shared history, fate and responsibility. (195)

Sacks advocated orthodox 'inclusivism' as a prescription for Jewish unity – accepting all Jews, while not necessarily legitimating their denominations

– and, as such, while his concerns about Jewish peoplehood are widely shared, his solutions have been more controversial. It is intriguing to speculate where, for example, anti-Zionist Jews might fit into his schema; does Sacks believe that Jews who do not support Israel should be included within this 'one people'?

The question as to where to 'draw the line' runs through the work of a growing number of proponents of the concept of 'Jewish peoplehood', which has emerged in recent years. Faced with the growing heterogeneity of the Jewish people worldwide, in particular divisions between inmarried-outmarried, secular-religious and Israeli-Diaspora Jews, Jewish thinkers and policy-makers have attempted to develop Jewish peoplehood into a conceptual, educational and policy framework. Advocates of Jewish peoplehood have attempted to reconcile the fact of plurality with a desire to maintain a common, unifying structure to bind together Jews around the world.

The roots of the concept can be traced ultimately to Judaism's venerable concern with *Am Yisrael*, the people of Israel. The Hebrew Bible tells the story of a covenant made initially with Abraham and his family and eventually with the people that came out of Egypt. The subject of Judaism is a collective subject and many Jewish rituals can only be practiced fully within a collective. Rituals, such as the Passover Seder meal – in which Jews are taught to identify themselves personally with those who came out of Egypt – embed peoplehood into the heart of Jewish practice.

In the twentieth century, Mordechai Kaplan's (1934) work on 'Jewish civilization' attempted to reconstruct Judaism as a kind of collective journey by a people otherwise divided religiously, culturally and nationally.[104] Jewish peoplehood, as it is used today, has a much more recent origin. Menachem Revivi and Ezra Kopelowitz date the use of Jewish peoplehood in Jewish communal strategic planning and policy-making to around the year 2000.[105] They explain the emergence of the concept as follows:

> ...the sudden take-up of the concept of Jewish Peoplehood by Jewish organizations stems from an ideological vacuum that developed in both the United States and Israel, beginning in the 1970s, but whose impact is only now being felt...The answers provided to the questions of Jewish meaning by

the 19th and 20th century ideological movements no longer capture the imagination of large segments of Jewry. The outcome has presented a serious problem for the leadership of Jewish organizations. Whether for fundraising, communal, educational or political work, all these organizations need to provide a convincing rationale for their actions or, over time, they will lose members and resources. Within this reality, the idea of Jewish Peoplehood is viewed as a possible avenue for organizations to reach out to their constituents. (xvii)

As such, Jewish peoplehood was developed as a response to the need to find ways to bring Jews together in an increasingly fragmented world. Organisations, such as the Jewish Agency, the Nadav Foundation and the UJA-Federation of New York, have made the promotion of Jewish peoplehood a central part of their work.

Scholars and thinkers have developed the concept into a more robust kind of ideology. Arnold Eisen, in an essay in the volume edited by Revivi and Kopelowitz,[106] sketched out the advantages of Jewish peoplehood as a concept:

'Nation' and 'religion' are each in their own way too all-encompassing. They demand more than many Jews are willing to identify with in terms of belief or behavior, and thus render significant portions of the population outsiders to a group which they know belongs to them and which they want very much to claim as their own. On the other hand, ethnicity and heritage are too narrow. They miss out on much of what makes Jewish identity attractive and even compelling to many Jews — a part of the self for which they are profoundly grateful and that many are profoundly disappointed not to transmit to the next generation. Only *peoplehood* seems just right. It betokens an identity in which religious as well as secular Jews, Israeli as well as Diaspora Jews, and traditional as well as liberal Jews (to list only a few of the many dichotomies), can feel equally at home. (2-3)

In other words, Jewish peoplehood is better than other modern concepts for drawing together the various aspects of Jewish identity and expression. It allows different kinds of Jews to use a common language and framework.

For its advocates, Jewish peoplehood is about more than simply finding a common conceptual framework. It is a framework designed to enable common identity and practice. As Erica Brown and Misha Galperin argue,[107] Jewish peoplehood is 'a sense of belonging to an extended family with a mission, a people with a purpose' (69). It is here that the concept becomes problematic. There is a tension between Jewish peoplehood as a unifying concept and Jewish peoplehood as a motivating concept. Those who cleave to a particular ideological standpoint may feel that if the 'purpose' of Jewish peoplehood is too specific, it threatens to compromise their own purpose. For example, in a 2011 article,[108] David Breakstone, vice-chair of the World Zionist Organisation, argued that Jewish peoplehood threatened the centrality of Israel:

> Zionism can accommodate to accepting the richness and viability of Diaspora Jewish life; it can't adjust to accepting that Israel is only another place where Jews happen to live. I am afraid that the "peoplehood" approach may be promoting such a worldview…. While teaching Jews in Israel that they are part of a people is vital, teaching Jews elsewhere that they are bound inextricably to this country is at least as critical. Zionist education encompasses both objectives. Peoplehood education may not.

At the other end of the spectrum, the Jewish peoplehood concept has been criticised for being too exclusive. A 2010 post on the blog of the UK Jewish radical group Jewdas,[109] similarly, argued that, by striving for unity, proponents of Jewish peoplehood ignore the vitality and importance of diverse Jewish ideologies:

> …this is the essence of Peoplehood theory, discarding all meaningful religious, linguistic, cultural, and philosophical elements, lest they offend anyone, Jewishness is reduced to a big ethnic love-in. Love your fellow Jew, the only mitzvah that remains…Judaism/Jewishness is without centre, diverse sets of cultures, practices and politics that are bound together only polemically in the service of particular ideological projects. But so what? Is that such a problem? From Mediaeval

philosophers to Kabbalists, Jews have frequently been more attached to their particular ideologies and communities than to the 'collective'. The strongest Jewish communities had the greatest diversity and argument, only the experience of 20th century hatred coupled with the fear of corrosive modernity has driven us to strive for an imagined unity.

The US writer Jay Michaelson argued in a 2010 article[110] that if support for Israel is central to Jewish peoplehood (as many of its advocates would argue) then the concept is inherently compromised. Discussing the decision by some Federations to exclude those Jews who don't support Zionism from their funding, Michaelson pointed out the contradiction with the Federation's professed aims of supporting Jewish peoplehood:

> One of the values of peoplehood is inclusion: creating a Jewish community where participation is open to people of different generations, different sexualities and gender orientations, different nationalities, different levels of education and so forth. But if we want a community that stands for something — for example, support for the existence of the State of Israel — then we are by definition excluding those who do not share that value. The stakes should be clear. If "we" as a community are committed to support for Israel, then it seems right that those opposed to Israel's very existence should not receive "our" financial support. But that commitment comes at the expense of another commitment to peoplehood and inclusion.

Advocates of Jewish peoplehood have attempted to deal with these difficult issues by reframing peoplehood as a common 'conversation' within a diverse Jewish people. Dr. Shlomi Ravid, director of the International School for Jewish Peoplehood Studies at Beth Hatefutsot, Israel, argued, in a collection of essays presented to the US General Assembly of the United Jewish Communities:[111]

> Our lead priority…is to focus on the building of Peoplehood capital. It assumes that the current level of Jewish social and cultural capital is in decline and needs enhancement. It calls for bringing Jews from throughout the Jewish world together to get to know each other, to develop a

conversation about each other and about their common heritage, values and future goals. It calls for both face to face encounters, joint projects as well as technology facilitated conversations. This process can initiate a sense of solidarity, of belonging to a larger collective and will eventually lead to the interpretation that will resonate with the people of the future. It will develop both Peoplehood capital and content. (2)

Similarly, Arnold Eisen argued in the same collection:

Facilitating the entry of Jews into common conversation will increase the chances that... bonding will occur and that it will survive the divisions which so beset [the Jewish people]. The conversation takes place one encounter at a time, each experience building on the next. Taken as a whole, they constitute, mark, and perpetuate Jewish Peoplehood — a never-ending project as each generation, community and Jew resolves, in turn, to make it last.[112]

This suggests that Jewish peoplehood can be created not through a common mission, but through a common form of communication. This is the version of Jewish peoplehood that I want to develop in the remainder of this chapter and the following chapter.

REFRAMING THE CONCEPT OF JEWISH PEOPLEHOOD

There is no doubt that the concept of Jewish peoplehood is deeply flawed in certain respects. Critics correctly note that if it is prescriptive then, inevitably, some Jews will be excluded, but if it is inclusive then it risks blandness and smothering distinctive Jewish ideologies and theologies. Jewish peoplehood advocates have, at times, excluded anti-Zionists and those who reject engagement with Israel as a central aspect of Jewish identity; conversely, they have not managed to appease those Zionists who see Israel as *the* centre of the Jewish people. In any case, the concept of Jewish peoplehood is not universally accepted throughout the Jewish world and, even in the US and Israel, it is largely a term used by policy-making elites.

Yet there is no doubt that the concept of Jewish peoplehood represents an important response to the problems discussed in this book. Jewish peoplehood advocates are concerned – as I am – that Jews are in conflict to the point where any kind of common ground between Jews becomes difficult. Jewish peoplehood is a concept that recognises both the inevitability of difference and the necessity of trying to find some kind of connection that can prevent differences from turning into balkanisation. As such, it can provide the grounding for the case that I am trying to make: that intra-Jewish conflict over Israel needs to be better managed.

The task is, therefore, to find a concept of Jewish peoplehood that will make sense to Jews on all sides of the Israel conflict. Jewish peoplehood needs to be reframed in a way that recognises the limitations of concepts of Jewish peoplehood that have been advocated in the last few years. In order to 'work', Jewish peoplehood needs to be a concept that almost any kind of Jew can buy into – including Jews who have no ideological or theological commitment to peoplehood and including those who do not see certain other Jews as 'proper' Jews.

At first sight this project seems impossible. Indeed, it is impossible, if the concept of Jewish peoplehood were to be based on some kind of Jewish ideology or theology. What I suggest, though, is that Jewish peoplehood can be reframed *not as ideology, but as self-interest*. Jewish peoplehood should be understood as *a common journey by Jews towards the protection of our self-interest as Jews*.

The concept of Jewish peoplehood I propose is a *pragmatic* one. It is based on two assumptions:

> 1. Those who identify themselves or are identified as Jews are inevitably connected to others who identify themselves or are identified as Jews – whether they like it or not.

> 2. Many of those who identify themselves or are identified as Jews will hold diametrically opposing views to others who identify themselves or are identified as Jews. These include views that some believe threaten the existential, moral or spiritual survival of Jews and Judaism.

My concept of Jewish peoplehood is not an ideal to be striven for. *Jewish peoplehood is simply a fact* in that any kind of identification as a Jew, inevitably, means being lumped in with other Jews. Even the strongest advocate of a purely secular Jewishness is, on some level, part of the same category as the most stringently observant Haredi Jew. Jewish peoplehood exists whether one believes in it or not.

Seeing Jewish peoplehood in this way throws a new light on intra-Jewish conflict. The problem is not that intra-Jewish conflict over Israel threatens to split the Jewish people apart irrevocably. Rather, the problem is that however much different kinds of Jews may be in conflict with each other, it is almost impossible for them to extricate themselves from each other. If this were not the case, conflict would be less of a problem, as different Jewish groups could go their own way and eventually form entirely different peoples with which cordial inter-communal relations could eventually be forged. This is, after all, what happened with the development of Christianity.

It follows, then, that Jews are faced with a simple choice: remain enmeshed in a perpetual conflict with those other Jews with whom one will always be connected, or try and find a way to live with the inevitable existence of other Jews whose views one abhors. Recognition of Jewish peoplehood is in every Jew's interest as it simply makes being a Jew a more pleasant experience. To accept the fact that other kinds of Jews exist and will always exist liberates Jewish existence so that it can become more than a perpetual and futile struggle to delegitimise other Jews. It frees up energy and time to devote to one's own Jewish journey. Of course, acceptance of the differences inherent in Jewish peoplehood does not mean that one should not try to convince other Jews of the rightness of one's own position. One can accept the existence of other kinds of Jews while still trying to ensure that there are as few of them as possible.

Even if the concept of Jewish peoplehood I outline is much more modest in its aims than that of other advocates, it still involves considerable commitment to make it work. Above all, it requires a commitment to make a special effort to improve one's relations with other Jews. To a degree, this can be done through simply ignoring other kinds of Jews. In fact, this is already the case with certain kinds of intra-Jewish relations. Haredi-secular Jewish relations outside of Israel are mostly neutral and unproblematic, as the two groups inhabit vastly different worlds. The most difficult conflicts are often between the most closely connected groups, such as the pro-Israel pluralists and the public supporters, discussed in chapter two. This is precisely where recognition of Jewish peoplehood is most difficult and potentially most useful. It can push Jews into appreciating that they have little choice but to work on their relations with other Jews who are, simultaneously, close to and far away from them.

RECONFIGURING JEWISH COMMUNITY

The concept of Jewish peoplehood I have outlined has implications for Jewish communal life. Any attempt to manage Jewish conflict over Israel has to address Jewish communal practices and institutions. Jewish community institutions are on the frontline of the conflict because many of its flashpoints are over inclusion and exclusion of individuals, groups and viewpoints.

Building on the pragmatic concept of Jewish peoplehood I have outlined, I suggest the following principles for dealing with difference (over Israel, but also, by extension, over other matters) in Jewish communities:

1. *The existence of differences over Israel should be recognised as a permanent feature of Jewish communities.*

Jews who espouse particular views on Israel need to accept that Jews who espouse opposing views will not go away and cannot simply be dismissed.

2. *Cross-communal Jewish institutions should avoid practices of marginalisation and the creation of pariahs.*

By 'cross-communal institutions' I mean institutions that do not formally require ideological/theological 'tests' for inclusion and that seek to serve Jews as a whole. This principle has two main aims. One is to ensure that Jews do not suffer the pain of being ostracised from other Jews. The other is to ensure that Jewish institutions do not spend endless amounts of time on ultimately futile attempts to suppress certain kinds of differences.

3 .*'Firewalls'* must be established to ensure that conflict over Israel does not intersect with and reinforce other kinds of conflict.

Conflicts and divisions over Israel need not appear in all communal settings. The issue of Israel does not have to be a touchstone for all kinds of communal activity.

While these principles seem modest, one implication of them is that Jewish communal institutions need to work to include those who reject or are strongly critical of Israel and Zionism. Given the opprobrium that anti-Zionists and even left Zionists face in many Jewish communal quarters, this is a difficult proposition. Indeed, the controversy that even the emergence of pro-Israel pluralism has generated demonstrates how even the most modest forms of inclusion are difficult to achieve.

As someone who identifies with the left, I am aware that my argument is open to the criticism that I am simply using the concept of Jewish peoplehood to make the Jewish community more congenial to those who also hold my views and also to those who are further to my left. However, I would stress that it isn't just sections of the left who are currently marginalised in the Jewish community. As I argued in chapter two, the religious right have a limited profile in the UK Jewish community, at least. The Jewish community I envisage is one that is more open to those on both the right and the left. The inclusion of one has to imply inclusion of all.

Even if the greater inclusion of those who are currently marginal may be hard for some to swallow at the moment, what is tolerable and intolerable in Jewish communities changes over time. As was the case with Zionism, what was once marginal, can become mainstream very quickly. As Donniel Hartman has argued, the 'boundary policy' of the Jewish people needs to be responsive to the reality on the ground:[113]

> That which is classified as intolerable must be shaped by the living reality that is the Jewish people. One may reject certain expressions of Jewish life, but the minute that that expression is the policy or ideology of more than a small minority of Jews, that rejection must remain within the confines of tolerance or tolerable deviance. (170)

The difficult transition towards a more inclusive Jewish community may be eased through reconfiguring the place of Israel in Jewish communal life. As I argued in chapter one, in the post-war period Israel became a point of consensus in the Diaspora. For communities increasingly divided by denomination, collective work on behalf of Israel – such as solidarity rallies, collecting money for Israeli charities and communal *Yom Haatzmaut* (Israel independence day) celebrations – became a precious unifying factor. Part of the problem with the situation today is that this strategy is becoming ever more unviable.

It follows then that in order to ease the Israel conflict, Jewish institutions that aspire to inclusion may have to pull back from some kinds of Israel-related activity. Celebratory, defensive and political engagement with Israel should be the job of specialist organisations with clear ideologies. The 'big tent' approach, which has been pioneered by pro-Israel pluralists, can only be a big tent covering pro-Israel organisations, rather than a big tent covering the community as a whole.

What I am arguing is paradoxical to some extent; if the Jewish community would be more open about its divisions, it would actually find it easier to come together. Acceptance that there cannot be a non-controversial, simple 'pro-Israel' position and that those who reject Israel cannot be suppressed is actually a liberating move. If Israel is recognised as a permanent source of division, then inclusive communal bodies can actually get on with working on areas of genuine consensus.

RED LINES

So, should anyone be excluded from Jewish communities? Although I am arguing for an inclusive Jewish community, I am not arguing that *anyone* should be included into any kind of Jewish institution, activity or event. For example, I am not suggesting that anti-Zionists be welcomed into Israel independence day celebrations. What I am arguing is that by concentrating Israel-related activity into certain spaces and institutions, a broader spectrum of Jews could be included into other kinds of spaces and institutions. In terms of criteria for inclusion, anyone who identifies himself/herself or is identified by others as a Jew should, in principle, be included in cross-communal institutions and activities. In some institutions this is already the case – Jewish welfare organisations do not formally exclude anti-Zionists – but, in others, those who reject Israel usually face a rough ride.

I do accept that some red lines are necessary and that some who identify as Jews or are identified as Jews should be excluded from most kinds of communal activity. This category would include only those who have actively and explicitly:

  • Rejected not just their own Jewish identity and also seek the dissolution of any kind of Jewishness.

  • *Explicitly* and actively embrace the discourses and practices of open anti-Semites who explicitly seek to destroy the Jewish people in its entirety.[114]

  • Whose anti-Zionism *explicitly* calls for the mass expulsion of all Jews from Israel.

  • Who embraces Holocaust denial.

The number of Jews falling into these categories is very small and includes notorious figures, such as Gilad Atzmon and Israel Shamir. However, not only do such people rarely wish to be part of Jewish communities, they are already mostly excluded, even from anti-Zionist Jewish circles. Messianic Jews – those who follow Christianity, including groups like Jews for Jesus – would also be excluded from most Jewish communal institutions and activities. While they rarely embrace anti-Semitism and their Zionism actually puts them in the Jewish communal mainstream, their proselytising for another religion, even with Jewish trappings, ultimately means they seek the dissolution of Jewishness in most of its forms.

However, even these red lines should not be inflexible. If a Jewish anti-Semite like Atzmon were to seek to attend a Jewish funeral for a family member, it would be unethical to refuse him entry. If a messianic Jew were to be a victim of an anti-Semitic attack, then he/she might arguably be entitled to Jewish communal support.

***

The proposals set out in this chapter are, in some respects, very modest and unambitious. While they are inspired by concepts of Jewish peoplehood, they ultimately reject the possibility that there can ever be a common, unified Jewish journey. At the same time, the proposals are also highly ambitious in that they require the inclusion in some communal settings of individuals who are today often treated as pariahs. Further, the proposal that cross-communal umbrella institutions retreat from some kinds of Israel-related activity effectively requires a sea-change in Jewish communal practice.

The proposals and analysis presented in this chapter only represent part of my argument. Even though divisions are here to stay and Jewish communal life needs to be reconfigured to cope with otherwise endemic conflict, relations between individual Jews can still be improved. In the next chapter, I will argue that the most important task for managing Jewish conflict over Israel entails working on the language and communication used among Jews.

NOTES

102 - See for example: Freedman, S. (2000). Jew vs. Jew: The Struggle for the Soul of American Jewry. New York, NY: Touchstone; Wertheimer, J. (1993). A People Divided: Judaism in Contemporary America. Hanover, NH: Brandeis University Press.

103 - Sacks, J. (1993). One People? Tradition, Modernity, and Jewish Unity. London, UK: Littman Library of Jewish Civilization.

104 - Kaplan, M. (1994) Judaism as Civilization: Toward a Reconstruction of American--Jewish Life. Philadelphia, PA: Jewish Publication Society.

105 - Revivi, M., & Kopelowitz, E. (2008). Editor's note. In M. Revivi & E. Kopelowitz (Eds.), Jewish Peoplehood: Change and Challenge (pp. xiii-xix). Brighton, MA: Academic Studies Press.

106 - Eisen, A. (2008). Four questions concerning Jewish peoplehood – and just as many answers. In M. Revivi & E. Kopelowitz (Eds.), Jewish Peoplehood: Change and Challenge (pp. 1-11). Brighton, MA: Academic Studies Press.

107 - Brown, E., & Galperin, M. (2009). The case for Jewish peoplehood: Can we be one? Woodstock, VT: Jewish Lights.[caps]

108 - Breakstone, D. (2011, July 24). Peoplehood vs. Zionism [Web log post]. Retrieved on June 1, 2013 from http://ejewishphilanthropy.com/peoplehood-vs-zionism/

109 - BaruchTrotsky. (2010, February 14). The big ethnic love-in [Web log post]. Retrieved on June 1, 2013 from http://www.jewdas.org/2010/02/the-big-ethnic-love-in/

110 - Michaelson, J. (2010, June 30). Peoplehood vs. Israel: The split at the heart of Jewish identity. The Jewish Daily Forward. Retrieved on June 1, 2013 from http://forward.com/articles/129089/peoplehood-vs-israel/#ixzz1vnX4Jb00

111 - Ravid, S. (2007). What is Jewish Peoplehood? And is it the Right Question? From Defining Peoplehood to Creating Peoplehood Capital. In K. Corbin, A. F. Plotkin, E. Levine, & G. Most (eds.), The peoplehood papers (pp. 1-2). New York, NY: United Jewish Communities.

112 - Ibid. 11

113 - Hartman, D. (2007). The boundaries of Judaism. London, UK: Continuum.

114 - Note that I do not necessarily include in this category those Jewish anti-Zionists who have joined pro-Palestinian coalitions, which include some Islamists who have embraced anti-Semitic rhetoric. While some Jewish anti-Zionists may arguably provide an alibi for anti-Semitism, most simply explain anti-Semitism away or ignore it, rather than actively embrace it.

CHAPTER SIX:
CIVILITY AND DIALOGUE

Any attempt to manage Jewish conflict over Israel, at some point, needs to grapple with questions of language and communication. The key issue is *how* Jews divided over Israel should communicate with each other. Language and other forms of communication are not neutral, for it is through them that conflict is either reproduced or mitigated.

In this chapter, I want to suggest that Jewish conflict over Israel can be managed through striving towards *civility*. Civility is about how we communicate, but it is more than simple politeness. Civility is an ideal, a practice for living alongside others. It is difficult to achieve without conscious efforts to do so. As I will go on to demonstrate, the practice of *dialogue*, as well as being valuable in its own right, can help to institute a more civil Jewish community.

THE VALUE OF CIVILITY

The concept of civility has its origins in the classical Greek and Roman city. The body of citizens (*civitas*) required a sense of civic virtue to ensure that citizenship and government could function. These origins in the city alert us to the central issue that civility concerns itself with the question: how do we live together amidst diversity and competing interests?

The historian Benet Davetian understands civility as follows:

> ...the extent to which citizens of a given culture speak and act in ways that demonstrate a caring for the welfare of others as well as the welfare of the culture they share in common.[115]

To the extent that all cultures require some form of care for others in order to function at all, some form of civility can be found in all times and all places. However, civility has been understood in different ways in different eras. Standards of civility have become more prominent and sophisticated in the western world since the medieval period. Norbert Elias's seminal work *The Civilising Process* traced the development of forms of bodily self-restraint and manners in the transition from medieval to early modern Europe.[116] What are now common, taken–for-granted standards of table manners, polite speech and the like, were initially developed within elite, courtly settings. Elias shows how behaviours, which may have once been strange and required teaching and enforcement, have now become internalised within the individual superego.

One implication of Elias's work is that standards of civility can not only change, but also spread outwards from the small groups within which they are developed until they become second nature. If standards of civility can be agreed on at an elite level with regard to how Jews deal with divisions over Israel, they can – in theory, at least – percolate into everyday practice and, eventually, be taken for granted.

One of the spurs to the development of modern standards of civility was social change. As medieval and early modern western societies developed increasingly complex forms of government and sources of social differentiation, so standards of civility enabled sophisticated forms of social distinction to emerge. While in this respect civility has always been tied into structures of power and forms of social exclusion, we should not underestimate how it allows individuals to use standards of behaviour to guard against the often frightening forces of dislocation that accompany times of rapid change. While different standards of civility may prevail in different strata of society – and the standards of lower classes may not be recognised as standards at all by those in higher classes – civility provides an important bulwark against the ever-present threat of social chaos.

In the last few decades, the more rigid and caste-like forms of differentiation between social classes have eroded, even if differentials of income and power have remained. The once-clear distinctions between standards of civility in upper, middle and lower classes – the forms of behaviours that Nancy Mitford could divide into 'U' and 'non-U' – have broken down to a significant extent. Class differences in accent, vocabulary and many other ways of acting are no longer as stark as before. This has not resulted in any kind of homogeneous contemporary culture – in fact, quite the opposite. The ease with which individuals can pick and choose identities and construct unique pathways through life, the proliferation of subcultures and small worlds, the rapidity and simplicity of movement throughout the world, the deep penetration of electronic communication into everyday life; all these developments have led to a world that is ever more fragmented, while, at the same time, closer together than ever. Marshall McLuhan's 'global village' is often a village of atomised parts.

This paradoxical, simultaneous closeness and distance can be seen with regard to divisions in the Jewish community over Israel. It is easier than ever to form new Jewish factions and groups; it is harder than ever for factions and groups to separate from each other fully. We are simultaneously pushed together and apart. In the Jewish community, as in the 'wider world', deeply engrained standards of civility may no longer be able to cope with the rapidity of change. It is no longer clear what civility is and, even if it were, who would enforce it?

Civility cannot be taken for granted anymore; rather, it needs to be made explicit and deliberately addressed. Some thinkers have started to revisit the concept, both to assess its contemporary relevance and to suggest how it may work as a contemporary ideal. Sociologist Richard Sennett, for example, sees civility as a 'craft' that must be worked on.[117] Like other crafts in the modern world, it has been neglected and debased in an era of industrialisation and mass production. For Sennett, the craft of civility is embodied in a form of communication in which 'you keep silent about things you know clearly but which you should not and do not say' (233). Crucial here is the use of the subjunctive voice and the existence of informal spaces that do not pressure or compromise participants. Civility both requires and facilitates the kinds of cooperation that 'enhances the quality of social life' (273). Sennett argues that '...we are capable of cooperating more deeply than the existing social order envisions' (280). But cooperation does not necessarily require fellowship and understanding. Rather, Sennett emphasises the importance of 'tough cooperation' with people one does not like or understand.

One of the difficulties of the craft of civility is that it is not 'automatically' produced by structures and organisations for which it might be seen as crucial. Communities are not necessarily civil places, even though they are based on cooperation. Civil society does not necessarily have civility embedded in it. Rather, as policy-makers have begun to realise, the practice of civility has to be nurtured in order for communities and cooperative structures to work better and achieve their full potential. A 2009 report by the Young Foundation defined civility as follows:[118]

> ...a learned grammar of sociability, that demonstrates respect (both felt or imposed by norms) for others and which entails sacrificing immediate self-interest where appropriate. (17)

For the authors of the report, civility is necessary for the better working of society:

> Civility can, as an unspoken language for interaction, provide the basis for achieving the 'good society' — through emphasis on qualities such as respect, empathy and compassion. Yet civility is not implicit and needs to be learned, made relevant, incentivised or often regulated. (21)

How to nurture civility is a difficult problem. In complex contemporary societies, rigid and clear standards of civility cannot be instituted outside of particular small groups. If civility cannot be precisely defined, there is a danger then that it will become little more than a vague injunction to be 'nicer' or more polite. Nonetheless, civility still remains a powerful ideal and, even if it risks vagueness, it is worth the effort to develop some kind of definition that will help to ground efforts to change behaviour.

DEFINING CIVILITY

Perhaps incivility is easier to define than civility. The symptoms of the Israel conflict in the Jewish community I highlighted in chapter four could all be seen as uncivil. Abuse, insults, anger, rudeness, personal attacks, marginalisation and perpetuating conflict – all of these are uncivil ways of communicating and acting. They are uncivil because they are based on a refusal to see the other as an individual alongside whom one can live and with whom one can interact and cooperate, as one whose welfare is of concern. That isn't to say that incivility is necessarily a permanent state – one can have bitter rows with close family and friends, after all – but each uncivil moment brings with it the risk of the permanent breakdown of any possible relationship. Of course, the Jewish community is resilient enough to survive members' incivility, up to a certain point, but it is endangered when incivility becomes the norm.

In contrast, civility should be understood as *a practice that maintains the possibility of relationship* between strangers, acquaintances, friends and family alike. A civil community is a community in which members are predisposed to develop relationships that are not conflictual.

Beyond this basic definition, I define civility as follows:

- *Civility is something of which almost all of us are capable.*

Even those who act in highly uncivil ways in some contexts will be completely civil in others. In fact, it is almost impossible to interact in the modern world without some capacity for civility. City life, in particular, is predicated on, at least, a minimum level of civility in order to be able to navigate the stresses and strains of living in close proximity to others. The only exceptions are the small numbers of people who, because of a communication disorder or mental illness or as a result of trauma, are incapable of interacting in the world on a daily basis.

- *Civility is a practice of communication.*

Civility is concerned with how we interact with others and interaction requires communication. Civil communication maintains the possibility of relationship and, while this may imply politeness, it is not simply reducible to it (politeness can be frosty). Rather, civil communication retains, at least, the theoretical possibility of relating on a more intimate level.

- *Civility requires subtlety and attention to tone.*

Civil communication is predicated on attention to the subtle craft of careful interaction. It requires an awareness of others and their distinctive ways of being in the world. As such, civility is displayed through attention to such nuanced and ineffable features of communication as tone, volume and nonverbal cues.

• *Civility is a process.*

Civility is about relationships and relationships require work to develop. This is why simple politeness cannot be the be all and end all of civility. However, civility cannot be legislated either. If civility is institutionalised in rituals or forms of words to the extent that it ossifies, it ceases to provide the possibility of connection. The quest for civility never reaches an end point.

• *Breakdowns in civility can be repaired.*

Just as there cannot be a permanent state of civility, so incivility cannot preclude the possibility of civility. Relationships are malleable – just as they can deteriorate, so they can be repaired.

• *Civility can be nurtured.*

At a basic level, civility is about individuals and the relationships between them. Individual practices of civility need to be nurtured, rather than imposed. This requires a 'light touch'. Civility can be modelled in the behaviour of others, rewarded within communities and organisations and advocated for by encouraging meaningful conversation. Civility can be encouraged within convivial spaces that enable our more civil selves. As Elijah Anderson argues in his book on public space in the city of Philadelphia: 'The public space of the cosmopolitan canopy encourages us to express our better selves and reminds us to keep our ethnocentric feelings in check.'[119]

PROMOTING CIVILITY

Recent years have seen a gradually growing awareness of civility. This has been spurred, in part, by the explosion of online discourse and the abusive forms of communication that often accompany it. In the US, in particular, some have argued that an increasingly polarised political scene has led to increasingly abusive and sometimes even violent communication.

The shooting of Congresswoman Gabrielle Giffords in Tucson in January 2011 which, at the time, was attributed, in part, to violent rhetoric by some American politicians and public figures (although, in retrospect, the connection has become less clear), caused some politicians, including President Obama, to call for greater civility in public life.[120]

It is in the US that the most concerted attempts to promote civility have taken place. One example is the Civil Conversations Project,[121] which was set up in response to the Gifford shooting. The project brings together 'thought leaders who are modelling new kinds of conversation and relationships across important differences' and makes these conversations available online. Another project, CivilPolitics.org, is a web-based resource and think tank that works to foster a more civil political environment. Its approach emphasises that disagreement itself is not problematic and that civility requires the kind of sophisticated approach I advocated above:

> Civility as we pursue it is *the ability to disagree with others while respecting their sincerity and decency.* We believe this ability is best fostered by *indirect methods (changing contexts, payoffs, and institutions), rather than by direct methods (such as pleading with people to be more civil, or asking people to sign civility pledges).*

Also in the US political sphere, the National Institute for Civil Discourse has tried to encourage elected officials to communicate more civilly through a campaign to encourage members of the public to contact their representatives when they see or hear their representatives using vitriolic language.[122]

It is unclear, though, how much effect such campaigns are having. In 2009, The Civility Project was set up jointly by a conservative Republican and a liberal Democrat. The creators wrote to all members of Congress and State Governors to ask them to sign the following civility pledge:[123]

1. I will be civil in my public discourse and behaviour.

2. I will be respectful of others whether or not I agree with them.

3. I will stand against incivility when I see it.

Despite the modest nature of the pledge, only three members of Congress signed and the project was disbanded in January 2011.

A number of attempts have also been made to promote more civil behaviour online. Wikipedia has a sophisticated and detailed section on civility in its code of conduct for editors,[124] summarised as follows:

> Stated simply, editors should always treat each other with consideration and respect. In order to keep the focus on improving the encyclopedia and to help maintain a pleasant editing environment, editors should behave politely, calmly and reasonably, even during heated debates.

How closely users abide by this code is hard to judge given the enormous size and scope of Wikipedia, but it remains the most developed and most prominent online civility code to date. Other civility codes have had more limited success. The 'Blogger's Codes of Conduct', proposed by Tim O'Reilly in 2007 and designed to promote civility by bloggers and in comment threads, attracted considerable discussion, but its lack of success is demonstrated by the fact that the webpage is no longer online.[125]

Civility, then, is on the agenda, at least sporadically, but it has yet to make a major impact on political and online discourse. Perhaps, as CivilPolitics.org acknowledges, the frequent focus on civility codes and pledges has only limited effectiveness, as nurturing civility requires a much deeper and subtle effort, in keeping with the subtlety of the concept itself. Efforts to promote and nurture civility might find more success if they focus on smaller spaces, such as the Jewish community.

CIVILITY IN THE JEWISH COMMUNITY

Jewish tradition can provide inspiration for the promotion of civility in Jewish communities and beyond for argument and disagreement are accorded a central place in the development of Jewish law and Jewish thought. To this day, the principle way that Talmud and other Jewish texts are transmitted is through discussion, in pairs (*chevruta*) or in groups. The Talmud itself, the foundational exposition of Jewish law (*halachah*), is a record of discussions and debates, rather than a set of fixed regulations. While there are views in the Talmud that are explicitly marginalised and pathologised (such as those of Elisha Ben Abuya), it is frequently the case that all sides in a particular set of debates are seen as valid – the debate itself is legitimate, even holy. Most famously, in the disputations between the schools of Hillel and Shammai, which run through the Talmud, both sets of opinion are treated as in accordance with God. However, in deciding on halachic rulings, it is the manner in which the debate is pursued that is crucial:

> R. Abba stated in the name of Samuel: For three years there was a dispute between Beth Shammai and Beth Hillel, the former asserting, 'The halachah is in agreement with our views' and the latter contending, 'The halachah is in agreement with our views'. Then a bath kol [voice of God] issued announcing, '[The utterances of] both are the words of the living God, but the halachah is in agreement with the rulings of Beth Hillel'. Since, however, both are the words of the living God' what was it that entitled Beth Hillel to have the halachah fixed in agreement with their rulings? Because they were kindly and modest, they studied their own rulings and those of Beth Shammai, and were even so [humble] as to mention the actions of Beth Shammai before theirs.[126]

The equal legitimacy of Beth Hillel and Beth Shammai is predicated on their both accepting a common set of assumptions. This passage, at least, does not imply that those who are considered outside the bounds of acceptable belief and behaviour should be treated with the same respect as Beth Hillel treats Beth Shammai. Indeed, Elisha Ben Abuya is so reviled in the Talmud that he is not referred to by name, but instead as *acher* (other). The concept of 'controversy for the sake of heaven' (*machloket l'shem shamayim*) draws clear lines between acceptable disagreement and unacceptable rebellion:

> A controversy for Heaven's sake will have lasting value, but a controversy not for Heaven's sake will not endure. What is an example of a controversy for Heaven's sake? The debates of Hillel and Shammai. What is an example of a controversy not for Heaven's sake? The rebellion of Korach and his associates.[127]

Jewish tradition doesn't just warn against rebellion, it also warns against the consequences of Jewish conflict. The Talmud suggests that, while the First Temple was destroyed as a result of Jews' 'idolatry, immorality and bloodshed', the Second Temple was destroyed due to *sinat chinam* ('groundless hatred') [128].The Jews of the Second Temple period may have been good Jews in terms of Torah observance; it was their relationships with each other that were poisonous.

Even though the boundaries of Judaism in Talmudic times may be too narrow for contemporary Jewish communities, the principle that arguments should be conducted in a manner that is kind, modest and respectful of opposing views is still an important one. If we see Beth Hillel as a model of civility, then the lesson is that an argument made civilly is an intrinsically better argument than an uncivil one. Some Jewish organisations have grounded a commitment to Jewish pluralism in explicit references to this tradition of civil discussion. Limmud, for example, has long seen the encouragement of 'arguments for the sake of heaven' as part of its mission.[129]

Another source of civility in Jewish tradition is the series of halachic injunctions against particular forms of harmful speech. *Hotzaat Shem Ra* ('spreading a bad name'), a form of slander or defamation through spreading untruths about someone, is a serious sin. *Lashon Hara* ('bad/ evil tongue') is another sinful form of speech that is derogatory, albeit truthful. Truthful speech is sinful, in this case, when it reveals negative points about another person without any kind of sincere attempt to address or heal them. Denunciations of *Lashon Hara*, together with denunciations of other kinds of gossip (*rechilut*) can be found as far back as the Torah (although this exact term is not used there) and the Talmud. The concept was most extensively developed in the work of Rabbi Yisrael Meir Kagan, known as the Chafetz Chaim, in the nineteenth century. Although the prohibition against *Lashon Hara* is hedged by exemptions for cases where sharing negative information can have a positive effect, the centrality of an ethics of speech is clear in Jewish tradition. Again, it provides the foundations for a form of civility that requires care in how one speaks to and of people with whom one disagrees.

These Jewish traditions have provided inspiration to those concerned with conflict between Jews. In 2005, a 'Jewish Bloggers Campaign for

Responsible Speech Online' was launched on the blog Jewschool, drawing on the work of the Chafetz Chaim as well as other Jewish sources, to implore Jewish bloggers to commit to developing a more responsible tone.[130] While the campaign never fully took off, it did show that Jewish tradition could be mobilised to ground an ethics of speech in a new medium. Further, in recognition of the need for more civil conversations within the Jewish community, some other Jewish blogs and websites have paid particular attention to developing robust comment policies, even if they have not always drawn on Jewish sources to do so.[131]

Another initiative, the Rodef Shalom Communication Agreement, was launched in 2011 and drew on a variety of Jewish sources to create a communication agreement designed for the discussion of difficult issues.[132] The agreement's preamble pledged:

> I agree to become a *rodef shalom* (pursuer of peace), a partner in the effort to transform society by changing the way I communicate with others and deal with conflict. I pledge henceforth to approach differences of opinion with an open and inquiring mind and to make every effort to avoid generalizing or demonizing those who disagree with me. I will try to be a force for changing bitter destructive disagreements to *machlokot leshem shamayim,* constructive conflicts for the benefit of all humankind.

The agreement grounds the work of the Pardes Centre for Judaism and Conflict Resolution. The Jerusalem-based institute, which developed the agreement, runs courses and programmes designed to promote methods of conflict resolution grounded in the study of Jewish texts.[133] Beginning in 2013, the centre has instituted 9 Adar as the 'Jewish Day of Constructive Conflict':

> Approximately 2,000 years ago, on the 9th of Adar, the initially peaceful and constructive conflict (*machloket l'shem shamayim*) between two dominant Jewish schools of thought, Beit Hillel and Beit Shammai, erupted into a violent and destructive conflict leading to the death of many (3,000 according to some sources). The day was said to be as tragic as the day the golden calf was created (Exodus 32:28).

This day was later declared a fast day (Shulchan Aruch, Laws of Fasts 580), however it was never observed as such. The PCJCR, together with institutional partners around the world, seeks to reinstate this somewhat forgotten day on the Jewish calendar, making it a day dedicated to the study and practice of constructive conflict, and other Jewish models of conflict resolution.[134]

In the US, the Jewish Council for Public Affairs (JCPA), together with a number of its constituent Federations and the Jewish Community Relations Council, has made a particular effort to promote civility. In 2010 the JCPA launched their 'Year of Civil Discourse', which paved the way for an ongoing Civility Campaign. The centrepiece of the campaign is a 'Civility Statement', backed up by online resources and public events and consultations designed to spread knowledge and discussion of the campaign. The statement reads as follows:

> In American society, especially in our diverse Jewish community, we value robust and vigorous debate about pressing issues. Such debate is one of the greatest features of our democracy and one of the hallmarks of our people. We revel in our tradition of debate: A frank and civil exchange of ideas helps to inform our decisions, provoke new ways of thinking, and sometimes even change our minds.

> And yet today, the expression and exchange of views is often an uncivil, highly unpleasant experience. Community events and public discussions are often interrupted by raised voices, personal insults, and outrageous charges. Such incivility serves no purpose but to cheapen our democracy. When differences spiral down into uncivil acrimony, the dignity of individuals and community is diminished, and our precious democracy is weakened. People holding diverse views cease to listen to each other. Lack of civility makes it more difficult, if not impossible, to open minds, much less find common ground.

> Therefore we as a community and as individuals, must pledge to uphold the basic norms of civil discussion and

debate at our public events. We do this not to stifle free expression of views, but rather to protect it.

We will discover civility in the guarding of our tongues and the rejection of false witness. We will find it wherever we show care for the dignity of every human being, even those with whom we may strongly disagree. We will find it by listening carefully when others speak, seeking to understand what is being said and trying to learn from it.

This pursuit has deep roots in Torah and in our community's traditions. Our Sages saw the fruit of arguments that were conducted *l'shem shamayim*, "for the sake of Heaven." They fervently believed that great minds, engaged in earnest search and questioning, could find better and richer solutions to the problems they faced. They refrained from insisting on uniformity. They sought to preserve and thereby honor the views of the minority as well as the majority. They did so through their understanding of the great teaching of *Eilu v'elu divrei Elokim chayim*, "both these words and those are the words of the living God."

As a community, we must commit ourselves and ask others to open their hearts and minds to healthy, respectful dialogue based on our love for our neighbors and our people.

We therefore agree to treat others with decency and honor and to set ourselves as models for civil discourse, even when we disagree with each other.

We commit ourselves to this course to preserve an essential element of a community – the ability to meet and talk as brothers and sisters.[135]

Like the other pledges and statements discussed previously, the JCPA statement draws on Jewish tradition and invites Jews to commit to its principles. Unlike the other pledges and statements, however, the JCPA statement is backed up by a large cross-communal institution with the potential to translate it into action.

The JCPA campaign was built on the back of a number of similar initiatives and resolutions among allied Jewish organisations.[136] The San Francisco Bay Area has been at the forefront of work in this area. In 2005, the Bay Area Jewish Community Relations Council initiated 'Project Reconnections' to work towards a more civil intra-Jewish conversation about Israel. The project involved relatively small numbers of Jewish community members in an ongoing process of dialogue which, ultimately, resulted in participants having a deeper appreciation of the views of others.[137] Similar projects, promoting civility in discussions about Israel and other contentious issues, have taken place in other US Jewish communities as well.[138] In 2013 the JCPA launched a new campaign for civil discourse, this time focusing on nurturing civility (again, using the concept of 'arguments for the sake of heaven') amongst American rabbis.[139]

In contrast, in the UK, no projects have been set up specifically to promote civility in discussions of Israel and other matters. However, there are mechanisms for intra-communal coexistence that can be drawn on to facilitate a more civil atmosphere. Since 1980, the growth of the Limmud conference, which provides a safe space in which people from all branches of the Jewish community can interact, has developed considerable expertise in finding ways to overcome entrenched communal divisions. Limmud has enabled speakers with all kinds of views on Israel to put on sessions and, while no speaker ever goes unchallenged, the strongly pluralist ethos of the conference mitigates much of the resulting tension. The 'Stanmore Accords', signed in 1998 by the heads of the major non-Haredi UK denominations, have been modestly successful in ensuring that denominational disagreements rarely erupt into public arguments these days. In 2010 Vivian Wineman, the President of the Board of Deputies, suggested that the Stanmore Accords could form the basis for a similar agreement to avoid public arguments within the Zionist camp:[140]

> He told a meeting on Israel at Hampstead Garden Suburb Synagogue last week: "An equivalent of the Stanmore Accords, where differences were acknowledged but treated with respect, would be of benefit not only to the groups themselves but to the community generally."
>
> Speaking afterwards, Mr Wineman said: "The level of Zionist debate is very strident at the moment. We are not

trying to stifle debate but to have it conducted in a more respectful atmosphere.

"It's unfortunate when someone argues, not simply that the other person is wrong, but calls them an idiot."

While nothing has yet come of this proposal, it does, at least, show that some Jewish communal leaders in the UK are concerned with issues of civility. Further, in 2013 the Board of Deputies issued a draft code of conduct, designed to deal with behaviour at Board meetings, warning Deputies against bullying, harassment and discrimination.[141]

THE LIMITATIONS OF CIVILITY

While the development of civility initiatives in the Jewish world is certainly a positive step, such initiatives often prove to be limited in their scope and impact. An important example of this is the Bay Area which, as I described previously, has been at the forefront of promoting civility. In 2010 the San Francisco JCRC helped to draft the San Francisco Jewish Federation's guidelines on what initiatives and organisations they would fund. The guidelines stated that they would not fund organisations that 'advocate for, or endorse, undermining the legitimacy of Israel as a secure independent, democratic Jewish state, including through participation in the Boycott, Divestment and Sanctions (BDS) movement, in whole or in part.'[142] The guidelines were, in part, a reaction to controversy in 2009 over the inclusion in the Federation-funded San Francisco Jewish Film Festival of films judged by some to be 'anti-Israel'. Progressive Jewish groups in San Francisco and elsewhere voiced heavy criticism of the guidelines.[143]

This controversy showed the difficulties of promoting civility at the same time as trying to marginalise 'delegitimization'. At the same JCPA national plenum at which the draft of the Statement on Civility was adopted, a resolution was also passed calling on the Jewish community to fight 'delegitimization' and BDS. Although this resolution, like the San Francisco guidelines, did not explicitly target Jewish pro-Palestinian organisations, the adoption of boycotts of settlement products by Jewish Voice for Peace and some other Jewish groups effectively places them beyond the pale. The question is whether calls for civility should extend to those outside the 'legitimate' camp. While the JCPA's statement on civility, like other Jewish-led civility campaigns, does not explicitly exclude anyone as a fit recipient of civil behaviour, at least some of those who support calls for civility do not wish to extend civil relations to those they deem totally beyond the pale. As one participant in one civility initiative in the US put it:

> Dr. Mike Harris, spokesman for the local branch of StandWithUs [a pro-Israel organisation]... says it's too soon to tell how useful the civil discourse effort will prove.
>
> On one hand, he said it is "absolutely necessary" for people to "get beyond the tension, so Israel can be talked about." But he considers Jewish Voice for Peace outside the bounds of the Jewish communal conversation, saying the group "does not accept the ground rules" of Israel as the Jewish state.
>
> "There is a conflict between the imperative for civil discourse and the imperative to name and shame those who are anti-Israel," Harris said.[144]

Calls for civility in Jewish debates about Israel are often limited ones. The desire for civility can be restricted to interactions with those who are seen to share certain basic values. The assumptions behind this attitude can be seen in a revealing 2011 post on the pro-Israel blog CifWatch.[145] The post responded to an article by David Yehuda Stern on the website Cartoon Kippah.[146] Stern was commenting on a war of words which was taking place on social media between CiFWatch and the pro-Palestinian campaigner Ben White. Stern argued that:

> ...both CIF Watch and Ben White have admirable goals but it is their aggressive, often intimidating rhetoric, that disengages the majority of the public from their important messages leaving all but the bitter taste of hate in the mouths of many who come into contact with their work.

CiFWatch's Adam Levick's response first took umbrage at the equivalence that Stern was making between CifWatch and White before rejecting the suggestion that civility could be an appropriate response to White:

As an Israeli citizen, I'd really like to know how I'm supposed to civilly respond to those, like White, who don't think my nation deserves the right to exist under any circumstances – within any borders.

And, similarly, I'm at a lost to understand how to calmly, respectfully exchange views with those who find antisemitism an understandable reaction to Israeli behavior.

The degree to which CiF Watch aggressively refutes anti-Zionist and antisemitic commentary – both by posts on our blog, and within the necessarily less expansive rhetorical parameters of social media such as Twitter – is informed by a quite sober understanding of Jewish history, and an intimate familiarity with the limits of reasonableness and the assumption of good intentions.

This blog certainly believes in what's known as "Big Tent Zionism", and we'll certainly continue to civilly debate those who don't necessarily share our views on how best to defend against the assaults on Israel's legitimacy – and, similarly, how most effectively to fight antisemitism – but, of course, the key word in the phrase "Big Tent Zionism" is, "Zionism".

I won't engage in a calm tête-à-tête with those who defend, rationalize or excuse antisemitism, nor those who find my nation's existence morally abhorrent, not worth fighting for, or in any way expendable.

In psychology there's a phrase called "fight or flight response", which refers to the human capacity, or lack thereof, to accurately identify threats and respond accordingly.

There is a time for compromise and a time to fight.

What is revealing here is Levick's assumption that acting with civility would compromise one's ability to 'fight'. Similar arguments are often made by those who feel that civility should be limited or redefined. Too much civility could, potentially, lead to communal conformity and a weakening of the Jewish community's ability to respond to dangers. One could make a parallel to the exposure of sexual abuse in communities, an action that requires direct and public confrontation, rather than civility. An argument that has been made to me privately, as part of the dialogue project discussed in the next chapter, is that civility consists of responding seriously to someone's arguments and asserting that the tone in which one does this is largely irrelevant. Another argument against civility is that it imperils passion, satire and humour. A civil world is assumed to be an overly polite, bloodless and staid one. As the cartoonist Garry Trudeau, creator of the long-running *Doonesbury* strip, argued in 2010:[147]

> Satire is unfair. It's rude and uncivil. It lacks balance and proportion, and it obeys none of the normal rules of engagement. Satire picks a one-sided fight, and the more its intended target reacts, the more its practitioner gains the advantage.

Despite these counter-arguments, I would maintain that civility is both necessary and should be extended as widely as possible. Further, civility *can* be reconciled with passion, satire and the need to combat one's enemies. One of the reasons that I maintain this is that, as I stated earlier, civility is not identical to politeness. Civility does not require one to listen passively to the other or even respect him/her. It only requires that one refrain from the kind of abusive and overly insulting behaviour that simply perpetuates conflict and makes living alongside one another impossible. The goal of the practice of civility is not to like and respect one another, but to make it tolerable for diverse individuals to live and interact in the same space. Civility does not mean that anger is illegitimate, only that it is what you do with that anger that counts.

In any case, a commitment to civility can actually make debating more effective and it does include a place for satire. The October 2010 'Rally to Restore Sanity', held in Washington DC and organised, in part, by satirist Jon Stewart, was aimed at the right-wing in US politics (particularly the 'Tea Party' wing), but it took aim, specifically at their uncivil and hyperbolic language:[148]

> We're looking for the people who think shouting is annoying, counterproductive, and terrible for your throat; who feel that the loudest voices shouldn't be the only ones that get heard; and who believe that the only time it's appropriate to

draw a Hitler moustache on someone is when that person is actually Hitler. Or Charlie Chaplin in certain roles.

The rally was marked by the use of satirical banners that teased the right while maintaining a civil tone: 'I disagree with you but I'm pretty sure you're not Hitler', 'Say no to hate, say yes to pancakes', 'You're entitled to your own opinion but not your own spelling' etc. In January 2011, one UK blogger proposed a 'mass trespass' on the comment threads *Guardian Comment Is Free*, which are notorious for their incivility:

> The idea is that people of mild temperament will shuffle gently onto CiF threads throughout the day, expressing their views in a thoughtful and respectful way. If nothing else, it will confuse the hell out of the regulars.

With thought and good humour, then, it is possible to be simultaneously civil and passionate while confronting opposing arguments. Calmly stating one's own position should be enough and there is no evidence to suggest that uncivil debate is more effective than civil debate.

However, one should not underestimate the difficulties that some Jews will have in expressing themselves civilly about Israel. As the CiFWatch post showed, it can be incredibly difficult to extend civility to those who one believes threaten one's deepest held values and indeed one's very survival. The problem is that the alternative – that of perpetual conflict – is not much more palatable. Feminist writer and pro-Israel campaigner Phyllis Chesler expressed, in an article in 2010 (updated in 2012), some of the anguish and ambivalence brought about by a simultaneous yearning for civility and disgust with opposing views:[149]

> Six years ago I first proposed a new kind of meeting of the twelve tribes..."So many Jews who hold passionate and opposing views have simply stopped listening and talking to each other," I wrote. "The silence is more awful than arguments. We must come together in order to strategize about our very survival."
>
> If such a conclave were indeed to take place, I believe we would need one psychiatrist for every three Jews present. I am not saying we are crazy. I *am* saying we are all so

> angry at each other, so hard, so sure of our own position - so stiff-necked, arrogant and self-righteous - that without professional help we would all walk out on each other, mid-sentence, blood pressure boiling, curses on our lips.
>
> I am asking us to envision doing something very difficult, very large. Can I actually sit in a room with J Streeters, or with Women in Black, or with others who demonstrate against Israel, sign petitions against Israel, arm the rogues at the United Nations with ammunition against Israel? Probablynot. I fear I'd walk right out.
>
> Moshe broke the first set of tablets at just such a moment. But he also begged God to forgive the Jews for the very sins that drove him to break the *luchot*.
>
> We are all in Moshe's position now. In Moshe's merit, and for God's sake, let us have less hate or even dislike for other Jews as we strengthen our resolve and gird our loins for battle.

This difficultly in dealing with the strong emotions that opposing views on Israel can raise means that civility cannot necessarily be achieved simply through exhortations to 'be civil'. Pledges and agreements may work as aspirations, but do not always manage to cut through the fog of conflict. As I argued previously, civility takes work, particularly when dealing with the deepest divisions between individuals. This work of nurturing civility can be strengthened through the practice of *dialogue*.

DIALOGUE

Dialogue is a process that can help engender civility, but civility and dialogue are not synonymous. Dialogue can produce a deeper form of civility, based on a more profound relationship with the other. Dialogue is different from debate. Whereas the goal of debate is to convince or 'defeat' others through the power of one's talk, dialogue's goal is to listen to and understand the other's position. Debate is not in itself a bad thing, when conducted in a civil fashion, but debate does not necessarily create or promote relationships of understanding. Dialogue may, in fact, make debate more effective as it allows for a better understanding of other positions and helps to mitigate the danger of debate turning into conflict. Dialogue involves recognition of the other's humanity, a recognition based on engaging with the deeper reasons as to why the other holds to particular arguments. It is predicated on vulnerability and imperfection, recognising that none of us is without flaws and emotions. Dialogue is both a means to an end, a way of easing and forestalling conflict, and an end in and of itself, a way of forming relationships.

Martin Buber's philosophy of dialogue is one of the most influential approaches to the concept and it is both influenced by and has been influential on Jewish thought. Buber differentiates between two modes of communication, 'I-Thou' (*Ich-Du*) and 'I-It' (*Ich-Es*).[150] The latter is monologic and the former is dialogic. In a dialogic I-Thou encounter, individuals engage with each other mutually as authentic human beings. In contrast, in an I-It encounter, individuals engage with each other as objects and, hence, do not really 'meet'. The I-Thou is rarer and more difficult in modernity than in previous eras, but it remains essential for human flourishing. For Buber, the I-Thou relationship is the model for and an instance of the human encounter with God.

The work of Emmanuel Lévinas provides a similarly influential philosophy of the encounter between individuals, which, like Buber's work, draws on and contributes to Jewish thought. Lévinas's 'Ethics of the Other' rejects the objectification of individuals in favour of an ethics based on face-to-face encounters.[151] The encounter is at once a transcendent connection with the infinite and also something that is rooted in human relationship. Lévinas's ethics of responsibility is grounded in the extraordinary yet everyday nature of this encounter with otherness, in which one comes face-to-face with an other who is both like oneself and utterly distinct.

The philosophies of Buber and Lévinas are part of a wider intellectual trend, begun in the twentieth century, that places dialogue and encounter at the centre of attempts to heal a divided and conflicted world. Philosophy and social theory from the twentieth century onwards have frequently put language at the centre of what it means to be human. We construct ourselves and our relationships with others through language and language is not a 'pure', unambiguous means of communication. 'Misunderstanding', far from being a kind of error, is, in fact, the condition of all communication. Language's slipperiness is such that we can never fully understand others or even ourselves. Language's paradox is that its amorphousness and ambiguity is such that we are always alone, yet, at the same time, language is an intrinsically social product and we are, therefore, fundamentally social beings enmeshed in webs of meaning that we do not create alone.

Psychotherapy and many other forms of therapy derive from Freud's innovation of a 'talking cure'. One doesn't have to be a follower of Freud or one of the many other schools of psychotherapy to recognise and appreciate the possibility that talk can nurture knowledge and healing. By turning our private, internal dialogue into 'public' talk with another, we open up the possibility of a more profound relationship with others and ourselves. This can take place in one-on-one sessions between a therapist and client, or – significantly, for our purposes – in group settings. In the Group Analysis tradition, as formulated by S.H. Foulkes, communication within groups is fundamental to human existence; groups can, therefore, be used to explore and change the ways that individuals relate to the world.[152]

One useful formulation of dialogue is that of David Bohm, who saw dialogue as a way of bringing people together to overcome the fragmentation, isolation and hopelessness of modern society.[153] Bohm's practice of dialogue involved small groups meeting together repeatedly over time. These groups were open-ended, with no fixed agenda and only used a facilitator at the start of the process:

> The object of a dialogue is not to analyse things, or to win an argument, or to exchange opinions. Rather, it is to suspend your opinions and to look at the opinions - to listen to everybody's opinions, to suspend them, and to see what all that means. If we can see what all of our opinions mean, then we are sharing a common content, even if we don't entirely agree. (p. 26)

Bohm emphasised that dialogue should not have a fixed outcome in mind. It should be a process of individual and collective self-knowledge predicated on the suspension of the purpose-driven communication and conflict that occurs 'outside' the group:

In the dialogue group we are not going to decide what to do about anything. This is crucial. (p. 17)

We are not trying to change anything, but just being aware of it. And you can notice the similarity of the difficulties within a group to the conflicts and incoherent thoughts within an individual. (p. 21)

This open-ended approach to dialogue has been followed by a number of projects and social movements (although not always directly influenced by Bohm's work). Although organisations, such as Art of Hosting, World Café and the Berkana Institute, do, ultimately, aim to transform the world through dialogue, at the heart of their work is not a rigid set of aims, but a powerful belief in the ability of human beings to grow closer through dialogue in safe and supportive settings. In a world dominated by rapid large-scale social change, globalisation and urbanisation, there is a need to make space for small-scale, localised decision-making based on people coming together to talk face-to-face. Thinkers and social activists, such as Paolo Freire and Ivan Illich, are among those who view the face-to-face practice of dialogue as one of what Illich called the 'tools for conviviality' necessary to develop a more human-scaled world.[154]

Aside from these lofty purposes, dialogue can be pleasurable in and of itself. While dialogue may seem an intimidatingly serious concept, 'conversation' is perhaps easier to 'sell' as a practice. Advocates of conversation, such as Margaret Wheatley and Theodore Zeldin, even though they might ultimately see conversation as a profound, world-changing practice, emphasise its ease, simplicity and humanity.[155] We converse every day, but by drawing attention to the practice's unnoticed potential, conversation can grow into something more.

While the advocates of dialogue discussed so far emphasise a small-scale, open-ended practice, dialogue is also at the heart of more focused attempts to resolve conflict. Dialogue plays a critical part in arranging ceasefires, truces and peace agreements in wars, as well as in settling legal disputes. Of course, these are usually not dialogues based on mutual recognition of vulnerability, but they do involve some kind of practice of listening and they do imply that conflicts, which are often started through divisive forms of communication, can also be resolved through communication.

To truly resolve conflict through dialogue, though, rather than by simply finding a concrete, mutually agreeable end to active hostilities, requires a much more open-ended, sustained kind of dialogue. Dialogue intended to bring about solutions to the most serious conflicts often takes place 'under the radar', confidentially and without a fixed outcome in mind. Conflict resolution is an expanding field of practice and scholarship with many different approaches and dialogue plays a central role in most of them.[156] The work of conflict resolution specialists in the world's most intractable conflicts, such as that conducted by the Oxford Research Group, usually takes place away from the spotlight of publicity.

One of the most prominent forms of dialogue, which takes place against a background of centuries-old conflict, is 'interfaith' dialogue. In the post-WWII period, in particular, a large number of initiatives have been set up to develop dialogue among the major world religions. Organisations, such as the Council of Christians and Jews, set up in the UK in 1942, have developed strong ties between religious leaders, in particular, based on regular dialogue and study. In the shadow of the Holocaust, Christian-Jewish dialogue has helped to heal the wounds caused by centuries of Christian persecution of Jews. The Second Vatican Council's Declaration on the Relation of the Church with Non-Christians (known as *Nostra Aetate*), promulgated by Pope Paul VI in 1965, explicitly rejected anti-Semitism and encouraged respect for other world religions. It was, in part, stimulated by, and, in turn, helped to stimulate, meaningful dialogue between Catholic and Jewish clergy. In more recent years as western societies have become more multicultural, interfaith dialogue has expanded to encompass other religions, particularly Islam. Organisations, such as the Maimonides Foundation and the Three Faiths Forum in the UK, have tried to develop ties between Islam, Judaism and Christianity based on recognition of their common 'Abrahamic' descent.

Interfaith dialogue is now common among clergy , although less so at the more fundamentalist ends of the spectrum. In the UK, the majority of non-Haredi rabbis are involved in interfaith work to some degree.[157] At the 'grassroots' level, however, interfaith involvement is more variable. In the Jewish community, some Orthodox rabbis, who are themselves involved in interfaith dialogue, have expressed misgivings about the involvement of the laity and less knowledgeable Jews. This may have less to do with fear of their engaging with non-Jews than with their not being Jewishly-equipped to be able to handle the challenges posed by engagement with the arguments of other religions. Former Chief Rabbi Jonathan Sacks has suggested that, while direct dialogue should probably be an elite activity, there is ample scope for shared interfaith activity among the grassroots:

> I distinguish between side by side and face to face relationships. Face to face is the thou and I. That is very demanding and maybe that will remain the property of the elite. However, side by side relationships are different. We recognise that we share certain problems, clearing the village green together, for instance, doesn't demand the leap of faith and vulnerability of face to face relationships.[158]

Sacks overestimates the challenge of interfaith dialogue for those outside the elite. While it is true that those who have had less education may have difficulties accurately representing their religion to others, one of the key principles of interfaith dialogue is that individuals participate as individuals, rather than as representatives. The human ability to forge connection through talk is not predicated on deep knowledge. That said, Sacks is correct to point out that interfaith relationships can be developed through shared activities as well as through face-to-face dialogue. It is also true that, historically speaking, interfaith activism has been largely dialogue-focused and that it is only relatively recently that serious attempts have been made to explore the potential of shared forms of social activism as a means of relationship building.

While interfaith dialogue and interfaith activism more broadly are incre-asingly important elements of religious life, including within the Jewish community, *intra*faith dialogue is barely developed. Some of the most serious religious conflicts take place *within* religions as well as between them. While ecumenical work has, during the last couple of centuries, made serious inroads into tackling Christian Catholic-Protestant-Ortho-dox conflict, other intrafaith conflicts remain acute and unaddressed. For example, violent Shia-Sunni conflict is a a major issue within the Is-lamic world. While other intrafaith conflicts are less violent, they are no less intractable. The Church of England, for example, is having extre-me difficulty reconciling its evangelical and liberal wings. In the Jewish world, Reform-Orthodox conflicts, to say nothing of the conflicts over

Israel discussed in this book, are extremely difficult to handle.

There are few organisations dedicated to intrafaith dialogue. Intra-faith dialogue is usually confined to umbrella bodies and ad hoc projects where religious leaders come together. The Anglican synod provides one forum for intra-Protestant dialogue, although its public nature often makes it ineffective. Sunni and Shia Muslims sometimes cooperate together in representative bodies in countries where Muslims are a minority. Dialogues over Protestant-Catholic conflict in Northern Ireland, together with other violent intrafaith conflicts, are often initiated by conflict resolution specialists, rather than by organisations that stress a common religious heritage. In the Jewish world, intra-Jewish dialogue is rarely promoted by dedicated organisations (one exception is described later). Rather, intra-Jewish dialogue happens informally or in the process of cooperating over issues of common concern. In the UK, Orthodox and non-Orthodox Jews have no dedicated dialogue organisation to bring them together, but their leaders work together within umbrella bodies as well as in confidential, informal and ad hoc meetings.

Speaking very generally, we can contrast interfaith activity, where dialogue is more developed and mutual cooperation less developed, with intrafaith activity, where dialogue is less developed and mutual cooperation is more developed. Just as more attention needs to be paid to developing shared activities between religions, so, too, does more attention need to be paid to dialogue within religions. In the Jewish community, one of the reasons why dialogue is important is that conflict over Israel, as we have seen, threatens intra-Jewish cooperation on other matters. Cooperation on matters of shared concern is much less effective as a way of bringing a divided community together if opposing sides define matters of concern in very different ways. Israel was once a way of uniting a divided religious community; without that unifying factor, the Jewish community is much less able to deal with other sources of division. Dialogue between Jews is, therefore, critically important as a way of coping with Jewish conflict.

While some of the Jewish civility projects discussed previously do promote dialogue between Jews, the most thorough attempt to develop intra-Jewish dialogue has been made by the Jewish Dialogue Group in the US. The group was founded in 2001 specifically to promote constructive conversations in the Jewish community about the Israeli-Palestinian conflict. It describes its work as follows:[159]

> The Jewish Dialogue Group is a non-partisan, grassroots organization that formed in 2001 to foster vibrant, respectful dialogue within Jewish communities about the Israeli-Palestinian conflict and other challenging issues. We create programs and materials that empower people to learn about one another across political divides, clarify their feelings and views, explore difficult ethical and intellectual questions, seek common ground, and strengthen relationships. We seek to make our resources available to all who need them.
>
> As an organization, we do not take positions on any issues, but focus solely on promoting dialogue. Our board members, volunteers, and advisors have many different political perspectives. We come from many different streams of Judaism: Conservative, Reconstructionist, Orthodox, Reform, Renewal, non-denominational, and secular.
>
> We have facilitated more than 300 dialogue programs, involving thousands of people, and we have trained dozens of facilitators. Our guidebooks and other materials have been used in synagogues, schools, organizations, and communities throughout North America, in England, and in Israel.

At the heart of the Jewish Dialogue Group's work is a rigorous methodology for facilitating dialogue. Their handbook, *Constructive Conversations about the Israeli-Palestinian Conflict*, produced in partnership with the Public Conversations Project, provides a detailed guide to their methodology.[160] The handbook draws extensively on Jewish traditions and Jewish texts to justify and ground the process. They define dialogue as follows:

> We define dialogue as a conversation in which the participants' primary goal is to pursue mutual understanding rather than agreement or immediate solutions. As participants pursue this goal, they sometimes decide to pursue other goals. For example, dialogue groups sometimes decide to become better informed together, or to build consensus about ways

that they can act on shared values while continuing to have significant areas of disagreement. (p. 11)

Listening, understanding and sharing are central to the methodology, but shared action is a possible outcome, too. The process is predicated on participants being unsatisfied with their previous conversations with Jews on Israel-Palestine and their wish for more fulfilling conversations:

[Our] dialogue programs invite people to move out of conversations that they find neither satisfying nor enlightening and into fresh, constructive, and wished-for conversations.

Therefore, we typically talk with potential participants to find out how they have experienced conversations (or the absence of conversations) about the divisive issue, and what kinds of conversations they would like to have.

When we ask these questions, we typically learn about unsatisfying conversations that are highly polarized and divisive—conversations from which some community members distance themselves, choosing instead to be silent in the presence of people who might have different views. And we often learn that the community would be enriched and energized if its members could find new ways of talking about their different perspectives. (15)

The handbook does not argue that debate is problematic *per se*. Rather, it asserts that dialogue can actually help debate become more constructive:

We do not intend to suggest that all debates are destructive. On the contrary, debates can be quite valuable and enlightening. Debate and advocacy are important tools in democracy. In long-standing conflicts, however — especially those that involve identity issues, histories of trauma, and a deep sense of threat to one's basic security and dignity — debate is often highly polarized and "stuck." It is in those situations that the "old" patterns make it difficult for people to explore a range of perspectives openly, to reflect deeply on their own perspectives, and to connect with each other across differences. Dialogue may help to prepare people for more constructive debate. (p. 16)

Although the group uses its own facilitators to run dialogues, the handbook is detailed enough to allow anyone who desires to facilitate their own dialogues to do so. It provides a set of guidelines and procedures designed to guide the process. The basic principles that structure the guidelines are:

1. We place a high premium on participant "ownership" of the conversation and on ensuring that the participants have clear and accurate expectations about what the dialogue is and what it isn't.

2. When we design the dialogue, we build a strong "container" through the use of a) communication agreements and b) structures for speaking, listening, and reflecting.

3. We pose well-crafted, purposeful questions in the crucial opening phase of the dialogue.

4. We facilitate in a manner that is responsive to participants' evolving goals and needs.

Point two is crucial. The Jewish Dialogue Group's methodology is carefully structured and depends on participants agreeing to abide by certain agreements, such as the following:

Regarding the spirit of our speaking and listening

1. We will speak for ourselves and allow others to speak for themselves, with no pressure to represent or explain a whole group.

2. We will not criticize the views of others or attempt to persuade them.

3. We will listen with resilience, "hanging in" when we hear something that is hard to hear.

4. If tempted to make attributions about the beliefs of others (e.g., "You just believe that because...") we will instead,

consider asking a question to check out the assumption we are making, *(for example, "Do you believe that because..." or "What leads you to that belief?").*

Regarding the form of our speaking and listening

5. We will participate within the time frames suggested by the facilitator and share "airtime."

6. We will not interrupt except to indicate that we cannot hear a speaker.

7. We will "pass" or "pass for now" if we are not ready or willing to respond to a question.

Regarding the broader community

8. When we discuss our experience here with people outside the group, we will not attach names or any other identifying information to particular comments unless we have permission to do so.

9. If we refer by name to other community members who are not present, we will show them the same respect that we intend to show each other. (p. 164)

The structured nature of this methodology is this model's greatest strength, but also, as I was to discover, its greatest limitation. Ruling certain kinds of talk 'out of bounds' enables the sharing of different opinions without the automatic descent into conflict. Such rules, particularly that of not criticising, are different from those of everyday talk and provide a way of stepping out of everyday conflict into a different space. Yet such preconditions for dialogue run the risk of excluding those who cannot or will not see the value of the process. The considerable 'buy-in' required from participants may put off those who are suspicious of the whole idea of dialogue. Dialogue of this kind is a skill that must be learned and not all are willing to make the effort to learn.

Dialogue, as the Jewish Dialogue Group understands it, is very different from that proposed by Bohm, as previously mentioned. Bohmian dialogue is based on creating an unstructured safe space in which those who participate can draw on their common ability to communicate meaningfully. The Jewish Dialogue Group model of dialogue is implicitly less confident in the human capacity to communicate. Yet both structured and unstructured dialogue can only work if participants make an active decision to take part in what can be a lengthy and difficult process.

Dialogue is not necessarily the answer to all conflicts. However, in order to have any chance of working, it requires willingness from participants and there is no guarantee that those with the most vociferous opinions and least civil tone will even take part. It is also hard to guard against the possibility that some participants may take part in bad faith. Participants in interfaith initiatives have on occasions been accused of using dialogue as a form of surreptitious proselytising (particularly in the case of Christians) or of whitewashing extremist views (particularly in the case of Muslims). But even if there is broad support for dialogue opportunities and everyone takes part in good faith, as the psychologist Peter T. Coleman has argued, the most intractable '5% of conflicts are not amenable to solution through a simple process of dialogue, but require a much more complex and subtle long-term process to work towards a solution.'[161] Dialogue aims at deeper engagement with others than simply finding out what their views are; it is about listening to the more complex and personal commitments, hopes and fears that motivate individuals. This can actually serve to clarify, rather than eliminate, the chasms that separate people. This clarification of conflict can help participants 'fight' more effectively[162] – but this result is far from the ultimate goal of resolving conflict.

NURTURING CIVILITY AND DIALOGUE IN THE JEWISH COMMUNITY

How can dialogue help bring about greater civility in the Jewish community? Civility and dialogue are both laudable ideals in and of themselves as well as potential means to resolve and manage conflict. Yet even if they might be intrinsically good, they are not always easy to achieve and, in any case, they sometimes stand in tension with other socially necessary practices, such as debate and the desire to fight for one's beliefs. Further, civility and dialogue are not the same thing and do not necessarily lead to one another. Civility, as I argued, can, at its most minimal, simply be a commitment to avoid abusive speech, rather than any commitment to the deep engagement that dialogue requires. It is important, therefore, to be realistic about what civility and dialogue can and cannot achieve. The kinds of deep divisions that have emerged in the Jewish world regarding Israel are unlikely to ever be anything other than difficult to navigate.

The civility in the Jewish community for which I am arguing is a civility that may help to *manage* rather than *resolve* the conflict over Israel. The practice of dialogue I advocate is one that helps to facilitate this form of civility. As in the previous chapter, when I advocated a minimal concept of Jewish peoplehood, here I am advocating a modest form of civility; a practice whose aims are :

- To prevent abusiveness

- To stem some of the hurt that Jewish divisions over Israel cause.

- To keeping channels of communication open.

Dialogue between Jews should work towards these aims, which are, I believe, achievable, if difficult.

Of course, these modest aims should not inhibit more extensive efforts to conduct deeper dialogues and build more robust connections between Jews. Perhaps one should think of a 'fast lane' and 'slow lane' in dialogue – everyone is capable of taking the slow lane, but not everyone is capable of taking the fast lane.

There is room for a plurality of initiatives that nurture civility and dialogue in the Jewish community. In fact, it is probably essential that there be a plurality of initiatives given that different kinds of people respond to different kinds of approaches. Some of the initiatives discussed in this chapter have shown great promise, but their impact has, so far, been modest. Initiatives, such as Project Reconnections and the Jewish Dialogue Group, have been transformative for some individuals in some sections of the community. Attempts to create broader coalitions, such as the JCPA's civility statement, appear to have been less effective outside of simply putting the issue of civility somewhere on the Jewish communal agenda.

Until such time as civility and dialogue become a higher priority across the Jewish community, there are things that individual Jews can do.

While 'top down' initiatives, promoted by large Jewish organisations, would be welcome, 'bottom up' approaches are also required.

STARTING WITH ONESELF

In the introduction to this book, I recounted one instance where I acted abusively towards a fellow Jew with whom I disagreed. As I stated, I am not always a paragon of civility and I cannot always listen to people with the patience that dialogue requires. Of course, I am not the only one. One of the starting points in nurturing civility, therefore, needs to be the recognition that *many of us are guilty of incivility (sometimes)*.

But being guilty some of the time doesn't mean I cannot push myself towards acting with greater civility. And while I am in no position to lecture people to be more civil, I can strive to demonstrate the kind of behaviour I would like to see in others. In the last few years, when I have engaged with Jews I disagree with about Israel, I have tried to act in a civil way, constantly trying to work towards dialogue and listening hard to others. At times, this strategy has born modest fruit.

In 2011 I entered a comment thread on the CiFWatch site, which is 'dedicated to monitoring anti-Semitism and combating the assault on Israel's legitimacy at *the Guardian* and its *Comment is Free* blog.[163] The original post revealed that *the Guardian's* online bookstore was selling copies of Gilad Atzmon's anti-Semitic tract 'The Wandering Who?' The post implied that this was part and parcel of *the Guardian's* tolerance of anti-Semitism, concluding '*The Guardian*: Your one-stop, hassle-free, 24/7 purveyor of antisemitism.' I pointed out that all other major online booksellers stocked the book, using the same blurb as on *the Guardian's* online store and, while there was certainly a case for asking *the Guardian* to stop selling the book, there was no particular reason to see *the Guardian* bookstore as any more tolerant of anti-Semitism than other online stores. A lengthy discussion ensued on the thread over *the Guardian*, anti-Semitism, censorship and how and whether people, like Atzmon, should be given a platform. Initially most comments were hostile to me, but with persistence and determination, the thread gradually resulted in a more productive dialogue between me and the other commenters on the site. By the end, Adam Levick, the editor of CiFWatch, had invited

173

me to contribute a piece on my attitude towards anti-Semitism to the blog. He did this knowing I was a leftist Jew with several pieces published on *Comment Is Free*. On this thread, as well as on others, and in private communications with Levick and other CiFWatch commenters, I have managed to develop what is, at least, a civil relationship, despite the gap separating our views on Israel.

In one small corner of the web, two protagonists in the conflict over Israel managed to find a civil way of communicating. In fact, it may be that writers, editors and communal leaders in the Jewish community have more common ground than they realise. Adam Levick, I am sure, faces a constant stream of online abuse for his stance, as does almost everyone who has published on the subject. In spite of this, my example demonstrates that a basis for common ground does exist, emerging from a mutual experience of being on the receiving end of incivility. Perhaps all it takes is a little bit of effort to establish a more civil tone in order to surprise other protagonists and lay the groundwork for more constructive dialogue.

NOTES

115 - Davetian, B. (2009). Civility: A Cultural History. Toronto, Canada: University of Toronto Press, p. 9.

116 - Elias, N. (2000). The Civilising Process (2nd ed.). Chichester, UK: Wiley-Blackwell.

117 - Sennett, R. (2012). Together: The Rituals, Pleasures and Politics of Cooperation. London, UK: Penguin.

118 - Buonfino, A., & Mulgan, G. (2009). Civility Lost and Found. London, UK: The Young Foundation.

119 - Anderson, E. (2011). The Cosmopolitan Canopy. New York, NY: WW Norton, p. 271.

120 - See for example: Cooper, H., & Zeleny, J. (2011, January 12). Obama calls for a new era of civility politics. The New York Times. Retrieved on June 1, 2013 from http://www.nytimes.com/2011/01/13/us/13obama.html?pagewanted=all&_r=1&

121 - The Civil Conversations Project. (n.d.) Retrieved on June 1, 2013 from http://www.onbeing.org/ccp

122 - The National Institute for Civil Discourse at the University of Arizona. (n.d.). Act now. Retrieved on June 1, 2013 from http://nicd.arizona.edu/act-now

123 - DeMoss, M. (2011, January 3). Letter to Senator Lieberman and Representatives Wolf and Myrick. Retrieved on June 1, 2013 from http://www.demossnews.com/resources/civility_project.pdf

124 - Civility. (2013, May 24). In Wikipedia, the free encyclopedia. Retrieved on June 1, 2013 from http://en.wikipedia.org/wiki/Wikipedia:Civility

125 - A brief summary can be found on Wikipedia: Blogger's code of conduct. (2013, March 30). In Wikipedia, the free encyclopedia. Retrieved on June 1, 2013 from http://en.wikipedia.org/wiki/Blogger%27s_Code_of_Conduct

126 - Eruvin 13b (Soncino translation)

127 - Pirkei Avot 5:17 (JTS translation)[proper ref?]

128 - Yoma 9b

129 - The latest version of Limmud's mission statement can be found at: http://limmud.org/home/mission/

130 - Mobius. (2005, November 22). Announcing the Jewish bloggers campaign for responsible speech online [Web log post]. Retrieved on June 1, 2013 from http://jews-

chool.com/2005/11/22/9608/announcing-the-jewish-bloggers-campaign-for-responsi-ble-speech-online/

131 - See for example the comment policy for the UK Jewish website Cartoon Kippah –http://cartoonkippah.com/comments-policy/ – and the US website Mondoweiss – http://mondoweiss.net/policy

132 - The Rodef Shalom communication agreement. (n.d.). Retrieved on June 1, 2013 from http://www.petitionbuzz.com/petitions/rodefshalom

133 - Pardes Center for Judaism and Conflict Resolution. (n.d.). Retrieved on June 1, 2013 from http://pcjcr.pardes.org/

134 - Jewish Day of Constructive Conflict. (n.d.). Retrieved on June 1, 2013 from http://us4.campaign-archive1.com/?u=50bba18218994413fc2e9e4e8&id=ec02014f23&e=baf5ff7734

135 - Jewish Council for Public Affairs. (n.d.). JCPA civility statement. Retrieved on June 1, 2013 from http://engage.jewishpublicaffairs.org/p/salsa/web/common/public/content?content_item_KEY=9249

136 - See the partial list given at http://engage.jewishpublicaffairs.org/p/salsa/web/blog/public/?blog_KEY=256

137 - Jeben-Elion, J. (2009, November 9). Learning how to argue. The Jerusalem Report, pp. 46-50.

138 - See for example: Kraft, D. (2013, January 1). Dialogue 101: Campus groups seek fresh conversations on Israel. Haaretz. Retrieved on June 1, 2013 from http://www.haaretz.com/jewish-world/jewish-world-features/dialogue-101-campus-groups-seek-fresh--conversations-on-israel.premium-1.500274

139 - Jewish Council for Public Affairs (2013, May 22) Dear rabbis... Retrived on June 1 2013 from http://engage.jewishpublicaffairs.org/o/5145/t/0/blastContent.jsp?email_blast_KEY=1249403. See also: Weintraub, M. (2013, May 9) Can We Talk? Building a Spirit of "Sacred Disagreement" on Israel Retrieved on June 1 2013 from http://www.hartman.org.il/Blogs_View.asp?Article_Id=1134&Cat_Id=275&Cat_Type=Blogs

140 - Rocker, S. (2010, June 3). Board urges less aggressive approach from Zionists. The Jewish Chronicle. Retrieved on June 1, 2013 from http://www.thejc.com/news/uk--news/32545/board-urges-less-aggressive-approach-zionists

141 - Dysch, M. (2013, May 17) No bullying allowed says Board of Deputies. The Jewish Chronicle. Retrieved on June 7, 2013 from: http://www.thejc.com/news/uk--news/107633/no-bullying-allowed-says-board-deputies

142 - Jaben-Eilon, J. (2010, June 11). Tough love. The Jerusalem Report. Retrieved on June 1, 2013 from http://www.jpost.com/JerusalemReport/Article.aspx?id=178152

143 - Snitow, A., & Kaufman, D. (2010, April 14). A chill in San Francisco. The Jewish Daily Forward. Retrieved on June 1, 2013 from http://forward.com/articles/127261/a- -chill-in-san-francisco/

144 - Fishkoff, S. (2010, December 14). On Israel, can U.S. Jews disagree nicely? Jewish Telegraphic Agency. Retrieved on June 1, 2013 from http://www.jta.org/news/arti- cle/2010/12/13/2742166/keeping-the-israel-conversation-civil-in-san-francisco

145 - Levick, A. (2011, November 20). Fight or flight? CiF Watch, David Yehuda Stern & Ben White [Web log post]. Retrieved on June 1, 2013 from http://cifwatch. com/2011/11/20/fight-or-flight-cif-watch-david-yehuda-stern-ben-white/

146 - Stern, D. Y. (2011, November 20). Words that destroy, words that build: CIF Watch and Ben White [Web log post]. Retrieved on June 1, 2013 from http://cartoonkippah. com/words-that-destroy-words-that-build-cif-watch-and-ben-white/

147 - Pilkington, E. (2010, October 26). Garry Trudeau: 'Doonesbury quickly became a cause of trouble'. The Guardian. Retrieved on June 1, 2013 from http://www.guardian. co.uk/books/2010/oct/26/garry-trudeau-doonesbury-40

148 - Rally to Restore Sanity. (n.d.). Retrieved on June 1, 2013 from http://www.rallyto- restoresanity.com/

149 - Chesler, P. (2012, October 22). Our daunting task. The Jewish Press. Retrieved on June 1, 2013 from http://www.jewishpress.com/indepth/opinions/our-daunting- -task/2010/08/11/0/?print

150 - Buber, M. (1970). I and Thou (W. Kaufman, trans.). New York, NY: Charles Scribner's Sons.

151 - Lévinas, E. (1999). Totality andInfinity: An Essay on Exteriority (A. Lingis, trans.). Pittsburgh, PA: Duquesne University Press.

152 - Foulkes, S. H. (1983). Introduction to Group-Analytic Psychotherapy. London, UK: Karnac.

153 - Bohm, D. (1996). On Dialogue. London, UK: Routledge.

154 - Freire, P. (1996). Pedagogy of the oppressed. London, UK: Penguin; Illich, I. (2011). Tools for Conviviality. New York, NY: Marion Boyars.

155 - Wheatley, M. (2002). Turning to one Another: Simple Conversations to Restore Hope in the Future. San Francisco, CA: Berrett-Koehler; Zeldin, T. (1998). Conversation: How Talk can Change your Life. London, UK: Harvill.

156 - For an overview of the field of conflict resolution, see: Ramsbotham, O., Woo- dhouse, T., & Miall, H. (2011). Contemporary Conflict Resolution (3rd ed.). Cambridge, UK: Polity Press.

157 - Kahn-Harris, K. (2009). Communities in Conversation: Jewish Involvement in Inter Faith Activities in the UK. London, UK: The Board of Deputies of British Jews Community Research Unit.

158 - Prospects (Woolf Institute: Spring / Summer 2007)

159 - Jewish Dialogue Group. (n.d.). Who we are. Retrieved on June 1, 2013 from http://www.jewishdialogue.org/about-us/who-we-are

160 - Herzig, M., & Chanin, M. (2005). Constructive Conversations About the Israeli-Palestinian Conflict. Watertown, MA: Public Conversations Project/Jewish Dialogue Group.

161 - Coleman, P. T. (2011). The Five Percent: Finding Solutions to Seemingly Impossible Conflicts. New York, NY: Public Affairs.

162 - For instance, some scholars have advocated dialogue with a listening to Islamist militants as a practice that will lead to a more effective strategy against them. See: Attran, S. (2010). Talking to the Enemy: Faith, Brotherhood and the (Un)Making of Terrorists. New York, NY: Harper Collins.

163 - Kahn-Harris, K. (2011, October 18). Re: At the Guardian's online bookshop, anti-semitism is shipped within 24 hours! [Web log comment]. Retrieved on June 1, 2013 from http://cifwatch.com/2011/10/16/at-the-guardians-online-bookshop-antisemi-tism-is-shipped-within-24-hours/comment-page-1/#comment-57624

CHAPTER SEVEN:
AN EXPERIMENT IN DIALOGUE

I n this and the following chapter, I recount my experiences in developing projects to encourage civil dialogue on Israel in the UK Jewish community. While I have considerable experience of working within the Jewish community, I am not a trained dialogue facilitator or conflict resolution specialist. I instituted the projects I will discuss in this chapter and the next as an 'amateur', a concerned individual. Although I have, subsequently, learned much more about this kind of work and developed a modest level of expertise, I am fully aware that 'professionals' in this area would do things very differently.

However, my lack of expertise, at least when starting out, should not disqualify me from this kind of work. The conflict over Israel needs to be managed through civil dialogue and this cannot be done through the work of experts alone. There needs to be a way for concerned communal activists to make a difference without extensive training. In this chapter and the next, I will recount the (not always simple) journey I made as I attempted to make a difference.

MY FIRST EXPERIMENT IN DIALOGUE[164]

Following the argument in the pub that I described in the Introduction, I started to work on two related processes. The first involved looking closely at the nature of Jewish conflict over Israel and finding a framework within which the case for action could be made. Chapters one to six are, in part, the fruits of this process. The second process was to search for a methodology for managing the conflict. My immediate sense was that the interfaith dialogue (of which I had some experience both as a participant and as a researcher) provided a possible model. I had seen for myself the transformative potential of interfaith dialogue and how it can lead to the formation of positive relationships between members of different communities. The question was how far the interfaith dialogue model would have to be adapted to serve as a basis for *intra*faith dialogue.

Sometime in 2007, I became aware of the Jewish Dialogue Group (JDG) in the US and its methodology (discussed in the previous chapter). This group offered a detailed guide for conversations on Israel that could be used without special training. I resolved to try out this methodology in the UK Jewish community and received encouragement from the JDG to do so. I had already initiated a project called New Jewish Thought that could provide a home for an effort to 'seed' dialogue groups across the UK Jewish community using the JDG methodology.

Two developments meant that my first effort to start a dialogue group went in a very different direction from that which I had originally planned. First, my efforts to find participants for the group were only partly successful. Despite producing a flyer and spreading it around the community, as well as running conference sessions and writing articles publicising the group, I received only a handful of responses. Eventually, I managed to recruit seven people with a reasonable spread of views about Israel. Yet the difficulty in doing so meant that I began to doubt the enthusiasm for the process at the 'grassroots' level of the community. My efforts did not seem to strike a chord with the community at large.

The second development was that, through a series of chance encounters, I was put in touch with a professional group analyst who works on conflict resolution in the Middle East. Gabrielle Rifkind, who directs the Middle East Security Programme for the Oxford Research Group, has many years of experience facilitating discreet dialogues and encounters between various parties in Middle East conflicts, including between parties without publicly acknowledged relations. Gabrielle was interested in my project and agreed to facilitate a number of sessions if I would convene and organise the group. Gabrielle's involvement meant that I set aside the JDG methodology and relied instead on her considerable experience. This left me free to act as the group 'rapporteur', recording its discussions, although, in later sessions, I began to participate actively in the group.

Six 2-hour group meetings were held between May and November 2008. While the JDG's methodology calls for highly structured sessions, Gabrielle chose to run the sessions in a more free-flowing way. She would pose questions for the group or suggest that we share our thoughts about a particular issue, but she was not prescriptive about the manner in which we should respond. On occasion, she would make comments on how individuals had responded to something and how the group was working. Details of the proceedings of the group were and remain confidential. However, the issues that came up within the group can be reported and their wider implications discussed. In this way, the group provided a highly productive 'experiment'.

Gabrielle Rifkind discusses her experience of this group in the foreword to this book. The following reflections are my own.

Membership and Purpose

The purpose of the group had been left deliberately fairly vague. The recruitment poster included the following details:

> Do you feel frustrated at the tone of debates about Israel in the Jewish community?
>
> Would you like to be part of a more respectful conversation?
>
> The group will offer an opportunity to speak candidly about our personal views and the experiences that have shaped them. Group members will aim to listen open-heartedly to others whose views and experiences are different from our own.

The open-ended framework was intended to enable the group to follow its own dynamic, rather than pre-judging where it should lead. However, the resulting ambiguities complicated the group considerably. As the group began to meet, it became apparent that members had differing expectations of what the group should be and differing understandings of what dialogue encompasses. Some group members saw themselves as being in the group primarily to listen and investigate group dynamics, whereas others were more concerned to ensure that their own points of view were put across within the group. Neither attitude was necessarily 'wrong', but the lack of consensus as to the purpose of the group did lead to tensions and difficulties in developing a productive dialogue.

The structure of the group was also an issue for some group members and, in particular, the role of Gabrielle as facilitator. A facilitator needs to be able to inspire trust among group members; this requirement would seem to preclude anyone who is closely identified with a particular posi-tion. I had thought that Gabrielle Rifkind would be ideal for the task due to her experience in Middle East conflict resolution. However, her experi-ence in facilitating dialogue with Hamas and other Islamist groups caused consternation for some group members when they found out about it.

Such conundrums cannot ever be completely solved. Perhaps the best way to navigate them is to see dialogue as something to be nurtured as the group runs its course, to view it as an ultimate goal rather than a starting point. Repeatedly, in the group, Gabrielle would encourage members to develop a different kind of perspective on interaction, to experiment with different ways of being heard and relating to others. The group, therefore, provided an opportunity for its members to do things differently.

Listening

The kind of deep listening that a dialogue group requires can only be achieved through a commitment to not interrupt, to not jump in immediately with criticisms and to not make unwarranted judgements about what the other 'really' thinks. Members should not be treated as representatives of anything other than themselves.

It proved extremely difficult to institute these listening practices within the group. Although the first and last two sessions were conducted in a relatively polite atmosphere, sessions two through four were fraught affairs. Some group members found it difficult not to interrupt and to talk when others were speaking. When some issues were raised, the group would collapse into angry accusations and counter-accusations. The group never fully achieved a mutually agreeable mode of communication that allowed for serious listening.

However, there were periods when group members did listen more seriously and intently. These tended to occur when discussion was focused on personal stories and experiences. Although some group members were more willing than others to share deeper emotions, hopes and fears, when members took ownership of their opinions, it allowed others to listen to them with more respect. Dialogue was most likely to break down when we focused on issues of policy, such as the nature of anti-Semitism or the future status of the West Bank settlements. Broadly speaking, the more impersonal the topic was, the more members saw each other as disembodied viewpoints, rather than complex human beings.

Perhaps the most striking finding in the group was how close to each other members were in their ultimate vision for Israel-Palestine. Almost all were sympathetic to the idea of a two-state solution. Although Zionism was criticised by some, it was never completely rejected. Rather, it was when discussion turned to questions of strategy, tactics and politics that bitter divisions arose.

Facts

One issue that recurred repeatedly throughout the sessions was the issue of facts and, more broadly, the status of truth. The various positions taken in the Israel-Palestinian conflict are marked by strikingly different narratives explaining the conflict and its history. It is common to justify one's position in terms of having the facts on one's side and to see those who disagree as being not just wrong, but also unwittingly or consciously untruthful.

Some group members took this absolutist position on the facts of the Israel-Palestinian conflict. This led to some passionate confrontations on issues such as the definition of anti-Semitism, the responsibility for the Palestinian refugee problem and the status of the settlements under international law. These confrontations would frequently degenerate into a series of assertions and counter-assertions as to who had the facts on their side. Larger issues would be cast aside in favour of struggles over minute questions, over individual incidents and over what one individual had said or done.

Boundaries

All prospective group members were told that the group would include people with whom they would vehemently disagree. No one made their joining the group conditional on certain people not joining the group. No one refused to attend further sessions when they discovered who else was joining the group and no one stopped attending after difficult sessions took place. The group was a success in that it managed to bring together people who would not normally associate with each other on a regular basis.

Of course, the group was set up with higher aspirations than simply putting people together in a room. Attempts to encourage people to engage in dialogue often came up against people's boundaries: the points beyond which members could no longer dialogue respectfully and effectively. Although no one ever walked out of the room, when boundaries were crossed the tone could become heated and angry.

Different group members had different boundaries. For some, it was the use of a certain term, the quoting of a certain source or the making of a certain point. One member found another member's use of the term 'Israel lobby' as being tantamount to anti-Semitism. For another, one member's question to the group as to whether Israel should exist was unacceptable. Other group members were happy to discuss almost anything in the group and had a high level of tolerance for any kind of argument being made. However, some of them took issue with *how* other members argued, rather than *what* they argued. In one particularly heated exchange, one member was accused of alienating other members (who agreed with him on many issues) because of the way in which he argued his case.

Almost all the group members were at times confronted with arguments and ways of arguing that they found hard to tolerate. To a certain extent, examining and testing boundaries was one of the aims of the group. However, it may be useful to distinguish between the boundaries that define *what* arguments may be tolerated and those that define *how* arguments should be made. Whereas raising one's level of tolerance for what kind of arguments are made can be a legitimate goal, boundaries over how arguments are made may be more worth preserving as they are likely to preserve the dialogic aims of the group.

Even though group members' boundaries created tension, members were able to reach agreement on other matters. In the penultimate session, alliances between members were made over non-Israel related issues, such as conspicuous consumption in the Jewish community. The divisions between group members over Israel were never so impenetrable as to prevent communication on all other matters.

Content

Perhaps the most striking feature of the group was how little Israel was actually discussed. In an early session, when each member was invited to describe what Israel meant for him/her, there was little detailed discussion of the country and individuals' relationships to it. Throughout the sessions, there was little engagement with Israeli arts, Israeli society, the Hebrew language, Israeli political culture and personal stories of visits to Israel. For most of the time, this was even true of those who had spent extensive periods of time in the country. Even when discussing the politics of the Israel-Palestinian conflict, many aspects of it, such as terrorism, the status of Jerusalem or the possible return of Palestinian refugees, were barely discussed.

So, in the twelve hours for which the group ran, what did we talk about? What appears to have been of most concern to the group was how to relate to the Israel-Palestinian conflict within Britain and, in particular, within the British Jewish community. It is here that the most intractable differences within the group were revealed. Whether and how Israel should be publicly criticised, how Jewish organisations should support Israel (or not), the responsibilities of Jews towards each other, what anti-Semitism is and how it should be combated – these were the issues that most engaged the group. While all of these issues relate to the Israel-Palestine conflict in some way, they have most direct relevance to questions of Jewish community – what it is and what it should be. Dialogue about Israel was, in fact, dialogue about Jewish community.

Divisions over how community was seen were profound. For some members, all those who wish to be part of the British Jewish community have an obligation to defend Israel publicly, whereas for others the obligation was precisely the reverse. Some were willing to define people as outside the community (even, for one member, as 'traitors'), whereas others were content to see the community as a more diverse space. It is perhaps the entanglement of Israel and Jewish community that makes for such intractable divisions. On reflection, it might have been better to encourage a separation of the two issues within the group. If the topic of community were discussed more abstractly, it might have been easier to engage in dialogue about it. If Israel were discussed more directly, it might have been possible to engage with the issues more dispassionately.

Structure

The JDG's method of conducting dialogue groups entails providing a strong structure designed to allow those who are not specialists in this work to convene and facilitate groups. This structure includes communication agreements, to which members have to adhere, detailed time-limited session plans and carefully designed stimulus material. In her own work in conducting dialogues in the Middle East, Gabrielle Rifkind also ensures that sessions are clearly structured. Group analysts and dialogue specialists refer to such structures as 'containers' for the group, intended to ensure that difficult issues can be raised without the group breaking apart.

Although I had acquainted group members with the JDG methodology and some of their literature prior to the start of the group, we did not follow such a structured methodology. This relative lack of structure had the advantage of giving the group the opportunity to set its own agenda. However, productive periods of dialogue were frequently interspersed with intense exchanges that sometimes spilled over into full-blown arguments. Gabrielle's subtle comments sometimes managed to diffuse such situations and she provided some challenging insights into the workings of the group and how members related to it.

In retrospect, while there were advantages in eschewing a tight structure for the group, it might have been preferable to have a more prescriptive framework. Communication agreements and structures that make members commit to pursuing respectful dialogue and hard listening would not have been foolproof, but would certainly have helped the group. Deciding on these agreements and structures collectively at the start of the series would have allowed members to buy in to the process. It also would have been helpful to have a stated goal for the group. Although I explicitly intended for the group to be an open-ended experiment, some sense of what was expected could have added some discipline.

Relationship to the wider community

A dialogue group is an artificial environment, unlike situations that occur in everyday life. In stepping outside normal contexts of interaction, group members have an opportunity to reflect on and experiment with how interaction takes place. Yet the illusion of the group as a space outside the community cannot always be maintained.

Given the relatively small size of the British community, it was inevitable that a number of the members of the group had had previous dealings with each other. Here the difference between interfaith and intrafaith dialogue becomes clearest. Dialogue within a community can involve people who may have long histories with each other and, even if they don't know each other, may feel they know them from their backgrounds, friends and family.

Most problematically, two of the group members had, in the past, exchanged confrontational e-mails with each other. While the group offered them the opportunity to develop a different kind of relationship, in practice, this never happened and they clashed repeatedly during the course of the sessions. Although I had said that members should not e-mail each other during the period that the group was running, in a moment of poor judgement, I relaxed this rule after the penultimate session. Subsequently, following a communal controversy in which both members were involved, the e-mail conflict erupted again, drawing in other group members. Following the last session of the group (which one of the parties could not attend) the war of words became more intense and spilled over into other online and offline forums.

While the group failed to prevent this conflict, this did not necessarily invalidate the group. In some respects, the presence of a real life communal conflict within the group provided a fascinating opportunity to learn how such conflicts are perpetuated. A group can provide a kind of microcosm in which community dynamics can be played out and analysed in miniature. In this way the group provided an invaluable sociological resource in the writing of this book, even if its success in achieving constructive dialogue was more erratic.

This sociological perspective is of use not just to sociologists, but also to anyone who seeks to understand how the Jewish community works. This perspective helps clarify the role that dialogue groups might be able to play in the wider Jewish community. Whatever happens when a group is run – and however successful members are in listening to and dialoguing with each other – a group is only a handful of people in a much bigger community. Its value lies not so much in the specificities of what happens inside the group (although this is clearly important), but in the new perspectives and skills it offers members in their interactions within the wider community. Although it is preferable that groups conduct constructive dialogues, even more troubled groups have a value in the light they shed on community dynamics. In this respect, there are no unsuccessful dialogue groups.

Dialogue and debate

Dialogue can also lead to communication problems. If listening is over-emphasised then there is a danger that dialogue will become simply a succession of monologues. The JDG's model seems to imply that group members should not be directly challenged in their views, but that members should respond to each other by explaining how their own position differs. While this has the virtue of being a very different way of communicating than usually occurs in the wider community, it has the potential to encourage solipsism. One group member argued that debate can be preferable to dialogue in that it does people the honour of taking their views seriously. Another went further and argued that s/he would be prepared to engage in debate with almost anyone, but would only do dialogue with those who shared certain common assumptions. In practice, the group tended to veer between dialogue and debate, sometimes listening and sometimes not, sometimes challenging and sometimes not.

MOVING ON

After the group finished, I spent a considerable amount of time reflecting on its lessons. One thing I clearly needed to rethink was the process of putting a dialogue group together. With few people interested in joining in the first place, I more or less accepted anyone who showed an interest. This was a mistake as the group ended up including some members who were unable to interact civilly with some of the others in the group. Clearly, the membership of a dialogue group needed to be put together with considerable care.

The highly structured approach of the JDG appeared to have been validated to the extent that the lack of focus and ground rules meant that it was often hard to prevent conflict from spiralling out of control. Gabrielle was, at times, taken aback by the ferocity of the conflict and, on one occasion, pointed out that she had run groups whose members were much more divided, yet still managed to maintain a civil discussion.

However, in her work in the Middle East and elsewhere, she had prepared more thoroughly and structured the groups more carefully. It was revealing that she had thought this approach would not be necessary with an intra-communal group. This was another sign that the methodology for dealing with intra-group conflict needs to be different to the methodology for dealing with inter-group conflict.

While everything pointed to adopting JDG's approach as the most appropriate way forward, in the end, I did not go down this route. The difficulty in recruiting group members had convinced me that, at this stage at least, there would not be much interest in a JDG-style exercise. In any case, I also began to feel that starting at the grassroots of the community might not necessarily be the best way of managing Jewish conflicts over Israel. I, therefore, completely changed my approach to developing civil dialogue in the Jewish community. In the next chapter, I describe this new approach and its results.

NOTES

164 - Some of the material in this section has been adapted from an earlier paper: Kahn-Harris, K. (2008, December). *An experiment in dialogue*. Published by New Jewish Thought. http://www.kahn-harris.org/writing/reports/an-experiment-in-dialogue2/

CHAPTER EIGHT:
MAKING PEACE IN THE JEWISH COMMUNITY, ONE DINNER AT A TIME

The more I researched the Israel conflict in the Jewish world, the more I became convinced that focusing on Jewish leaders and opinion formers was a more urgent priority than the grassroots community. Some of the worst instances of Jewish conflict over Israel occur in the public sphere amongst high profile figures. Although the distinction between leadership and grassroots is not clear-cut, it is at least plausible to think that a more civil conversation at a high level of the Jewish community might influence a more civil conversation at the grassroots level. Further, those who run Jewish institutions have the ability to set parameters of civility within their organisations.

I started again with a completely different approach that was less reliant on existing models of dialogue. The new approach would be both more and less ambitious in its aims. It would be less ambitious as it would not set up groups that met multiple times, nor would there be a fixed structure. It would be more ambitious in that part of the aim was to leverage conversations amongst high profile Jewish leaders to create change across the community.

Initially, the aim of the process was to create a consensus for a 'communication agreement' on how we talk about Israel in the UK Jewish community, to be signed by leading figures in the Jewish community from across the communal spectrum. The way I would create this consensus would be through convening confidential dinners at my house in which participants from different sides of the debate could discuss the agreement in a convivial environment. The agreement was modest in its ambitions: largely a commitment not to use certain kinds of language (e.g., accusations of Nazism), in keeping with the kind of civility I advocated in the previous chapter. However, after only a couple of dinners, it was clear that, not only were there wide differences over what should be in such an agreement, but also that some key figures would not sign such an agreement on principle, as they do not sign *any* public statements, petitions or letters. What emerged instead was a

191

much more open-ended process that, while it had no tangible outcome, was probably much more useful.

THE DINNER PARTY PROJECT

From 2009 to 2011, my wife, Deborah, and I hosted 13 dinners at our home, involving a total of 72 guests. These guests included chief executives of Jewish organisations, rabbis, leading activists in campaigning organisations concerned with Israel-Palestine and anti-Semitism, academics, journalists and writers. Together, the guests represented a broad cross-section of Jewish opinion on Israel, including most of the positions described in chapter two. The majority held positions towards the middle of the spectrum (although their disagreements with others were no less marked). This is partly because, numerically speaking, these are the most popular positions in the Jewish community, but also because, for reasons I will discuss later, there were often difficulties in getting other guests to sit down with people who held more radical positions. The guests also included some non-Jews, who held positions within the Jewish community and organisations concerned with Israel, or were important figures in the wider discussion over Israel-Palestine.

The most difficult challenge in hosting the dinners was coming up with an appropriate guest list. There needed to be enough difference within each group to ensure that guests engaged with opposing views. No guests should feel out on a limb and no viewpoint should be over-represented. Guests needed to be pushed gently to sit down with people with whom they had not sat down before and who would challenge them, but not pushed so far that they felt compromised. I met up with some of the guests beforehand to explain the process and find out where their 'red lines' were. The care and delicacy with which dinners had to be put together led to numerous logistical difficulties in finding mutually convenient times. It also led to some frustration when carefully wrought guest lists were scuppered when one or another guest cancelled at the last minute.

All of the dinners were confidential, under 'Chatham House Rules'; guests could say they'd been to dinner, but not who the other guests were, and they could quote something that had been said, but not who said it. I took no written record of anything that happened at the dinners and had no set agenda. I started each dinner by explaining why I think the Jewish community is facing difficulties because of Jewish conflict over Israel and then I opened the conversation to the other guests. I would participate in the subsequent discussion as a fellow guest and did not actively chair it. However, I did reserve the right to step in if a conversation was becoming too heated or off-topic. I also made one rule: that there should be one conversation round the table, rather than a collection of conversations between individuals. Since there were usually six to eight people at the table, including my wife and I, an intimate group conversation was possible. The resulting conversations lasted two to three hours. There was no follow up, except for thanking guests by e-mail the next day. The one-off format was deliberately chosen so as not to pressure guests into a regular commitment they may not have desired.

The format of the dinners was thus very different from the highly structured framework of the Jewish Dialogue Group or some other conflict resolution and dialogue methodologies. I tried to put as little expectation and pressure on guests as possible other than to come along and talk to others. The aim was to try and create a *convivial* space in which civil conversation could be developed. Across the dinner table, away from the stresses of the public sphere, it might be possible to see how another kind of relationship with those with whom one disagrees might be possible.

In attempting to establish this convivial space, we paid great attention to how we hosted and provided for our guests. While my wife, Deborah, was not party to the process of recruiting the guests, she was an equal partner in planning and hosting the dinners. We made a decision, from the start, that we would put a considerable amount of effort into the food. If at all possible, we wanted everyone to eat the same meal. We tried to provide food tailored to the needs of the person round the table with the most restrictive dietary needs. On more than one occasion, this meant producing vegan food or food that would not interfere with a particular set of allergies. Although the level of *kashrut* we follow in our kitchen was acceptable to most – meat-free, fish eating, using vegetarian ingredients where possible – for a couple of dinners, we bought in kosher takeaway food to ensure that no one had any worries.

We also tried to produce food that showed evidence of care and attention. This meant avoiding such standard Jewish community fare as grilled salmon with new potatoes, in favour of less expected recipes (or at least, less expected in the Jewish community). These included Mexican tacos, gazpacho, smoked cod's roe with ricotta and broad beans, savoury Scottish porridge with smoked haddock and Sephardi-style red mullet. We offered home-baked bread and pies on a number of occasions. The amount of time spent preparing such dishes made an obvious statement about the importance we attached to the dinners and the value of our guests. Food was intended to be more than 'background noise' and, instead, the focus of a shared experience.

Of course, the danger of serving non-bland food was that those who didn't like a particular dish might find the dinner as a whole less agreeable. It is, perhaps, no coincidence that one of the few rows we had occurred at a dinner where we served a fairly indigestible lentil dish that had burned. On another occasion, one guest, whose views had left him in something of a minority, was also the only one who disliked one of our dishes.

The location of the dinners in our home was also intended to promote conviviality. We have a relatively small dining table and the physical closeness helped to heighten intimacy. The presence of our children's toys and other sentimental objects was a reminder of the intimate, private world that we all possess. Neutral public spaces as venues for dialogue are not anchored in this way, encouraging the separation of the public and the private person. Our dinners tried to nurture the private side of public figures.

Of course, it was possible that hosting the dinners in our home simply predisposed people to be polite, rather than intimate. The desire not to offend or embarrass a host who has clearly made a big effort may have led guests to bury their less civil feelings. To an extent, this was not a problem as a polite conversation is, at least, an improvement on the angry conver-sations that often take place about Israel. But it's also true that the desire not to disrupt the evening and embarrass the hosts may have suppressed some of the more difficult conversations that arguably need to happen.

Every one of the 13 dinners was different. The unique composition of each evening created a unique dynamic and a unique set of preoccupations. We discussed a broad range of aspects of the Israel conflict from many different angles. This was, in and of itself, a success to the extent that we avoided the simple repetition of the arguments that are so familiar in public debates over Israel. Amidst the diversity, though, a number of themes recurred throughout the dinners.

A General Willingness to Take Part – With an Unwilling Minority

My first attempt at an intra-Jewish dialogue group was marked by a difficulty in recruiting enough participants through advertising, rather than approaching people directly. In contrast, I actively recruited guests for the dinners, 'designing' particular dinners around particular combinations of guests. The vast majority of people I approached expressed a willingness to come, although it was sometimes not possible to find a mutually convenient date. It is hard to tell whether, had I been proactive in this way with recruitment for the first group, I would have had more success. It is possible that the leaders and public figures who attended the dinners were more engaged with the issues and saw a greater need to come, but this cannot be confirmed one way or the other.

I used a variety of approaches to invite guests. Particularly at the start of the process, I met up with some prospective guests to explain my plans. Some guests I approached via e-mail 'out of the blue'. To recruit others, I drew on personal or professional ties. Although I am far from a famous Jewish figure, I was able to draw on my modest reputation as a sociologist and writer in the Jewish community to solicit participation. By the time of the last few dinners, I could point to my track record of running dinners; by this point, some prospective guests had heard of the project before I even approached them.

When I first approached potential guests, I did not immediately share the names of other possible guests. Particularly when inviting combinations of guests with an especially strong possibility for conflict, it was better to seek buy-in to the principle of the dinner in general before asking a prospective guest to attend a specific one. Most of the time, this approach worked and only very occasionally did someone, who agreed to attend in principle, balk at sitting down with a particular individual at a particular dinner. There was also a very small contingent that refused to attend any dinner at all. Most cited time pressures (which of course might have been a polite excuse), one or two explained that they found the prospect of the dinner much too stressful as they were trying to disengage with the whole issue of Israel and another handful disagreed in principle with the project as they could not see themselves ever sitting down with their opponents.

Although those who refused constituted a small minority, this group might have been larger had I not been careful in choosing whom I invited together. One of the lessons of the previous dialogue group was that some combinations of individuals would almost certainly lead to conflict. Despite this, it was still possible to ensure that most of the people I wanted to invite could be fitted into one dinner or another. However, I could not find a way of including a number of people, partly because some would not have agreed to sit down with them and partly because I thought their presence would simply lead to a protracted row. These were mostly, but not exclusively, some of the more radical Jewish anti-Zionists (although, I did manage to include a few anti-Zionists whose positions were more nuanced).

The problem with this approach is that it gave an effective veto to those who treat others as pariahs. It meant that discussion of the basis on which people are excluded from the Jewish community conversation proceeded without at least some of the excluded ones, effectively reproducing that exclusion. Another issue was that some of those who refused to come were those who are most frequently embroiled in Jewish conflicts over Israel. This is related to a more general challenge that most kinds of dialogue and conflict resolution projects face – how and whether to include the most intractable and bellicose individuals. There is always a danger that dialogue could simply become a pleasant pastime among those whose views are relatively close together and/or who are friendly enough to get along with most people. I wanted to ensure that guests at the dinners would be challenged, to some degree, to find a way of relating to people with whom they would vehemently disagree. But how far to push this? Are arguments necessarily always a bad thing or can they lead to some kind of understanding if they are managed the right way?

Whether or not I pushed guests hard enough to attend, there were certainly plenty of different opinions expressed at each dinner. Indeed, some dinners included those who had debated and, even argued publicly, in the past. Some of the most well-known, even notorious, Jewish figures in the Israel debate attended. This may or may not have been an achievement, in and of itself, but it was certainly a promising starting point.

A Mostly Civil Atmosphere

The dinners were mostly civil in that guests worked together to engage with each other and establish relationships based on communication and listening. In the intimate space of our crowded dinner table, guests listened to each other and communicated in a different way than they might do elsewhere. Although, of course, guests did propose arguments with which others disagreed, there was relatively little of the 'point-scoring' that so often characterises public debates on Israel. Guests' private behaviour sometimes contrasted with their public image in striking ways. People who are renowned for their strong views and the emphatic way in which they pursue them were often much quieter and more nuanced at our dinners.

Some dinners went beyond mere civility towards establishing a convivial, friendly and even light-hearted atmosphere. There was often laughter, joking and affectionate teasing. The effort we made to cook interesting dinners did help here, particularly when guests had drunk a glass or two of wine (no one ever came close to being drunk, though). Passing dishes and taking breaks to say whether they wanted cream or ice cream with their desert often broke any lingering tensions and reminded guests that they were at someone's home.

Conviviality was the flipside of the intimacy that is one of the drivers of Israel-related conflict among Jews. Intra-community conflict emerges, in part, from the sense of uncomfortable closeness to those whose beliefs seem to threaten one's very existence. But this closeness also allows Jews, when they wish to, to establish connections with other Jews. Playing 'Jewish geography' before the meal helped to find common frames of reference and common histories. Even when pairs of individuals had a history of public conflict, it was sometimes possible, in the space of the dinner table, to see it as a kind of game that should not damage one's private relationships. Even some fairly notorious pairs revealed an unexpected near-affection.

The 'chemistry' that made some dinners work better than others was hard to pin down. At one dinner, in particular, there were considerable *longeurs* in the conversation and an awkward tone to proceedings. This was not necessarily due to ideological differences and the dinner never came close to an argument. Perhaps some groups of people are simply more difficult to gel into a cohesive unit than others. The reasons for this cannot be predicted in advance and may not even be possible to pin down after the event.

When Civility Breaks Down

There were two dinners when civility broke down. In both instances, the arguments were between two individuals who had a previous history of conflict. In neither instance was the ideological divide between them enormous, indeed all parties were of the left. What appeared to happen was that existing grudges were not left outside the dinner. Significantly, one of the parties had needed considerable persuasion to attend the dinner and after the dinner continued to express his scepticism towards the process. His view was that civility consisted of responding seriously to the content of someone else's arguments and he rejected the relevance of attending to tone when speaking.

Both arguments were diffused, to some extent, by me adopting the role of facilitator rather than participant and suggesting that we moved on to other matters. Since the other guests at the dinner had not joined in the argument, it was possible to sideline the pairs-in-conflict by ensuring that the other guests took a more active part. Eventually the atmosphere cooled off, although there was still considerable tension for the rest of the dinner.

The question is whether these two arguments constituted a 'failure' of the process. On the one hand, to the extent that the dinners aimed to create a space for a more civil conversation, arguments were not welcome. On the other hand, arguments can, at times, be productive, if they lead to greater insight into the ways communication breaks down. In group analysis, a facilitator would topicalise and examine such an argument so as to offer the opportunity to move forward in a less conflictual way. At neither of the dinners was I able to do this and it would, probably, have been impossible given the one-off, unstructured nature of the groups and my lack of formal training.

As with my first attempt at a dialogue group, I was left wondering whether it had been unwise to invite pairs with a history of conflict to the dinners. The dinners certainly needed to contain sufficient diversity to enable a challenging conversation. In any case, in a small community, it would not have been easy to invite guests who were entirely unknown to each other. Perhaps, though, it would have been preferable if, as far as was practical, the divisions between guests were restricted to matters of ideology, rather than divisions created by previous histories of personal conflict.

Areas of agreement

Outside of those two dinners, the great majority of guests did buy in to the process in that they agreed with my assertion that there was a problem that needed to be addressed. At the start of each dinner, I explained my view that conflict over Israel was causing distress and fragmentation in the Jewish community. Very few guests dissented from this view, although some stayed noticeably quiet. The agreement extended from left to right and those who did dissent were not confined to any one position.

It was noticeable that those who agreed with my position included some who have received a degree of notoriety for the zeal with which they express their views. The desire for civility would seem to extend to those who have been accused of incivility themselves. Some of them rejected the accusation that they are uncivil and argued that it is their opponents who are guilty. Sometimes there was a sense of being trapped into incivility by one's attackers, there being no choice but to fight fire with fire.

What came through strongly from many guests, particularly from those with a high public profile, was the hurt and distress that the conflict had caused them. Perhaps the most valuable role that the dinners played was to give guests a space in which to bear witness to the toll the conflict can take. It showed guests that others from different views also shared the difficulties they faced. That doesn't mean that they could agree on the causes of or the solutions to the problem, but, at the very least, they were compelled to view the conflict and the incivility it causes in a broader way.

The dinners also subtly encouraged guests to see each other as fellow participants in a common enterprise. While of course they differed substantially from each other in their views, they were all deeply engaged in Israel and (with the exception of the small number of non-Jewish guests) with being Jewish. As I argued previously, the flipside of the closeness that generates intra-communal conflict is the closeness that binds community members together. The dinners tried to nourish this closeness, with a certain degree of success. One of the most gratifying aspects of the dinners was when guests, on different sides of the divide, discovered unexpected connections, such as friends in common and similar upbringings and histories. The dinners provided a space in which guests could, for a time at least, emphasise and even enjoy these commonalities.

Topics of Conversation

As previously mentioned, to some extent, *how* we talked at the dinners was as important, if not more important, than *what* we talked about. One of the most striking aspects of the dinners was how little we talked about Israel itself. In fact, there was only one dinner where we talked about Israeli politics and the chances of Israeli-Palestinian peace in much detail. It is possible that at some dinners the guests had actively avoided directly addressing Israel given that there were others round the table who held radically diverging views. At others, though, the principle differences were clearly less about Israel itself than about how Jews in the Diaspora should relate to it.

For the most part, conversations at the dinners concentrated on the UK Jewish community and the UK in general. There was considerable discussion of Jewish communal politics and the intricacies of how the UK Jewish community related to Israel. Particularly notorious incidents and individuals were examined from different angles. It became very clear that the Israel conflict has deep and personal repercussions relating to how guests live their lives both as Jews and as people living in Britain. This is particularly the case for those with a high public profile. Whatever guests disagreed about – and they disagreed about many things – most could agree that the Israel conflict was far from trivial in its consequences.

Despite this widely shared sense of the conflict's significance and a widely shared sense that it had impacted on them personally, most guests had not discussed this issue or even thought about it much previously. Particularly striking was one of the dinners where we hosted senior *madrichim* (leaders) from the main Zionist youth movements.

Despite knowing each other well and representing movements with different ideologies, they had never before discussed the nature and impact of Jewish differences regarding Israel. More generally, many guests expressed gratitude at the chance to engage with an issue that had been worrying them.

Just as talking about Israel at the dinners often meant talking about how Israel affects the UK Jewish community, so a range of other issues were brought to the table. One issue was anti-Semitism, which for many guests was inextricably linked to the question of Israel. Anti-Semitism was just as sensitive an issue as Israel itself and, in some cases, in fact, even more sensitive. The rights and wrongs of accusations of anti-Semitism weighed heavily on guests' minds. Other issues that arose included denominational differences in the Jewish community, multiculturalism and British politics.

When conversation did address Israel directly, it was striking how often guests on all sides expressed great ambivalence, a position frequently at odds with their decidedly non-ambivalent public statements. Many of those who spent much of their time defending Israel in the public sphere or running 'pro-Israel' activities were privately concerned about or even horrified at Israel's settlement policy and the rise of the Israeli right. Conversely, many guests who were known as critics of Israel or supporters of Palestinian rights were critical of aspects of the pro-Palestinian movement and its tendency, at times, to tolerate forms of anti-Semitism. That guests often felt ambivalent and held nuanced positions in private did not necessarily weaken their public commitment to particular forms of activism, but it did mean that those who take contrary or opposite positions to them had the opportunity to see them as more rounded individuals.

A Stimulating, But Tiring Process

The conversations at the dinners bore witness to the toll the conflict can take on people. Guests were often anguished and exhausted by the constant efforts to hold their end up in an unending struggle. For the most part, the dinners were not exhausting in this way as they did not involve the same style of 'no-quarter-given' debating. However, the dinners were often intense, as we discussed sensitive and often emotional issues. While a civil conversation about Israel is certainly an improvement from conflict, it does not provide an escape from the constant concern about Israel that envelops so many Jews.

The same goes for organising the dinners. The process was fascinating, exciting, difficult, enervating and frustrating. It was never dull. It was always hard work, whether going through the delicate process of putting guest lists together and inviting people, deciding on menus and cooking or hosting the actual conversations.

One can have too much stimulation. At the end of 2011, I decided to put the process on hold. I had not lost faith in the value of the dinners and I had many more people I wanted to invite. However, both my wife and I had taken on heavier workloads, making it hard to find the considerable time needed to run the dinners. The process has not been completed – indeed, it is an unending process that can never be completed – and I hope to resume it at some point. I did feel, though, that I had enough experience to demonstrate the value of the process and its wider applicability.

Legacy of the Dinners

Despite the intense and time-consuming nature of the process, the dinner party project was very modest in its aims. One-off dinners cannot, on their own, transform the way the Jewish community talks to itself about Israel. What they can do, however, is raise the issue and offer guests a vision for a different way of interacting. As such, it is very difficult to evaluate the precise 'impact' of the dinners on the Jewish community. Certainly, I received many e-mails and letters after the dinners to express guests' thanks and their thoughts on the process; most of them were very positive about the project and wished it every success. Yet even guests who bought into the process most strongly would, outside the dinners, face the same intractable problems in the wider community that make civil dialogue about Israel so difficult.

I was not prescriptive about what the lessons of the dinners should be and that meant that, to some extent, guests could draw conclusions with which I might disagree. However, I did write a number of articles in the Jewish and wider press that used the example of the dinner party to suggest that Jewish divisions over Israel could and should be improved. There were a few specific instances of guests going on to make policy recommendations based on their experiences at a dinner. For example, one senior communal leader, who attended a dinner, has spoken publicly a number of times about the need to develop better relations between sections of the Jewish community currently divided over Israel. In their 'We Believe in Israel' toolkit, published in 2011, the British Israel Communication and Research Centre (BICOM), one of the staff members of which had attended a dinner, suggested that dinner parties could be used in Israel advocacy:

Dining for Israel

One of the most effective ways to engage people in a discussion about Israel is to invite them into your own home for dinner.

We would suggest you invite a mixed group with half the guests being supporters of Israel who will be pa-tient enough to spend time trying to convince the other half who should be people who are undecided. The JC ran an interesting article about organising din-ner parties to discuss Israel, which is well worth reading: http://www.thejc.com/lifestyle/lifestyle-features/42738/ how-easedivisionsover-israel-have-a-dinner-party [This is a reference to an article I wrote on the dinner party project] Remember this is all about relationships. People are very flattered to be invited to dinner. Don't underestimate your own influence. Most people want to be asked. Most people are not hostile to Israel. Unless you reach out you will never be able to persuade people of Israel's case and it leaves the field clear for our and Israel's opponents' messages.

This recommendation was emphatically not in the spirit of the dinners I organised. I did not organise them in order to provide a forum to convince others of my beliefs and guests were not invited to persuade others about their beliefs. Nonetheless, BICOM's recommendation does recognise that civil debating is more productive than confrontational debating and in this modest respect it represents an advance on some advocacy strategies.

Probably the most far-reaching impact of the dinners has been personal. Not only has it pushed me to find ways of developing civil dialogue with people holding a whole range of views, it has also deepened and broadened my connections across the Jewish community. Through reaching out to people I did not know and getting to know better people with whom I was already acquainted, my relationships across the Jewish community became more profound. I came to see myself as one person among many others struggling to deal with the conflict over Israel. This has had a direct impact on how, as an occasional writer on Israel and its impact on the Diaspora, I have positioned myself. Those with whose views I disagree now have a human face. This works in reverse as well. I have been struck by how, when I have made interventions in public debates on Israel, I have not been criticised, in some quarters, with the same ferocity that others, who hold similar views to me, have faced. I am probably no more respected for my opinions than I was before the dinners, but I am, at least, at little more human in others' eyes.

THE WIDER RELEVANCE OF THE DINNERS

The dinners I hosted were part of one idiosyncratic project. Although I was influenced by projects and writings on the practice of civility and dialogue, the dinners themselves were not initially inspired by anyone else. However, as the project developed, I became aware that the dinners mirrored the work of other projects and that there was a whole literature on the power of food-based hospitality and civility.

Dinner parties don't always have a good reputation. One common phenomenon discussed in Jewish discourse is 'dinner party anti-Semitism'.[165] That is the anti-Semitism supposedly expressed by the 'chattering classes' who are critical of Israel, but do not recognise their lazy stereotypes of Jews as anti-Semitic. The dinner party is here, and elsewhere, seen as a forum for smug, ill-thought-through platitudes and prejudices. In TV shows such as *Come Dine With Me,* dinner parties are portrayed as bitchy, hypocritical and ridiculous. In countless comedy sketches, dinner parties are the epitome of middle class absurdity and pretension.

Look deeper, though, and it is clear that, at dinners and other occasions when people come together over food, powerful possibilities for civility emerge. Roy Strong, in his history of 'grand eating', shows how, since the Middle Ages, elaborate dining and feasting have been important tools in the development of norms of civility within the nobility and later the bourgeoisie.[166] More generally, convivial conversations in small groups have been at the heart of cutting-edge thinking and social change at many points in history – from Greek symposia, to eighteenth century French salons and English dining clubs to the Algonquin round table.[167] For the radical thinker, Ivan Illich, table-based conversations were as important in his work as his writing; the table was the crucible in which a new future could be formed. As he argued in 1996:

> I do think that if I had to choose one word to which hope can be tied it is *hospitality*. A practice of *hospitality* — recovering threshold, table, patience, listening, and from there generating seedbeds for virtue and friendship, on the one hand — on the other hand radiating out for possible community, for rebirth of community.[168]

Hospitality is an important value in religious thought and eating together is a common way for religious communities to create fellowship with one another. All the major world religions have traditions that value hospitality and the provision of food.[169] For example, the story of Abraham providing food to three strangers at Mamre in Genesis Chapter 18 is a demonstration of his fitness to be a patriarch and prophet. In the Islamic world, hospitality to strangers is accorded a high value and, during Ramadan, communal breaking of the fast is an important ritual. In Christianity, the Eucharist and its antecedent in the Last Supper, place shared eating at the centre of ritual practice, what Dietrich Bonhoeffer called the 'Fellowship of the Table'.[170]

The centrality of food in Jewish tradition and Jewish culture is widely recognised. The intricate laws of *kashrut* ensure that food is something that cannot be consumed thoughtlessly; it is an object of care and attention. Most Jewish festivals are associated with the eating of particular foods. The onset of Shabbat is marked by eating together in the home. On Passover, the *Seder* table is the central ritual at which Jews commune with other Jews, both those physically sitting at the table with them and the wider Jewish people with whom Jews are symbolically connected in the past and present. There is a strong tradition of inviting strangers to join in the Seder (the Haggadah states 'Let all who are hungry come and eat'). On Sukkot, the tradition of eating together in the Sukkah becomes a way of inviting the Jewish past into the present through symbolically inviting illustrious *ushpizim* (guests) to the table. In Hassidic Judaism, a *rebbe* connects with his followers at his table (*Tisch*); the sharing of his food becomes the sharing of his wisdom and spirituality. The Jewish table is, therefore, both symbolically and literally a space at which Jews become closer to each other and to God.[171] Recently, various Jewish projects have used food as a way of bringing Jews together, both for its own sake and in the pursuit of a more ethical and spiritual relationship to consumption.[172]

At the present time, I am not aware of any other projects that have used food and the table as a resource for dialogue and conflict resolution between Jews. However, in interfaith dialogue, the potential of eating to bring people of different religions together has been recognised. For example, the UK-based Dialogue Society has produced a number of guides on using dinners and festivals in interfaith work.[173] For example, Ramadan is sometimes used as an opportunity for non-Muslims to join Muslims in breaking the fast together.

More generally, a number of projects have used dining, hosting and the table to promote connection, civility and conviviality in a fragmented world. The US-based organisation Eat4Peace, which aims to 'diminish stereotypes, prejudice, and discrimination and to spread the word of peace to every corner of the earth' encourages people around the world to 'learn about another culture and experience a way of life different than your own' by eating a meal from a different culture every year on April 11th.[174] In the UK, The Big Lunch promotes getting together to eat lunch with neighbours on one day every year.[175] Hosting, eating together and conviviality also provide the central metaphor for some initiatives, such as Art of Hosting[176] and Conversation Café,[177] which promote dialogue.

Dining together does not have to have an explicitly lofty purpose to be valuable. The artist Jim Haynes has hosted a dinner at his flat in Paris every Sunday for over 30 years, free to anyone who wants to come, for the simple pleasure of meeting others.[178] There are many such quirky contemporary salons that allow people to enjoy the pleasures of meeting people in private settings over food or some other common activity.[179] Similarly, in recent years many 'underground' and 'pop up' restaurants have emerged, often taking place in people's homes.[180] Part of their attraction lies in their domestic setting, allowing guests to interact with each other and the hosts.

Without being conscious of it at first, the dinners my wife and I hosted at our home were part of a much broader movement that draws on the potential of hosting and eating to nurture civility and conviviality. This movement has deep roots historically and cross-culturally in the practice of eating together as a way of affirming and repairing social relationships. These deep roots also extend into Jewish tradition and culture, both past and present. What I had, initially, thought of as an experiment in dialogue turned out to be simply a particular version of a tried and tested practice. As such, the successes of the project can also be found elsewhere, and its limitations, too.

LESSONS

The lessons of this and the previous chapter are twofold. First, formal dialogue groups, while they can make an important contribution to developing better Jewish relations regarding Israel, need to be handled very carefully. While professional training in group processes and facilitation skills may not be necessary, at the very least 'amateurs' should look carefully at the practices used elsewhere and try to learn from them. The second lesson is that more informal means of improving Jewish relations may be available to most of us. The dinners my wife and I hosted had a modest, but discernible impact on their guests and us as hosts. They did not require specific training: only care, attention and hard work.

This second lesson provides a significant ray of hope into the bleak picture of Jewish conflict I have painted in this book. Yes, Jews are in conflict over Israel and much else besides, but the tools to ameliorate this conflict are not out of reach. Jews and other human beings create conflict and pain through practices of communication – and we can heal conflict and pain through the very facility to communicate that causes the problems in the first place.

NOTES

165 - See for example: Koenig, R. (2009, March 5). You're Jewish? You can't be English. NewStatesman. Retrieved on June 6, 2013 from http://www.newstatesman.com/society/2009/03/jews-anti-friend-syria-dinner

166 - Strong, R. (2002). Feast: A History of Grand Eating. London, UK: Jonathan Cape.

167 - Davetian, B. (n.d.). The history and meaning of salons. Retrieved on June 6, 2013 from http://www.bdavetian.com/salonhistory.html

168 - Ililich, I., & Brown, J. (1996, March 22). We the people, KPFA. Retrieved on June 6, 2013 from http://www.wtp.org/archive/transcripts/ivan_illich_jerry.html

169 - Kearney, R., & Taylor, T. (Eds.) (2011). Hosting the Stranger: Between Religions. London, UK: Continuum.

170 - Smith, C. (2012, March 22). Bonhoeffer on the Fellowship of the Table. Retrieved on June 6, 2013 from http://www.patheos.com/blogs/slowchurch/2012/05/22/bonhoeffer-on-the-fellowship-of-the-table/ caps

171 - Berrin, S. (Ed.) (2012, March). The Jewish table – Complete issue. Sh'ma: A Journal of Jewish Responsibility, 42(688). Retrieved on June 6, 2013 from http://bjpa.org/Publications/details.cfm?PublicationID=13758

172 - See for example: Jewish Food Experience. (n.d.). About: Welcome to our table! Retrieved on June 6, 2013 from http://jewishfoodexperience.com/about/

173 - Dialogue Society. (n.d.). Publications. Retrieved on June 6, 2013 from http://www.dialoguesociety.org/publications.html

174 - Eat4Peace. (n.d.). Retrieved on June 6, 2013 from http://eat4peace.com/

175 - The Big Lunch. (n.d.). Home. Retrieved on June 6, 2013 from http://www.thebiglunch.com/

176 - Art of Hosting. (n.d.). Home. Retrieved on June 6, 2013 from http://www.artofhosting.org/home/

177 - Conversation Café. (n.d.). Welcome to Conversation Café! Retrieved on June 3, 2013 from http://www.conversationcafe.org/default.htm

178 - Haynes, J. (n.d.). Home. Retrieved on June 6, 2013 from http://www.jim-haynes.com/

179 - Sandra, J. N., & Spayde, J. (Eds.) (2002). Salons: The Joy of Conversation. Gabriola Island, Canada: New Society.

180 - One of the most prominent British secret restaurateurs is Kerstin Rodgers, aka Miss Marmite Lover, who has recounted her experiences running her restaurant in: Rodgers, K. (2011). Supper Club: Recipes and Notes from the Underground Restaurant. London: Collins.

CONCLUSION:
THE WAY FORWARD

Whatever the impact of the dinner party process may or may not have been on the UK Jewish community, and whatever its wider lessons might or might not be, they did help change one particular person – myself. While I am still a person capable of flashes of anger and scorn, I have learned to love civil dialogue more than I ever could have imagined. I loved the intimacy of the dinners, I loved listening to people's views, I loved hosting people in my home, I loved the connections I made with people across the Jewish community. The process of dialogue has convinced me both that there is a problem in how Jews relate to each other on the question of Israel and that there are ways of addressing the problem.

The final draft of this book was completed in the summer of 2013. The book's completion marks the culmination of a process that began for me in 2007, with the argument in the pub I discussed in the introduction. The dialogue group, discussed in chapter seven, met in 2008 and the dinners were held between 2009 and 2011. These past six years represent a particular period in time. In Israel-Palestine they have seen wars in Lebanon and Gaza and a period of stasis in the peace process. In the UK and other Diaspora Jewish communities, they have seen increased conflict over the question of Israel, together with a cautious opening up of new spaces for Jews to discuss and share their concerns over Israel.

While no author wants their book to date too quickly, it would be gratifying to think that the issues discussed in this book will quickly become anachronisms. If conflict over Israel in the UK and other Diaspora Jewish communities were to die down, either because of some kind of resolution to the Israel conflict itself, or because of an acceptance of differences in Jewish communities, no one would be happier than I – even if my book played no part in this process.

This is unlikely to happen, though. There are no imminent signs of resolution in the Israel-Palestinian conflict, or in the Jewish conflict over Israel in the Diaspora. The future is extremely hard to predict. We can, though, point to one issue that, depending on how it unfolds, will determine the nature of Diaspora Jews' engagement with Israel. That is, the issue of how and whether a two-state solution to the Israeli-Palestinian conflict might come about. For a number of years, the principle of the two-state solution has been endorsed by much of the Israeli political class and by much of the community leadership in the Diaspora Jewish communities. There is, however, a growing consensus, in the centre and centre right of Israeli opinion, at least, that under the present circumstances, no deal with the Palestinians can be reached and that to immediately withdraw from the occupied territories, in whole or in part, would be unwise from a security point of view. The greater part of the government coalition formed in March 2013, while it has not officially rejected a two-state solution, is not convinced of its immediate necessity and viability. Further, within the coalition, the HaBayit HaYehudi party and significant sections of Likud-Beiteinu are committed to the annexation of large sections of the territories and oppose the formation of a Palestinian state. On the Palestinian side, the split between Fatah and Hamas and the ongoing crisis of leadership in the West Bank has meant that it is unclear whether any Palestinian leader has the authority or will to make a final settlement to the conflict with Israel. It is thus highly uncertain whether a two-state solution is possible in the near future and what kind of two-state solution the Israeli and Palestinian leadership and publics would or would not settle for in the medium to long-term. The combination of the Israeli government's 'in principle' acceptance of the two-state solution and its indefinite deferment has, in fact, been a significant factor in the maintenance of the limited consensus that exists across the mainstream of the UK Jewish community. As long as Israel keeps the possibility of the two-state solution formally on the table, but does not enact it, there is at least the possibility of some kind of relationship between all the various Diaspora Jewish Zionist positions on Israel. The pro-Israel, pro-peace left can keep their hopes alive that a full withdrawal to the green line might take place, and the neoconservative and religious rights can hope that any withdrawal from the territories will be minimal and any Palestinian entity will be limited in its power. As long as there is no final agreement and Israel does not officially set its borders, most Zionist visions remain viable, at least in theory. Ambiguity is useful both to Israel diplomatically and to Diaspora Jews communally.

The question is how long this state of ambiguity will continue. Any kind of resolution to the Israeli-Palestinian conflict will bitterly upset at least some sections of both Israeli and Diaspora Jewish opinion. Whether the fallout from any kind of resolution to the Israeli-Palestinian conflict will make Diaspora Jewish conflict worse than it is currently is difficult to predict. We can, at the very least, point to two developments that are likely to follow should Israel formally and permanently rule out the possibility of the two-state solution. First, there is likely to be a movement of some or all pro-Israel, pro-peace Jews towards radical Jewish and even anti-Zionist positions. It is also possible that a new position will develop, of left wing Jews who were once supporters of two states who have concluded that the two-state solution is no longer possible, but who do not wish to embrace the one-state solution either. There may, in fact, be considerable creativity in developing post-two-state visions that attempt to reframe the Zionist belief in Jewish sovereignty. The second consequence is that the global Palestinian solidarity movement (and the campaign for BDS that goes with it) would receive a considerable boost in popularity, drawing in support from those outside the radical left. Self-defined Jewish supporters of Israel would be even more isolated than they are now from mainstream non-Jewish opinion.

Given that these possible future developments would cause turmoil in the Jewish community, it is at the very least prudent to put in place strategies that can help manage the conflict now and are robust enough to deal with the conflict as it might develop in the future.

So what is to be done?

The primary task is this: *we need to start work – now.*

We need urgently to start attending to the conflict as it is today and as it might be tomorrow. We need to treat Jewish conflict over Israel as an issue of vital concern; one that should be high on the communal agenda. The 'we' to whom I am referring here is not just Jewish community leaders, policy-makers and opinion formers, although they are clearly critical. Rather, the conflict over Israel should be on the agenda for all Jews. We cannot go on like this.

More specifically, I want to outline three agendas for managing the conflict. These agendas reiterate and expand on recommendations made in previous chapters.

Agenda One: Reconfiguring the Place of Israel Within the Jewish Community

In chapter five, I suggested three principles for dealing with divisions over Israel in the Jewish community:

1. The existence of differences over Israel should be recognised as a permanent feature of Jewish communities.

2. Practices of marginalisation and the creation of pariahs should be avoided by cross-communal Jewish institutions.

3. 'Firewalls' must be established to ensure that conflict over Israel does not intersect with and reinforce other kinds of conflict.

Putting these principles into action requires moves that will be difficult and painful, but not impossible, for many in the Jewish community to come to terms with:

• *The inclusion, at the very least, of those who no longer define themselves as Zionists within some Jewish communal settings.*

• *Making space for the open articulation of religious right wing views, including the views of those who support the permanent annexation of the occupied territories.*

• *Retreating from using support for Israel as a way of developing cross-communal cooperation.*

This does *not* mean that I am advocating that all British Jews should stop supporting Israel. In fact, I am advocating the reverse; British Jews should be more open and public with their political engagement with Israel, which for many will mean supporting what Israel does. A community that accepts that there are and will always be fundamental differences in how Jews relate to Israel politically will be one that lives with itself more civilly. Politics is not the problem; it is the denial of politics and the rendering of some political positions as beyond the pale that causes intractable conflict. Political systems can provide ways of living with and managing conflict.

The public supporters and other centrist Zionists will have most difficulty developing this political stance, but they can derive inspiration from Zionism pre-1948 in their efforts. At that time, there was no consensus within Jewish communities that Zionism was the right direction to take and there was no consensus within the Zionist camp as to what Zionism should be; different Zionist and non-Zionist streams openly and politically contended with each other. This politicised environment did not weaken the fight for a Jewish state; instead, it sharpened Zionist's motivation, eventually resulting in the birth of Israel. Diaspora Zionists today will ultimately find life easier if they commit to fighting for the vision of Israel they would like to see, rather than pursuing an illusory dream of a non-politically consensual Zionism.

My vision is, therefore, for a Jewish community that moves in two directions at once: looking in one direction, Jews of all kinds share a common space and cooperate over a range of common issues; looking in the other direction, Jews pursue different political divisions within a common space of political contestation.

Agenda Two: Embedding Organised Processes of Civil Dialogue in Jewish Communities

A Jewish community of this kind will have to confront tensions between political divisions and communal inclusion. A shared commitment to civility can mediate and soothe these tensions. The kind of civility I advocated in chapter six allows people committed to different political divisions to mitigate the distress that the presence of others can generate. A commitment to minimal civility within political space can provide the basis for a more thoroughgoing form of civility within cross-communal space.

This commitment to civility will not come about without significant effort. The kinds of agreements and exhortations that were discussed in chapter six can play a modest role here, particularly if community leaders and opinion formers worked harder to set an example. However, in order to heal the wounds that the conflict has perpetuated and in order to create lines of communication that can manage future conflict, more systematic processes of dialogue need to be developed and implemented. There are, as I have shown, a variety of models for conducting dialogue and all of them can, potentially, be of use. What is important is that Jewish community institutions support dialogue, both in financial/organisational terms and by highlighting it as a practice that should be part of the fabric of Jewish communal life. Serious investment in civility and dialogue projects will help develop capacity.

In the US, as we have seen, there has been a growing awareness among some Jewish organisations of the need for civility in discussions over Israel and of the role that methods of dialogue can play in this. Pro-Israel pluralists in the UK Jewish community have recognised the need for safe spaces in which Jews can share their diverse views about Israel. However, most of the time, the civility and dialogue advocated by mainstream Jewish communal institutions have been directed towards Zionists only. While this is difficult enough as it is, it does not go far enough. The vocal and growing number of Jews who do not see themselves as supporters of Israel should not be excluded from those with whom one should be civil and who should be civil in return.

Agenda Three: Taking Responsibility for the Conflict

The first two agendas address the role that Jewish community leaders, opinion formers and institutions can play in ameliorating the conflict. 'Top down' work of this kind can, if conducted carefully, trickle down to influence the conflict at the grassroots. The reverse is also true. The conflict is perpetuated by the myriad arguments that occur in public, private and semi-private settings and managing it will require an effort that can spread through all these settings. That will only happen if enough Jews take on the individual and collective responsibility for the conflict and for working through it.

Responsibility does not mean guilt. Although some people do play a greater role in perpetuating conflict and find it more difficult to be civil, the conflict is too diffuse and widespread to trace it back to any particular individual or individuals. Rather, taking responsibility means making an active effort to play one's part in developing a more civil conversation over Israel.

Jewish organisations have a particular role to play here. Jewish organisations, especially those that rely totally or in part on volunteers, often rely on their most active and committed members. The kinds of activism that take place at the sharp end of campaigning concerning Israel are often the most challenging and bruising. Organisations can, therefore, become reliant on those who are most able to withstand the incivility of the conflict. In some cases, this means those who are themselves least able to be civil. In this way, the least civil voices can, effectively, become the public voices of organisations. Jewish organisations need to take responsibility for monitoring and managing those empowered to speak on their behalf to ensure that incivility is curtailed. It may be necessary to find ways of supporting those who are less resilient in conflict situations to ensure that those with more civil voices are empowered.

In this book, I have tried to take responsibility for my own behaviour when it has fallen short of the standards I have set for myself. Undoubtedly, I will fall short again at some point, but I am at least trying to work hard to avoid doing so and to make amends when necessary. I have also recounted my experiences in promoting civility through private dinners and on comment threads. These were areas where I was in a position to make some sort of difference. Everyone has different skills and different spaces through which they can make a difference. A proliferation of individual efforts would embed the search for a way to live with divisions over Israel into the very fabric of the Jewish community.

A FINAL WORD

I am sure that many readers will disagree with aspects of this book. Some may see the situation with regard to Jewish divisions over Israel as less serious than I do. Some may apportion blame in one or another direction more than I do. Some may simply feel that conflict and incivility are just a fact of life. I am also certain that there will be strong disagreements with the recommendations made in this and previous chapters. In particular, I am aware that the inclusion of those who are not Zionists into the Jewish community is completely taboo for some.

Whilst I will commit to listening carefully to those who disagree with my analysis and recommendations, there is one criticism against which I will defend myself most strongly. That is the criticism that my argument is too idealistic and naïve, my recommendations hopelessly impractical. I have based this book's arguments and recommendations on what I believe to be a *pragmatic* approach. As I argued in chapter five, the case I make for attending to Jewish conflicts over Israel is based on a consideration of the self-interest of Jews and the Jewish community. Jewish divisions over Israel are inevitable and will not go away. Jews cannot avoid the incursion of Jews with opposing views into their lives. Given this situation, Jews need to deal with the conflict that arises with other Jews if they wish to live fulfilling Jewish lives. We don't have to like or even respect each other; we just need to be able to live alongside each other without constant conflict.

Ultimately there is no choice – whether we like it or not, we have to work towards dealing with the Jewish community's uncivil war; to do otherwise is to risk further turmoil within the community that so many of us hold so dear.

POSTSCRIPT:
FOR THOSE WHO ARE NOT JEWISH

The Jewish conflict over Israel is a particular manifestation of a more general conflict over Israel. If anything, the conflict is even more vicious outside the Jewish community, although it, perhaps, lacks the intimate and personal nature of conflict in this small world. This book has addressed conflict between Jews and how to ameliorate it, but this does not mean that conflicts over Israel that do not exclusively involve Jews should not be addressed. Further, the case I made in chapters five and six, that Jews need to make a particular effort to develop civil forms of dialogue between themselves, should not be taken to imply that civil dialogue is unnecessary elsewhere.

In fact, I believe that this book has relevance beyond the Jewish community. The conflict over Israel is so toxic that steps need to be taken to address it more generally. The process of civility and dialogue, I suggest in this book, could be applied more widely. However, what works (or does not work) between Jews may not always work more generally and vice versa. Responses to conflicts need to be sensitive to context.

It may be, though, that if Jews can show that they can live with their differences over Israel, it will inspire other communities to develop constructive ways to deal with their own conflicts. At the very least, a more civil Jewish community would remove one aggravating factor in the global conflict over Israel.

INDEX